The World of Reptiles and Amphibians

The World of Reptiles and Amphibians

GENERAL EDITOR: JOHN HONDERS

PEEBLES PRESS

New York: London

First published 1975
by
Peebles Press International
U.S.: 10 Columbus Circle, New York, N.Y. 10019
U.K.: 12 Thayer Street, London, W1M 5LD

ISBN 0-85690-038-9

Distributed by
Walden Books, Resale Division, in the
U.S. and Canada
WHS Distributors in the U.K.. Ireland.
Australia, New Zealand and South Africa

Printed and bound in the U.S.A.

A

ADDER *Vipera berus*, or Northern viper, is a representative of the large family of venomous snakes known as the Viperidae. Adders are variable in colour and pattern but are most commonly cream, yellowish or reddish-brown with black or brown markings. They nearly always have a dark zigzag pattern down the middle of the back. These markings and the short, rather thick body, together with the copper coloured iris and vertical pupil make this snake easy to recognize, at close quarters. The adder occurs farther north than any other snake in Europe and Asia. It occurs within the Arctic Circle in Scandinavia and ranges well into southern Europe, where it tends to inhabit cooler mountainous areas. Dry, open moorlands and heaths, sunny hillsides and open woodland are its preferred habitats. Adders mate in April and May, and the young are born (usually free of the egg membrane) in August and September. They hibernate for much of the winter but may emerge early to bask in sunshine on warm days in February and March. In keeping with their northern distribution, they cannot tolerate very hot sun and retreat into shade during the hottest part of summer days. They hunt lizards and small mammals mainly in the evening and at night. Adder venom, like that of most of the Viperidae, is dangerously toxic to humans, especially small children. FAMILY: Viperidae, ORDER: Squamata, CLASS: Reptilia.

AESCULAPIAN SNAKE *Elaphe longissima,* a large, slender, non-venomous snake, $4\frac{1}{2}-6\frac{1}{2}$ ft ($1\cdot5-2\cdot0$ m) long, with a small head and a long tapering tail. Its colour is brown, rarely black (melanic) and most of its scales are striped with white. There is a pair of yellow patches on each side of the neck. The belly is light yellow and there is a distinct dark stripe from the eye to the corner of the mouth. Young individuals have dark brown blotches on the back. The scales of the mid-body are in 23 (seldom 21) rows and there are 212–248 ventral plates. There are three geographical races or subspecies known as *longissima, romana* and *persica* respectively. The Aesculapian snake ranges across Europe but is not found in the British Isles, the Iberian Penin-

sula, Scandinavia and countries north of the 50° parallel. It is also found in Turkey, Armenia, the Caucasus and on the southern shores of the Caspian Sea. Its habitat is forest with clearings and rocky slopes with shrub or bush vegetation. The Aesculapian snake is an excellent tree-climber. When young, it feeds on lizards, as an adult, on rodents, moles and shrews, young birds and eggs. Females lay clutches of 5–8 eggs and the hatchlings from these are $8\frac{1}{2}-10$ in (22–25 cm) long. The snake is named after Aesculapius, son of Apollo and Coronis, mythical founder of the science of medicine, who is usually represented with a large snake coiled around his staff. FAMILY: Colubridae, ORDER: Squamata, CLASS: Reptilia.

AGAMIDS, a large family of lizards living in the Old World. Agamids differ from most lizard families in their teeth, which are acrodont. That is, the teeth are fixed by their bases on the summit of the ridge of the jaw. The post-orbital temporal line on the skull is complete. The tongue is short, thick and

East African agamid lizard.

slightly forked. Agamids are small to medium-sized lizards with powerful claws. They live on the ground, in rocks or in trees. Their limbs are fully developed. The scaly skin very often consists of small spines which appear mainly on head and tail. Tail autotomy is completely absent in agamids. The ability to change colour depending on temperature and emotional changes is well developed. Most agamids feed on insects and other small invertebrates. A few are omnivorous, others mainly herbivorous. Nearly all agamids lay eggs, only a few species of the genera *Phrynocephalus* and *Cophotis* being oviparous.

There are approximately 35 genera of agamids with 300 species. The focal point of their distribution is the oriental region but from there they have spread to Africa, the Indo-Australian Archipelago and Australia. They did not reach Madagascar, which is inhabited by the iguanas that are otherwise confined to the New World. Nowhere in the world do agamids and iguanas occur together, as the former always drove out the latter. The agamids only reached the borders of temperate zones in the Old World: in Europe, the hardun *Agama stellio* is to be found in the southern part of the Balkan peninsula and a few species of *Agama* and *Phrynocephalus* are found in the central Asian steppe.

About 60 of the 300 species of *Agama* live in southwest Asia and Africa. With their dorso-ventrally flattened heads and strong limbs the medium sized agamas look like typical lizards. They live on the ground, among rocks or on thick tree trunks. Some of the rock dwellers have taken to living in the walls of houses, like the African *Agama agama*.

The many species of the Toad-headed agamids *Phrynocephalus* live in the deserts and semi-deserts of Central and West Africa. Although the colouration and markings of back and head of these tiny lizards contain some surprising colours they match their surroundings perfectly. Their behaviour also seems to fit their desert environment. They can quickly bury themselves in sand by wriggling their flat bodies from side to side.

5

The Flying dragons of the genus *Draco* found throughout the Indo-Australian Archipelago are small tree dwelling agamids. On each side of the body which is supported by five or six pairs of extended ribs there is a flap of skin or 'flying skin' that can be spread. This flying skin works like a parachute and enables the Flying dragon to glide from one tree to another, often covering considerable distances. The flying skin and also the erectable throat pouch frequently show striking colours, especially in the males which display them during courtship or in territorial dispute. When taking off from a tree the dazzling colours can be seen clearly and are surprising even to the human eye. The Flying dragons are insectivores, the predominant part of their food being ants that are caught with the tongue and crunched with the teeth.

The Angle-headed agamids *Gonyocephalus* are slightly bigger tree dwelling agamids ranging from Southeast Asia to New Guinea and in Australia and the South Sea Islands. The species of the genus *Calotes* are also tree dwellers and are common in tropical and subtropical Asia. None of these, however, shows any special adaptation to tree living comparable to the Flying dragons. In contrast to ground dwelling agamids the bodies of the tree agamids are slightly flattened from side to side. The change of colour in some of these species is quick and distinctive. The bloodsucker *Calotes versicolor* got its common name from the brilliant red that appears on the head during courtship and territorial dispute. The red colour can change to an unobtrusive brown within seconds if the lizard loses a fight and is ready to flee.

Amongst the most impressive of the agamids is the Water lizard *Hydrosaurus amboinensis*. With a length of about 3 ft (90 cm) it is a giant in its family. On its tail it sports an enormous rigid crest which is supported by the spinal column. Nothing is known of its function. The Water lizard and also lizards of the genus *Physignathus* roam the forest trees in search of food and will drop into the rivers in moments of danger and escape by swimming or walking under water. The Australian Frilled lizard *Chlamydosaurus kingi* is about the same size as the Water lizard. Its skinfold is supported by the tongue bone and can be raised like an enormous cape. This colourful frill together with the wide open mouth are displayed at any enemy. The contrasting colour of the mucous membrance emphasizes this threat posture. Sometimes when fleeing at high speed the Frilled lizard runs on two legs.

Australia has a great variety of remarkable agamids. The Bearded lizard *Amphibolurus barbatus* can inflate its spiny throat pouch and assume a similar threat posture to that of

Bearded lizard in threat posture, with mouth open and throat pounch inflated, displaying its 'beard'.

the Frilled lizard. The moloch or Thorny devil *Moloch horridus* of the Australian semi-deserts is protected by big pointed thorn-like spikes that give this little lizard a most bizarre appearance. Contrary to its common name the moloch is a completely harmless lizard that feeds mainly on ants. Relying on its protective colouring a moloch will sit quietly next to an ant trail and pick up a few insects with its tongue from time to time. As it is very dependent on certain types of ants the moloch is probably the most specialized of all species of agamids.

The Spiny-tailed lizards of the genus *Uromastix* from the desert belts of West Asia and North Africa are specialized in a different manner (see mastigures). Spiny-tailed lizards are mainly herbivorous, at least when adult, and search for the sparse flowers, fruits and leaves of the semi-desert. They also feed on dried parts of plants. They are active during the day and spend the nights and unfavourable seasons of the year in burrows which they dig themselves or in crevices in the rock. FAMILY: Agamidae, ORDER: Squamata, CLASS: Reptilia.

AJOLOTE *Bipes biporus*, is one of three species of worm-lizard native to Mexico and southern Baja California. The soft skin of its body is folded into numerous rings and this, with its cylindrical body, gives it a close resemblance to an earthworm. Its eyes are covered with skin but it has two forelimbs each with five toes well equipped with claws. Few specimens were known to science until recently. Nothing is known of its breeding habits. FAMILY: Amphisbaenidae, ORDER: Squamata, CLASS: Reptilia.

ALLIGATOR LIZARDS, about five species of *Anguid lizard living in Central America and the southern part of North America.

ALLIGATORS, an ancient, relict group of crocodilians comprising only two species out of a total of over 30 forms in the order Crocodylia. They are distinguished from crocodiles by the pattern and arrangement of the teeth, and, not so reliably, by the shape of the snout. In the alligator the lower row of teeth project upwards into a series of pockets in the upper jaw so that when the mouth is closed, the only teeth exposed to view are the upper teeth. This gives the alligator an appearance of 'smiling' when viewed from the side. The crocodile, on the other hand, normally has both rows of teeth exposed when the jaws are closed, and the teeth intermesh with one another. Particularly prominent is the enlarged tooth fourth from the front which may even extend above the line of the upper jaw giving a constricted appearance immediately behind the nostrils. So the crocodile's 'smile' resembles a toothy leer.

Alligators are found only in two widely separated parts of the world: the upper Yangtse River valley in China and the southeastern United States. One theory is that the less aggressive alligator—which will run away from man—was once almost world-wide in distribution. but the more recent crocodiles have successfully weeded out the alligator throughout its range to where it is now found only in two relict 'islands'.

The more efficient crocodile, faster growing and consuming more food, but not as long-lived as the alligator, may have been simply a keener competitor for food. However, the alligator can withstand cold more successfully than the crocodile. When water temperatures drop below 65°F (18°C) an alligator still surfaces for air, whereas the crocodile when exposed to cold water sinks and drowns. This explains the occurrence of the alligator in relatively colder regions. In North America, the American crocodile has successfully survived in extreme southern Florida, but its numbers are severely affected by cold spells. Alligators, however, range from southern Florida, north into the Carolinas and west to Texas.

Although the crocodile is now the most numerous and widespread of the crocodilians throughout the tropics, the alligator family has come up with perhaps an answer to the crocodile: the caiman. Caimans are even smaller than crocodiles and a number of species occupy the northern regions of South America and appear to be spreading out in a slowly radiating pattern into the regions

Young alligators look almost benign.

American alligator *Alligator mississipiensis*.

7

occupied by crocodiles. With an appetite and temperament to match that of the crocodile, it is conceivable that these 'new-comers' may eventually replace a large number of the crocodiles over a great part of their range.

Man, however, has had a crushing effect on the populations of all crocodilians, primarily regarding hide-hunting. During the period 1880 to 1894, for example, $2\frac{1}{4}$ million alligators were slaughtered. Although the alligator is protected in the USA by most of the states in which it is found, it has been illegally hunted and its hides sold to markets in northern states in such numbers that it is doomed to extinction unless efforts are taken to curtail this smuggling and poaching.

The Chinese alligator is protected by the government of China but there is no recent word on whether its numbers are increasing. In fact, it has been said that the Buddist priests hold the alligator in high regard, and will quietly liberate captured specimens if they have the opportunity.

The name 'alligator' is thought to be derived from the Spanish word *el lagarto*, meaning 'the lizard'. In Latin America, many smaller forms of crocodilians are called *lagarto*. The larger forms are called *cocodrilo*.

In years past, baby alligators were gathered by the thousands and sold in pet stores in the United States. This resulted in a rapid decline in alligator populations, whereupon many states in the south began protecting small alligators or at least controlling their export. Although baby alligator traffic has been halted, baby Spectacled caimans have been sold by pet stores in even greater numbers, with the result that some South American countries have become alarmed at this drain on their natural populations of caiman and are gradually placing these species under protection and control.

Crocodilians of any kind make poor pets. They are usually unpredictable in temperament, especially if their enclosure is heated to the extent where they can efficiently digest food. Normal household temperatures are generally too low for proper assimilation of food by the baby crocodilian, and although it may be quite lethargic and unaggressive in this state, it will usually develop and grow quite unnaturally, resulting in deformed jaws, a humped back, or even death within a few months. Even zoological parks have difficulty in providing necessary •heat requirements, food with the proper balance of nutrients and minerals, exposure to adequate dosages of the proper lighting and necessary space for adequate growth.

Alligators will feed on practically anything moving that wanders close enough to be snatched up and will conveniently fit into their mouths. They are strictly carnivorous, and prefer to gulp down food in smaller, whole portions. However, if necessary, an alligator can dismember a larger animal by

American alligators in water.

thrashing the victim back and forth or suddenly rotating over and over several times to 'unscrew' a portion. Typically, baby alligators feed on insects, worms, crustaceans and small fish. Later they take frogs and perhaps small rodents. Four-foot (1·2 m) long individuals feed on larger fish, lizards, baby turtles, and rat-sized rodents. Eight-foot (2·4 m) alligators feed on rodents, some larger fish, and an occasional unwary bird. Larger individuals may even be lucky enough to snatch up a small wild pig or stray dog, although their food consists primarily of large rodents in the wild. Alligators play an important part in controlling rodents in such out of the way areas as swamps and canals where they would otherwise destroy vegetation and water levels in areas even far removed from the alligator's habitat. The stomach of an alligator also contains stones, pebbles, and even hard, man-made objects that aid in breaking down food particles for digestion, much like the gizzard in a bird.

Alligators, in the wild construct underground dens at least portions of which are

filled with water. In fact, one method used by collectors for locating alligators is to probe with a long pole into the soft earth along a river bank. It is easy to tell when the pole enters a large, open cavern and contacts an alligator. At egg-laying time in the spring, a female American alligator constructs a large mound of mud and vegetation about 5–7 ft (1·5–2·5 m) wide at the base. 20–70 hard-shelled eggs $3\frac{1}{3}$ in (8·5 cm) by $2\frac{1}{2}$ in (6·5 cm) are laid in a cavity in this, and are then covered with more debris and sealed in by the restless activity of the mother. The peeping of hatching young after approximately 10 weeks of natural incubation will encourage the female to tear open the nest and help release the eight-inch (20 cm), brightly coloured black and yellow young which will then make for the nearest water and are then given some protection by the female for the next few months.

Alligators have been known to attain large sizes in the past, and some records claim individuals over 20 ft (6 m) in length (in which case, such individuals probably weighed well over half a ton). A 19 ft (5·8 m) specimen was shot in Louisiana a generation ago. Today, 10 ft (3 m) specimens are a rarity, and 8 ft (2·4 m) individuals are uncommonly hard to find in the wild.

Chinese alligators are not known to exceed a length much over 6 ft (1·8 m).

Except in moments of danger or when seizing prey alligators are slow-moving. Even their bodily processes work slowly, which is perhaps why they have been known to reach the age of 75 years. Crocodiles, on the other hand, are not known to live much beyond 30 years.

In contrast with true crocodiles, the two ribs on the first cervical vertebra (the atlas) of an alligator diverge only a little. Moreover, alligators have bony plates not only on the back but also on the belly beneath the large horny scutes. Whilst with true crocodiles there is generally only a single transverse series of occipital scutes and not more than six nuchal scutes, these are usually far more numerous in alligators.

True alligators of the genus *Alligator* are characterized by having the nasal cavity longitudinally divided by a bony septum. This septum is also visible in the living animal because the hump of the nose exhibits a clear longitudinal sub-division. The other genera of alligators (in the broader sense) which do not have this bony septum are referred to by the collective name 'caiman' although they probably do not form a natural group like the genus *Alligator*.

The typical characteristic of the Mississippi alligator is the relatively long but very flat and broadly rounded snout. On the top, a few rudimentary bony ridges extend parallel to one another from the base up to the hump of the nose but the front corners of the eyes are not interconnected by a transverse ridge. In the midline of the back there are generally eight longitudinal rows of large scutes. The keels of the two central longitudinal rows of scutes along the top of the tail run parallel to one another right up to the end and do not curve outwards.

A very sad part is played by commercial interests. Since the skin of the belly of the Mississippi alligator is only sparsely ossified, it is well suited for the manufacture of bags and other leatherware; even coats are made of alligator leather. A rather ingenious souvenir industry has caused the slaughter of countless young animals in order to prepare them and, with tasteless paintwork and ornamentation, sell them as souvenirs. The author of this article even saw at an American airport two small alligators which had been dressed up as a bridal couple, the male in tails and tophat and the female in a wedding dress and veil! FAMILY: Alligatoridae, ORDER: Crocodylia, CLASS: Reptilia.

ALLIGATOR SNAPPING TURTLE

Macroclemys temmincki, the largest freshwater turtle in the United States and one of the largest in the world. Reaching a weight in excess of 200 lb (90 kg) it is sluggish and heavily armoured, frequenting the bottoms of lakes and rivers. It is unique in possessing a built-in fishing lure: a fleshy appendage on the floor of the mouth that resembles a twitching worm. Fishes, attracted by this lure enter the mouth and are swallowed by the turtle. The ruse is enhanced by the dull colouration and rough shell, which is usually heavily covered with algae and serves to render the turtle invisible. FAMILY: Chelydridae, ORDER: Testudines, CLASS: Reptilia.

AMBYSTOMATIDS, North American Mole salamanders, are sturdily built broadheaded, medium-sized salamanders. They include the Marbled salamander *Ambystoma opacum* which may attain a length of 5 in (12·5 cm) and is terrestrial. It lives on hillsides near streams from New England to Northern Florida and westwards to Texas. Breeding takes place in autumn, fertilization is internal and the eggs are laid in shallow depressions on land, usually guarded by the female until the next heavy rain, when they hatch. In very dry conditions they may not hatch until the following spring. In most other ambystomatids, such as the Spotted salamander *Ambystoma maculatum*, which has the same range as the Marbled salamander, courtship takes place in water with an elaborate ritual. The sperm are released in a packet, or spermatophore, which the female picks up with her cloaca. The Spotted salamander breeds in the early spring when it may be seen in fairly large numbers making their way to the breeding ponds. After breeding they return into 'hiding' until the next spring and

for the rest of the year they are secretive and rarely seen. The eggs hatch in 30–54 days releasing larvae of $\frac{1}{2}$ in (1·25 cm) long. After 60–110 days the external gills are resorbed, metamorphosis is complete and the animal becomes terrestrial at a length of 2–3 in (5–7·5 cm). Adults grow to a length of 9 in (22·5 cm).

The Tiger salamander *A. tigrinum* may grow to 13 in (32·5 cm) which makes it amongst the largest of the terrestrial salamanders. It derives its name from the yellow or light olive bars on its upper surface. It has a similar distribution to the Marbled and Spotted salamanders except that it is a lowland form. Its eggs are laid in deep-water ponds, metamorphosis is completed quickly.

Another familiar Mole salamander is the Frosted flatwood salamander *A. cingulatum*, $4\frac{1}{2}$ in (11·25 cm) long, named for the greyish dorsal markings on a black background which suggest frost on leaves. The second part of the name refers to distribution of the species in the wire-grass flatwoods between North Carolina and northeast Florida.

The Ringed salamander *A. annulatum* is generally only found in the mating season after heavy rain when it may be seen in shallow pools, from Central Missouri to West Arkansas and Eastern Oklahoma. For the rest of the year it is difficult to find despite its comparatively large size of 8 in (20 cm).

The majority of salamanders, including the ambystomatids, are usually voiceless. A notable exception is the Pacific 'giant' salamander *Dicamptodon ensatus*, which occurs in the moist coastal forests from British Columbia to Northern California and may reach a length of 12 in (30 cm). It makes a low-pitched bark or scream, especially when disturbed. As its name suggests this is a large

Tiger salamander, largest terrestrial salamander, one of the so-called Mole salamanders.

The Marbled salamander, smaller than the Tiger salamander, is sometimes found on hillsides.

species. In contrast to the slender, graceful appearance of the other ambystomatids this form has a clumsy build, yet it can apparently climb well and has been found several feet above the ground in small bushes or on sloping tree trunks. Almost all ambystomatids have well developed lungs but the Olympic salamander *Rhyacotriton olympicus,* 4 in (10 cm) long, has extremely small lungs. It inhabits mountain streams of the coastal forests of Oregon and Washington.

The genus *Rhyacosiredon* is known from four species which occur at the southern edge of the Mexican plateau.

Neoteny (breeding in the larval state) is not uncommon in the Ambystomatidae, the best known example being the axolotl, the permanent larva of *Ambystoma mexicanum*. It is found around Mexico city and keeps well in captivity. Some species of salamander are habitually neotenous in one part of their range and not in another. For example, in the eastern subspecies of the Tiger salamander metamorphosis takes place within a few months, but in the western subspecies metamorphosis often fails to take place, the animals breeding as larvae. The major factor which contributes to the neoteny is a lack of iodine in the water.

The ambystomatids (family Ambystomatidae) together with the plethodontids (family Plethodontidae) form the suborder Ambystomatoidea, the largest group of tailed

amphibians with some 27 genera and in excess of 200 species. FAMILY: Ambystomatidae, ORDER: Caudata, CLASS: Amphibia.

AMNIOTES. Vertebrates can be classified into two groups, the anamniotes and amniotes. The former comprises fishes and amphibians, the latter the reptiles, birds, and mammals. The feature which separates the two groups is the type of embryonic development. The typical anamniote embryo forms within a simple gelatinous egg capsule and a moist environment is essential for development. Consequently, even the most terrestrial frogs and salamanders must return to water to breed or at least ensure moist surroundings in which to lay their eggs. The typical anamniote egg has a moderate amount of yolk as a food store and a feeding larval stage is necessary for the completion of development. In contrast the amniote egg of reptiles, birds, and egg-laying mammals can develop on land under the most arid of conditions and the larval stage is eliminated. The egg is covered by a calcareous or leathery shell porous enough to allow the gaseous exchange essential for embryonic respiration but resistant to egg desiccation. Furthermore the amniote embryo develops three extra-embryonic membranes: the yolk-sac enclosing the large food store vital for protracted growth and the elimination of a larval stage, the allantois which is an organ of respiration

and excretion, and the amnion which forms a protective shelter over the embryo. The cavity between embryo and amnion is fluid filled so that the embryo carries its own aquatic environment within the egg and the need for a moist external environment is removed.

The first amniotes were the primitive reptiles which evolved in the Carboniferous period. It is likely that the amniote egg evolved at this time as a means of assuring a predator free environment for incubation rather than in association with a general trend towards terrestrial life. In the early Carboniferous the fresh waters abounded with carnivorous fishes and amphibians whereas the land was essentially free of predators apart from the relatively small number of semiterrestrial amphibia. The aquatic amniote could therefore temporarily leave the water to lay its eggs on land and incubation could continue in comparative safety. Today for similar reasons many completely aquatic frogs leave the water to construct elaborate nests on land away from severe egg and larval predation. Being anamniotes, however, a moist nest is essential for development.

The reptiles, the birds and the egg-laying monotreme mammals demonstrate the basic pattern of amniote development and freed from the necessity of a damp environment for embryonic development they have dispersed widely. In the higher mammals, where the egg is retained in the maternal uterus, the extra-embryonic membranes become variously modified to unite with maternal tissue to form a placenta. The marsupial mammals represent an intermediate grade between the egg-laying monotremes and the higher mammals for in the great majority of species a placenta is lacking and precocious young are born which must continue their development within the parental marsupial pouch.

AMPHICOELA, a suborder of amphibians with amphicoelous vertebrae, considered to be primitive. The vertebrae, which are quite unlike those of any other amphibian group, are concave at each end. There is only one family with two genera, *Leiopelma* from New Zealand, with three species, and *Ascaphus* of the North American and southwestern Canada known only from a single species. All are small seldom exceeding 2 in (5 cm) in length. They live in cool places. Archey's frog *Leiopelma archeyi* lays its eggs under stones and its larvae develop within the egg capsule, so there is no free-swimming tadpole. The young hatch as miniature frogs, require no surface water but move around in the damp earth and vegetation. Hochstetter's frog *L. hochstetteri* lays its eggs in small tunnels close to or sloping into water. Usually the male stands guard over the eggs. The embryos develop a long tail which is used to rupture the egg capsule and allow the larva to escape. The larva respires through the skin of the abdomen and the tail until the lungs develop sometime after hatching.

The Tailed frog *Ascaphus truei* is so called because it has a posterior projection which superficially resembles a tail. It is, however, part of the cloaca, the chamber into which the gut and urino-genital systems empty, so it forms a common exit for both reproductive and excretory matter. The cloacal projection in the Tailed frog is used to insert the sperm into the female during mating, which is unique among frogs. Tailed frogs are voiceless and this is correlated with their life in swift-moving streams where a call would be unheard because of the noise of the water. The tadpoles become attached to rocks soon after hatching by a triangular adhesive organ which prevents them from being carried away by the swift currents. Tailed frogs can endure cold and are usually found in areas where the water temperature does not exceed 40°F (5°C) even on a summer's day. In captivity they need to be kept in a refrigerator. FAMILY: Ascaphidae, ORDER: Anura, CLASS: Amphibia.

AMPHISBAENIDS, or worm-lizards represented by some 125 species in Africa, South America and Mexico. One species of the genus *Blanus* is found in Europe; one *Rhineura* in the United States and several in the West Indies. Three species of *Bipes,* found in Mexico and Lower California, are unique among the amphisbaenids in having diminutive, but well developed forelegs. With this exception all worm-lizards present essentially identical features. They closely resemble earthworms in their long and cylindrical body, with the integument arranged in rings separated by shallow grooves. Their movement, unlike that of snakes or legless lizards, is in a straight line and the animal can move backwards or forwards with equal ease. There are no external ear openings, the eyes are covered with scales and, when visible, appear as dark spots. Only the left lung is present. The exact relationships of worm-lizards are not clear. Although long grouped with reptiles, there is considerable doubt whether these animals actually are lizards or, for that matter, reptiles.

Amphisbaenids are inoffensive and spend their lives in underground burrows, beneath forest litter or in the nests of ants and termites. Association with ant colonies is common, and in parts of South America, the local peoples (which believe the animal to be a venomous snake) refer to it as *mai das saubas* or 'mother of ants'. Little is known of the feeding habits of these animals, examination of the stomach contents revealing little other than ants and termites. Captive examples of the large, tropical American species *Amphisbaena alba,* however, readily accept from a dish shreds of meat mixed with beaten raw egg yolks. The same species will also actively chase and consume live crickets. *Rhineura* feeds on small spiders and earthworms.

Both oviparous and ovoviviparous species are known, but the majority of species probably lay eggs, live births being recorded for only a few African species.

Completely defenceless when exposed, worm-lizards resort to a ruse, often used by animals, of imitating something else. Thus, several species raise the tail from the ground and by waving it about give a reasonable impression of an alert snake. Such behaviour is apparently successful for many native peoples consider the animals venomous or at least aggressive.

Modern worm-lizards appear to have remained essentially unchanged since they first appeared many millions of years ago. The fossil record dates to the Eocene. Then as now, most of them were small animals, seldom more than 1 ft (30 cm) in length. Several species attain a greater size, however. *Amphisbaena alba,* previously mentioned, reaches a length of 18 in (46 cm) as does *A. fuliginosa,* also from South America. *Monopeltis,* an African genus, is considered to be the largest known, attaining a length in excess of 2 ft (60 cm). FAMILY Amphisbaenidae, ORDER: Squamata, CLASS: Reptilia.

AMPHIUMAS, among the largest amphibians in the world, also called 'Conger eels', 'Congo eels or snakes', 'Ditch eels' or 'Lamper eels' depending on the region and individual whim. The same names are applied without much discrimination to other elongated aquatic animals, whether they be true eels, sirens, or true lampreys. To avoid confusion, the scientific name Amphiuma is used as the common name.

The amphiumas are elongated salamanders. The three very similar species are distinct enough from all other salamanders to be placed in a separate family Amphiumidae. Superficially they resemble eels in size, proportions and colour and it is easy to understand how the two could be confused, particularly if seen moving through a mass of weeds. The movements, however, are different. Amphiumas are more apt to crawl slowly and thrash wildly when disturbed.

Amphiuma, North American salamander, almost legless.

Amphiumas have a cylindrical body, averaging about 24 in (60 cm) and may reach 46 in (116 cm). The tail, if undamaged, is approximately $\frac{1}{4}$ the total length and tapers to a point. The most distinctive anatomical feature is the presence of two pairs of small legs, with 1–3 toes according to species, which are totally useless for propulsion. The head is long, pointed and compressed from the top. The colour is dark, uniformly brownish grey or slate grey above and lighter below. In contrast to the eel, there are no gill openings or fins behind the head, and no external gills as in the sirens. Vision is probably very poor, the eyes being very small.

Because of the close similarity of all amphiumas they were formerly considered to belong to one species *Amphiuma means*. Now three species are recognized. The least known is the One-toed amphiuma *Amphiuma pholeter* which was described only in 1964. This is the most degenerate of the family, being the nearest to becoming blind and legless. It does not seem to attain as large a size as the other two. The head is shorter, more rounded, with even smaller eyes. The limbs are proportionally shorter, and have only one digit. It is brownish grey, with little difference in shade from top to bottom but usually there are lighter mottlings. It is presumed that the range of the One-toed amphiuma extends through the swamplands of Florida's west coast. The Two-toed amphiuma *Amphiuma means,* with two toes on each limb, is larger, up to 36 in (90 cm) long. Its dark grey colour changes gradually to the lighter grey below. It ranges along the coasts from Virginia through all of Florida and west through Southern Missis-

sippi. The Three-toed amphiuma *Amphiuma tridactylum,* up to 40 in (100 cm), is usually brownish grey above and lighter grey below, with an abrupt transition between the two. It has three toes on each limb. Its range extends up the Mississippi Valley to the southern border of Illinois and west into eastern Texas.

Amphiumas are found in warm, weedy, quiet bodies of water in the lowlands of southeastern and gulf-coastal plains of the United States and into the Mississippi Valley as far north as Missouri. They are mostly active at night searching for small aquatic animals. Besides soft-bodied prey like worms and insect nymphs, their powerful jaws enable them to crush snails and subdue crayfish. An occasional frog or fish is caught with a surprisingly fast strike. They may occasionally come out on land on wet nights.

Little is known of the reproductive habits, courtship if any and mating procedures being unrecorded but fertilization is internal. In the Two-toed amphiuma fairly large elliptical eggs, $\frac{1}{3}$ in (8 mm) in diameter, are extruded like a row of beads connected by a continuous gelatinous string. The eggs may number 48 or more and are sometimes guarded by the female who stays with them in a sheltered hollow during the long incubation period of several months. The eggs hatch in about five months into 2 in (5 cm) long larvae which metamorphose and lose their external gills when 3 in (7.5 cm). During growth the legs, which start off well developed, fail to keep pace with the rest of the body.

Amphiumas adapt well to captivity, being long-lived and hardy and learning to feed readily from the hand even during the daytime. Nevertheless, they are not very popular

either as public exhibits or as pets. They hardly ever move but tend to fight each other and other animals and occasionally bite when handled. The natural enemies of the amphiuma are the Rainbow snake *Abastor erythrogrammus* and the Mud snake *Farancia abacura*. Both are found in the same area as the amphiuma, the distribution of the Mud snake in particular being practically the same as that of the amphiuma and it may largely depend on amphiumas for food. FAMILY: Amphiumidae, ORDER: Caudata, CLASS: Amphibia.

ANACONDA *Eunectes murinus,* the largest of the non-venomous snake family Boidae. One of the more aquatic boas, it inhabits swamps and slow moving rivers in the northern parts of South America to the east of the Andes. It is the largest of living snakes, for although its length is a little less than that of the Reticulated python of Asia it is proportionately much thicker.

Its reputation as a man-eater is largely undeserved. A large anaconda may be capable of devouring a child but such occurrences are rare. It generally shuns human habitations and preys chiefly on birds and small or medium-sized mammals such as rodents and peccaries. Fish and caimans are also included in its diet.

Like all boas the anaconda is ovoviviparous, the female giving birth to as many as 72 living young, each measuring about 3 ft (1 m) in length. FAMILY: Boidae, ORDER: Squamata, CLASS: Reptilia.

ANAPSIDA, subclass of the Reptilia comprising two orders: the Cotylosauria and the Testudines. The diagnostic anapsid feature is the presence of a complete roofing of bone on the skull behind the orbits. In all other reptilian groups the skull in this region is variously perforated for the passage of jaw muscles. This group includes the oldest and most primitive of all reptiles, the cotylosaurs or 'stem reptiles'. From them all other reptiles evolved. The cotylosaurs are first found as fossils in the Carboniferous and became extinct in the Permian. The tortoises, turtles, and terrapins constituting the Testudines, although preserving the anapsid skull pattern, are separated on many features from their cotylosaur ancestors. The oldest chelonian is of Triassic age.

ANGUID LIZARDS, a family of small to medium-sized lizards usually classified in seven genera with about 75 species. This family comprises standard lizard-like forms and limbless, snake-like ones, presenting a problem in classification. In the skull the temporal arch is complete and the teeth are solid, not hollow, and attached to the inner jaw bone. The tongue is protrusible and can be withdrawn into a case-like sheath. Nearly

Harmless snake-like Scheltopusik lizard.

all anguids have a skin armour of overlapping scales with bony plates beneath them. Many anguids have particularly long tails that can be shed by autotomy, in moments of danger. The lost tail is regenerated in a few weeks, but it never grows as long as the original tail and is supported by an unjointed cartilage bar so autotomy cannot occur again in the regenerated tail.

The distribution of anguids is discontinuous. A number of species are found in Central America and on the Caribbean islands, but many of these have only a small range, and some are so rare they are known only from the original specimens from which they were named. In America the anguids range from British Columbia in the north to Argentina in the south but they are absent from large areas in between. There are only two genera with very few species in Europe, northwest Africa and western and southeast Asia, but amongst these we find the *Slow worm *Anguis fragilis* the best known of the family. There are no anguids in Africa south of the Sahara or in Australia.

Six species of *Ophisaurus* are found in the Old World and five in America. They are relics of a once abundant genus and fossils can be found in places where *Ophisaurus* no longer occurs. The Scheltopusik *O. apodus* with a length of about 3 ft (90 cm) is the most impressive of the genus and of the family and can be found from the northern part of the Balkan peninsula through Asia Minor and the Caucasus to Turkestan. Like all species of *Ophisaurus*, the Scheltopusik is legless, snake-like and its body well armoured with a great number of bony scales. There is a furrow on each side of the body enabling the lizard to move its otherwise rather rigid body sideways. Insects alone are not enough to feed a strong Scheltopusik; it also eats snails and small rodents, crushing these with its powerful jaws. A lot of people fear the Scheltopusik more than any snake and even believe it, incorrectly, to be poisonous. The other *Ophisaurus* species of the Old World live in comparatively restricted areas. The New World Glass snake lives in the central and southern part of Northern America and in Mexico. As far as is known all *Ophisaurus* species lay eggs.

About 30 species of the Alligator lizard *Gerrhonotus* can be found in North and Central America. Their body structure is more primitive than that of the snake-like anguids. In *Gerrhonotus* the limbs are well developed, the head and body are protected by scales. Alligator lizards are ground dwellers, but some species are able climbers making use of their tails. Their food consists of insects which they stalk and seize, leaping at them from a short distance. Alligator lizards may be viviparous or oviparous.

Less well-known are the galliwasps of the genus *Diploglossus*. They are rather shapeless

anguids with small but well developed legs. There are about 30 species in Central America, South America and on a few islands of the West Indies. A number of species have only rarely been found and it is probable that some of the island species have become extinct already, perhaps exterminated through the introduction of predators. The differences in colouration between adult and young is often quite remarkable. The young Brazilian *Diploglossus fasciatus* has striking transverse black and white stripes but in the adult the stripes are lengthwise.

Finally the South American Snake lizard of the genus *Ophiodes* has to be mentioned. There are four species in the open plains south of the Amazon basin. They are very snake-like, the front limbs being absent but one-toed flaps remain of the hind legs. Unlike Glass snakes the Snake lizards have no side furrows.

FAMILY: Anguidae, ORDER: Squamata, CLASS: Reptilia.

ANKYLOSAURS, Cretaceous dinosaurs belonging to the Ornithischia. These quadrupedal herbivores demonstrate the greatest degree of armour plating found in dinosaurs. Some reached a length of 20 ft (6 m) and in all the much flattened head and trunk were protected on their upper surface by a mosaic of bony plates. Commonly the tail had a flexible armour of bony rings and in some species long bony spikes for defence projected from the shoulder and tail regions. The teeth were weak or absent. The group had a world-wide distribution. Well known forms are *Polacanthus* from England and *Nodosaurus* from North America.

ANOLE, American lizard-like reptiles of the family Iguanidae. There are 165 species, of which the best known is the Green anole *Anolis carolinensis*. Anoles, which are also known as American chamaeleons from their ability to change colour rapidly, range from 5–19 in (12·5–47·5 cm) in length. The toes of anoles are armed with small sharp claws and have adhesive pads of minute transverse ridges which enable them to cling to rough and smooth surfaces alike. The Green anole is active in daylight and moves continuously and rapidly searching for insects in bushes and trees. Male anoles have a reddish throat sac which is extended to deter rival males from encroaching on another's territory. FAMILY: Iguanidae, ORDER: Squamata, CLASS: Reptilia.

ANOMOCOELA, amphibians belonging to the suborder Anomocoela with procoelous vertebrae and lacking ribs. The single family Pelobatidae has members in Europe, North America and Asia. They are known as Spadefoot toads because of their ability to burrow using a crescent-shaped horny projec-

tion on the side of the foot with which to dig. The Western American form *Scaphiopus couchi* lives in semi-desert regions and may burrow several feet underground to avoid desiccation. The European spadefoot *Pelobates fuscus* lives in sandy areas and on capture emits a secretion which is said to smell of garlic, hence its German name 'Knoblauchskröte', Garlic toad. ORDER: Anura, CLASS: Amphibia.

ANURA, tailless amphibians, including frogs and toads, which are the most successful of living amphibians, with some 250 genera and around 2,600 species. They are widely distributed throughout temperate and tropical regions except for a number of small islands in the Pacific. Some species live in the inclement conditions of Patagonia and others within the Arctic Circle in Europe.

Living frogs and toads have short squat bodies, large eyes and long hindlimbs. The length of the hindlimb is partially due to the presence of an 'extra joint' formed by the elongation of certain ankle bones. The presence of large hindlimbs is a major difference

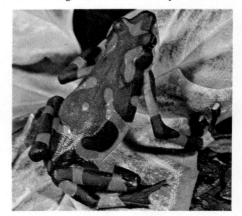

Atelopus varius, member of the Anura.

between the anurans and the tailed amphibians or Caudata, the salamanders and newts, in which the limbs are small and of roughly equal size. The other group of living amphibians, the caecilians or Apoda, are limbless. The distances covered by leaping frogs has been of considerable interest, as in the 'frog-jumping' contests in North America. Tests have shown that smaller frogs can generally jump greater distances relative to their size than the larger frogs. For example the large bullfrog *Rana catesbeiana* can leap a distance equal to nine times its own length, whereas the smaller Sharp-nosed frog *Rana oxyrhyncha* can cover a distance equal to 40 times its own body length.

The anuran vertebral column has usually only nine vertebrae and the first of these has two small areas (facets) which articulate with the hind end of the skull. The last vertebra, termed the sacral, usually bears lateral extensions which articulate with the pelvic girdle. Behind the sacral vertebra is a rod-shaped

Hemisus marmoratus, a digging Anura.

bone, the urostyle, which is thought to be derived from a number of fused, post-sacral, vertebrae. Ribs are usually absent.

The term 'toad' tends to be used in an ambiguous way; it should be restricted to the family Bufonidae, the true toads. Toads are usually more plump and less graceful than frogs and have relatively shorter hindlimbs. They have a large parotid gland just behind the head on either side and the skin frequently has a granular or warty appearance. Frogs lack parotid glands and their skin is fairly smooth.

Anurans are largely dependent on water for reproduction. Fertilization is usually external and the eggs are laid in a gelatinous mass as spawn. The life history usually involves a free-swimming stage, or tadpole, which swims by means of a tail that is lost during metamorphosis. Some anurans have departed from the usual type of life history. For example, Archey's frog *Leiopelma archeyi* (family Ascaphidae) lays its eggs under stones, the larvae developing within the egg capsule, omitting the free-swimming stage and hatching as miniature frogs.

Mating in frogs and toads involves amplexus, or gripping of the female by the male, so that the sperm may be shed onto the eggs as they leave the female. Frogs may remain in amplexus for a number of days and a single male may undergo amplexus with a number of females at different times. Anurans often lay large numbers of eggs and a single female Marine toad *Bufo marinus* (family Bufonidae) may produce as many as 35,000 eggs. In unmated females the eggs are usually resorbed. Anurans often develop secondary sexual characteristics, that is, features which apart from the structure of the male and female reproductive system serve to distinguish the sexes. Generally the females are larger than the males. The males usually have stouter forelimbs than the females and the male forelimb is often specially modified to grasp the female during amplexus.

A characteristic of frogs and toads is the presence of a tympanic membrane on either side of the head, behind the eye. This is sensitive to air-borne vibrations and performs much the same function as the ear-drum in mammals and is correlated with the ability of frogs and toads to produce sounds. The Caudates and apodans are generally voiceless and lack a tympanic membrane, but are thought to perceive vibrations in the sub-stratum either through the lower jaw or the forelimbs. The voice in anurans also tends to

be a secondary sexual characteristic since it is usually more fully developed in the male than in the female. The sounds are produced by a well developed vocal apparatus and are often amplified by the resonance of large vocal sacs. The calls of anurans differ in pitch, duration, frequency and harmonics and each species has its own particular call, although the sounds produced by closely related species are often very similar. The call of the male is largely used to attract the female at breeding time but may also be used to establish a territory. The male bullfrog takes up a 'calling station' each night at a particular spot. His call serves to warn others of his territory. Occasionally frogs which breed in spring also call at other times of the year. The Squirrel frog *Hyla squirella* (family Hylidae) has a distinctive call when the rains come in autumn, so is often termed the Rain frog. Not all frogs and toads have a voice and the Striped mountain toad *Bufo rosei,* of South Africa, has neither voice nor tympanic membrane. The Tailed frog *Ascaphus truei* (family Ascaphidae) which inhabits swift-moving mountain streams is also silent.

One of the largest anurans is the Roccoco

Dicroglossus pictus.

toad *Bufo paracnemis* of Brazil which is 10 in (25 cm) long, whereas the tiny Grass frog *Hyla ocularis* is about $\frac{3}{4}$ in (1·8 cm) in length.

The anurans have a long geological history. They were probably in existence in the Carboniferous period 340 million years ago and can be traced back with certainty 230 million years to the Triassic form *Triadobatrachus* (=*Protobatrachus*). This had a skull similar to that of modern frogs but the trunk was longer and ribs were present. *Vieraella* from the early Jurassic, 180 million years ago, had a skeleton remarkably similar to that of the modern forms and most modern anuran families seem to have been in existence since the Cretaceous, 130 million years ago. This suggests that modern anurans have evolved from long-bodied forms but unfortunately we can say little of the very early ancestry of the anurans, which is true also of the caudates and apodans. This makes it extremely difficult to decide whether the anurans, caudates and apodans are closely related to each other or whether any two are closer to each other than to a third. Current opinion favours the view that the three modern amphibian groups have probably evolved from a common ancestor and should be considered as a natural group, the Lissamphibia.

The classification of frogs and toads has

always presented problems. The feature which seems to be most useful is the structure of the vertebrae. On this basis it is generally agreed there are five anuran suborders with 12 families.

It is generally supposed that the families Ascaphidae, Discoglossidae and Pipidae are the most primitive. ORDER: Anura, CLASS: Amphibia.

APODA, or caecilians, limbless worm-like amphibians which burrow in the ground in tropical countries. See caecilians.

ARCHOSAURIA, a subclass of the Reptilia sometimes referred to as the 'Ruling reptiles' because of their dominance of the land faunas of the Mesozoic. The group comprises five orders: the Thecodontia from which all other archosaurs and birds evolved, the Saurischia and Ornithischia together including all dinosaurs, the Pterosauria which took to the air, and the Crocodilia.

In such a large and diverse group it is difficult to select diagnostic characters but archosaurs have in common a skull with two openings on each side behind the orbits for the passage of jaw muscles, and teeth that are set in sockets. Bipedal locomotion is a noted feature in several separate evolutionary lines and a number of forms are armoured. The

group was primitively carnivorous but some descendant lines evolved herbivorous dentitions.

The archosaurs originated in the Permian, reached their zenith in the Mesozoic and then suffered wholesale extinction, the only order to survive into the Age of Mammals being the Crocodilia.

ASP *Vipera aspis,* also known as the Aspic viper or June viper, of southern Europe, looks like the European adder or viper except that the tip of its snout is turned up, making a spike. The name has been misapplied to snakes elsewhere. See cobra. FAMILY: Viperidae, ORDER: Squamata, CLASS: Reptilia.

ATELOPODIDAE, a small family of frogs found in Central and South America. They are contained in the suborder Procoela and are most closely related to the toads (Bufonidae). They are distinguished from toads by the structure of their shoulder girdle; the two halves, instead of overlapping at the front as they do in toads, are fused down the midline, while another part of the shoulder girdle, the sternum, is missing.

There are only two genera, *Atelopus* and *Brachycephalus,* the former comprising about 25 species which are widespread in

Hylarana albilabris, a little Anura.

The Anura *Phrynobatrachus plicatus* is a frog that looks like a treefrog.

Central and South America while the single species of *Brachycephalus, B. ephippium,* is found in southern Brazil.

Externally also they are readily distinguished from toads, many of them having long bodies with very thin long legs. In some species the snout is beak-like while in others it is square, as though the tip had been cut off. The pupil of the eye is horizontal and the ear disc is not visible.

The skin is poisonous and many species of *Atelopus* are brightly coloured. Zetek's frog *A. zeteki* from Panama is golden yellow with black spots and, perhaps because of its poison, is quite fearless, making no attempt to escape when approached. It is active during the day and its colour makes it very conspicuous. The Green mosaic frog *A. cruciger,* from Venezuela, on the other hand, it patterned with green and is well camouflaged as it sits on the mossy banks of streams.

A. stelzneri from Uruguay is black with orange hands and feet. When frightened it suddenly bends its head and legs backwards displaying its brightly coloured hands and feet. This warns its attacker of its poisonous nature. In this species the female, as well as the male is able to call. The eggs are laid in temporary rain pools and the tadpoles hatch out after only 24 hours.

The Gold frog *Brachycephalus ephippium* is a remarkable little frog. When fully grown it is only about $\frac{3}{4}$ in (20 mm) long, and only one of the fingers on each hand is well developed, the others being reduced to small lumps. Two of the toes on each foot are similarly reduced. It has a short, toad-like body with large bony knobs behind the eyes. It also has a large bony plate set in the skin of its back. This fits across the back like a saddle and is fused to

A pair of brilliantly coloured frogs *Atelopus varius* of tropical America.

the underlying vertebrae. Its function is uncertain but it is probably protective because this frog moves very slowly. Its skin is smooth except over the bony plate and is brilliant orange above and chrome yellow below. Its eyes, although not particularly large, are very conspicuous since they are completely black. The tadpoles of this species are similarly a bright orange colour but are very much larger than the adult.

The adults live on the forest floor under leaves and fallen tree trunks in the mountain forests of southern Brazil, coming out in large numbers in rainy weather. ORDER: Anura, CLASS: Amphibia.

AXOLOTL *Ambystoma mexicanum*, neotenous larva of the Mole salamander, is confined to certain lakes around Mexico city. It measures 4–7 in (10–17·5 cm) in length and is usually black or dark brown with black spots, but white or pale pink albino forms are common. The legs and feet are relatively small and weak while the tail is long. A fin runs from the back of the head along the animal's back to the tail and then under the tail. Breathing is by three feathery gills on either side just behind the head and immediately in front of the forelimbs. During mating the male attracts the female by an elaborate courtship display as he secretes certain chemicals from abdominal glands and makes violent movements of the tail, thought to serve in dispersing the chemicals. Sperm is deposited in a packet or spermatophore which the female picks up from the bottom with her cloaca. Fertilization is therefore internal. The female lays 200–600 eggs in April-May and the young hatch 2–3 weeks later, reaching their maximum length by the winter when they hibernate. They eventually become sexually mature and are able to breed while still in a larval condition. That is, they are neotenous. The axolotl was assigned to a separate genus *Siredon* until it was discovered that under certain conditions it could lose its external gills and larval characteristics and metamorphose into an adult salamander. The neoteny of the axolotl seems to be due to a deficiency of iodine in the water.

In fact the word 'axolotl' is Mexican for 'water sport' and the animal is eaten as a delicacy.

In some instances the term axolotol may be

The axolotl can be made to turn into a typical salamander.

This is what the axolotl looks like when made to 'grow up'.

used in a more general way for the neotenous larvae of other salamanders. For example, the larvae of the Tiger salamander *Ambystoma tigrinum*, which develop in cold water at high altitudes, fail to metamorphose and are often referred to as the 'axolotl' of the Rocky Mountains.

The axolotl keeps well in captivity but must have moving prey and will ignore still dead food. Axolotls cannot usually be kept together however, since they are liable to bite off each other's gills, pieces of tail or feet. FAMILY: Ambystomatidae, ORDER: Candata, CLASS: Amphibia.

Atelopus varius ambulatorius.

B

BANDY-BANDY *Vermicella annulata,* a small venomous snake found throughout most parts of continental Australia, from the wet coastal forests to the central deserts. Up to 3 ft (0·9 m) long the bandy-bandy is a slender, small-headed snake with up to 70 alternate black and white bands along its length. It is a burrowing snake which forages above ground at night, feeding on insects, small lizards and especially Blind snakes. It is, however, not regarded as dangerous to humans or domestic animals because it has small fangs and a mild venom. When threatened the bandy-bandy exhibits a distinctive behaviour pattern in which it throws its body into a series of stiffly-held loops. FAMILY: Elapidae, ORDER: Squamata, CLASS: Reptilia.

BASILISKS, lizards of the genus *Basiliscus* containing several species inhabiting Central America and ranging as far north as central Mexico. They live along the banks of the smaller rivers or streams where they bask during the day or sleep at night on bushes that overhang the water. Basilisks are slender lizards with long slim toes and tail and the males are often adorned with crests.

Speed is the chief means of snatching up food (insects and small rodents or birds) and escaping enemies. When attempting to escape basilisks head for water and run across it. A fringe of scales along the lengthy rear toes provides support as they dash over the surface. Basilisks are known as tetetereche in some parts of their range as this resembles the sound they make when running on water. Another name is the Jesus Cristo lizard for the ability to 'walk on the water'. As its speed slackens, however, the lizard begins to sink and must swim in conventional manner like any other lizard.

Most colourful and largest of the basilisks is the rare Green crested basilisk *Basiliscus plumbifrons* of Costa Rica. The male has a large, ornamental crest on its head, another along its back and one on the tail, the use of which is not fully known unless it is used to threaten other males.

Basilisks hatch from $\frac{1}{2}-\frac{3}{4}$ in (c. 2 cm), nearly round eggs that may be white or brown and are buried by the female in damp sand

Bandy-bandy, relatively harmless Australian snake.

near stream banks. Hatching takes 18–30 days (normally 20–24 days) and the tiny youngsters are replicas of the adults except they have no crests. Basilisks are normally some shade of brown with white or yellow bands or mottling. In the Green basilisks, the young are brown with only a trace of greenish tint to the lighter markings on neck and sides.

The basilisk, South American reptile, named after the legendary monster of Europe, best known for its running on water.

They turn green after approaching $\frac{1}{3}$ of the adult size, and the males begin rapidly developing a crest when $\frac{2}{3}$ grown.

In the Banded basilisk *Basiliscus vittatus,* the colouration is variable. It is dark brown in the daytime, but when resting at night on branches over streams, the lateral bands are vivid yellow or white. In captivity, the basilisk seems to lose its ability to undergo such drastic colour change between night and day. No such colour change ability has been noted in captivity with the Green basilisk, and it appears to be a vivid green at all times. FAMILY: Iguanidae, ORDER: Squamata, CLASS: Reptilia.

BATRACHIA, an obsolete name for the Amphibia.

BLIND SNAKES or Worm snakes, are among the most primitive of living snakes. The 300 species are grouped into two families, the Typhlopidae, which contains the vast majority of the species, and the Anomalepididae. Blind snakes occur throughout the tropical and sub-tropical zones and extend also into South Africa and the southern region of Australia, but not Tasmania. They have reached numerous oceanic islands. All Blind snakes are harmless; most are quite small and worm-like, though a few reach a length of 2 ft (61 cm) or more. Even the longest specimens seldom have a girth greater than finger width, apart from a few African species which may have a diameter of up to 1 in (2·5 cm). Blind snakes have poorly developed teeth, on the mobile

Tail end of Blind snake *Typhlops*, showing spine.

upper jaw only. Vestiges of the hindlimbs are sometimes present.

Blind snakes feed on a variety of small soil animals, such as worms, termites, and ants and their eggs and larvae. They are nocturnal and live underground, or under large flat stones, rotting logs or stumps, or in termite nests. The Blind snake is adapted for burrowing. The head is small and narrow, and unlike most snakes, has no movable bones in the cranial part of the skull. The snout is blunt and projecting, with a tiny mouth on the ventral surface, so the whole head is a most efficient structure for forcing a passage through the soil. There is little change in diameter throughout the length of the body. Blind snakes do not develop broad scales on the ventral surface of the body, which in other land snakes assist in locomotion. Instead their firm, round body is covered with small, smooth, highly polished scales that offer a minimum of resistance to the soil as the animal forces its way through. Further, the tail is very short and ends in a small, sharp spine, which is pushed into the soil and provides a purchase when the animal is moving forward. If a Blind snake is caught it will struggle to escape, and in so doing may press the tail spine into its captor's hand. This will inflict no more than a very mild and perfectly harmless prick, but has given rise to the belief among some peoples that Blind snakes are dangerous and have a sting in the tail.

The eyes of Blind snakes are small and very poorly developed, and each appears as a dark spot covered over by a transparent scale. Probably they can only distinguish between light and darkness. Many Blind snakes, and especially the females, have a pair of large scent glands in the tail from which, when disturbed, they produce an evil-smelling liquid. Its primary purpose is probably to attract members of the opposite sex, though it can also be used as a weapon of defence. FAMILIES: Typhlopidae, Anomalepididae, ORDER: Squamata, CLASS: Reptilia.

BOAS, non-venomous snakes that bear their young alive. See Boidae.

BOIDAE, a non-venomous family of snakes containing about 80 species of boas, pythons and their relatives. The family is generally considered to be primitive, having retained several features found in lizards but absent in the more advanced snakes such as the colubrids and · vipers. A pelvic girdle is nearly always present, although much reduced, and the hindlimbs are usually present, at least in the male, in the form of claw-like cloacal spurs. Boids also retain the coronoid bone in the lower jaw, another lizard feature that is absent in higher snakes. Most boids have two functional lungs of which the right is much larger than the left. In this respect they

Royal python hatching from egg.

are intermediate between the lizards, which usually have two lungs of equal size, and the higher snakes in which the left lung has disappeared.

There are four subfamilies: the Loxoceminae, Pythoninae, Boinae and Bolyeriinae.

The Loxoceminae contains a single species, the Loxocemus python *Loxocemus bicolor,* a small semi-burrowing inhabitant of the lowlands of Central America. Earlier zoologists placed this controversial snake either with the Sunbeam snake *Xenopeltis*

unicolor or in a family of its own but recent research suggests its affinities lie with the boids.

The seven genera that form the Pythoninae inhabit the warmer regions of the Old World from Africa to Australia. They differ from other boids in having a separate supraorbital bone in the skull, a feature unknown in any other group of snakes. All pythons lay eggs, as many as 100 in a clutch in some species, whereas all boas bring forth their young alive.

The boas, subfamily Boinae, are divided into 15 genera most of which inhabit the warmer regions of the New World. The four genera occurring outside the Americas are the Sand boas *Eryx,* of northern Africa and western Asia, the Pacific boas *Candoia,* of New Guinea and the Pacific islands, and the two genera *Acrantophis* and *Sanzinia* of Madagascar. Because of their disjunct distribution some experts consider the boas to represent three distinct subfamilies of separate origin whose apparent similarity is due to parallelism rather than to a common ancestral stock.

The fourth subfamily, the Bolyeriinae, contains two species, *Bolyeria multocarinata* and *Casarea dussumieri,* both of which are found only on Round Island, a small island near Mauritius in the Indian Ocean. They are

An arborial member of the genus *Boa,* Cook's tree boa *Boa cooki.*

the most advanced of the Boidae, having completely lost their pelvic girdle and hindlimbs. In addition their left lung is much more reduced than that of any other member of the family. They are believed by some to be descended from the forerunners of the higher snakes.

Probably the best known boa is the Boa constrictor *Boa constrictor* an inhabitant of Central America, tropical South America and the Lesser Antilles. Primarily a surface dweller, it may be found in a variety of habitats ranging from tropical rain-forest to semi-desert regions. It is divided into eight subspecies, each having its own area of distribution. Many stories have been written about the great size and prowess of the Boa constrictor but in reality it is only the fifth largest of living snakes, having a maximum length of a little over 18 ft (5·5 m). Its food consists mainly of small mammals and the occasional bird and lizard. Like most boas its prey is killed by constriction before being swallowed whole.

The habitat of the boids is varied, ranging from arboreal to fossorial and semi-aquatic. Some species, such as the Boa constrictor, the Rainbow boa *Epicrates cenchria* and the Royal python *Python regius,* are surface dwellers. These tend to inhabit scrubland and wooded regions where their blotched or reticulate pattern forms an excellent camouflage. There are seven species of *Epicrates*, six of which inhabit the West Indies. The only mainland member of this genus, the Rainbow boa is primarily a surface dweller feeding on small rodents, but it has been known to climb trees and devour bats. It rarely exceeds 4 ft (122 cm) in length and is called the Rainbow boa because of the bright green and blue iridescent sheen reflected by its scales.

The arboreal species include the South American Tree boas *Corallus*, the Malagasy

Sand boa *Eryx jaculus.*

This python clearly shows the notch in the upper lip through which the tongue is protruded.

tree boa *Sanzinia madagascariensis* and the Papuan tree python *Chondropython viridis*. These are often blotched like the surface dwellers but two species, the Emerald tree boa *Corallus caninus,* of South America, and the adult of the Papuan tree python have acquired an effective camouflage in their bright green colour with whitish markings. This is an excellent example of parallelism, where two unrelated species acquire a similar appearance as an adaptation to a similar environment. These two species are also alike inasmuch as the young differ from the adults in being yellow or pinkish brown with darker markings.

All arboreal boids have prehensile tails as do many of the surface dwellers. Some species such as the Asiatic Rock python *Python molurus* appear to be at home in several different habitats, spending much of their time in or near water yet retaining their ability to climb trees.

The Ground boas *Tropidophis* number 15 species most of which inhabit the West

Royal python curled in a ball, its defensive posture.

Indies. They are ground dwellers, feeding on frogs and lizards. The Cuban ground boa *Tropidophis semicinctus* possesses the defensive habit of voluntarily bleeding at the mouth. At the same time the eyes become ruby red.

The anaconda *Eunectes murinus* is the most aquatic member of the family, inhabiting swamps in the jungles of the northern parts of South America.

Many of the smaller boids are burrowing or semi-burrowing. The Sand boas, the Rosy boas *Lichanura,* the Rubber boa *Charina bottae* and the Calabar ground python *Calabaria reinhardtii* fall into this category. They are all small, rarely exceeding 3 ft (91 cm) in length and all have a short thick tail. They spend their time burrowing in sand, loose earth or forest litter. The Rubber boa inhabits western North America where it preys on small mammals and lizards. When threatened it defends itself by rolling up into a tight ball with its head concealed beneath the coils. Its short, blunt tail, which bears a superficial

resemblance to its head, is then raised above the ball and waved about to distract the enemy from the more vulnerable parts of its body.

The five remaining New World genera are all small, burrowing or semi-burrowing, and little is known about their habits. One species, *Exiliboa placata* was not discovered until 1967.

The ten known species of Sand Boa, genus *Eryx,* of North Africa, southern Europe and western Asia, rarely exceed 3 ft (91 cm) in length and inhabit desert and semi-desert regions. They are burrowers with short thick tails and feed mainly on lizards.

Boids prey chiefly on small mammals although most species will also take birds and reptiles. Most pythons and a few boas are provided with special sensory labial pits on the scales bordering the mouth. These are believed to act as heat-detectors, in the same way as the loreal pits of the pit-vipers, enabling the snake to locate prey which is too well camouflaged to be seen. In nocturnal species, such as the Cuban boa *Epicrates angulifer,* which feeds mainly on bats, these pits are particularly advantageous.

The burrowing species are not endowed with labial pits and their eyes which are of little use in a subterranean habitat are reduced in size. In locating their prey they rely more on their modified inner ear which, as in all snakes, is adapted to pick up vibrations passing through the ground. Their prey consists of small mammals and lizards.

The majority of boids rely on their cryptic colouration for protection. The adult Cook's boa *Corallus enydris cookii* bears a superficial resemblance to the deadly fer-de-lance *Bothrops atrox,* thereby probably discouraging some of its predators. Some ground dwellers, such as the Royal python *Python regius* and burrowers, like the Rubber boa, protect themselves from predators by rolling up into a ball with the head concealed by the coils of the body. See anaconda and pythons. FAMILY: Boidae, ORDER: Squamata, CLASS: Reptilia.

BOOMSLANG *Dispholidus typus,* large African Tree snake with three enlarged grooved fangs in the upper jaw below the eye. It is the most venomous of the back-fanged snakes and its bite can prove fatal to man. 'Boomslang' is Afrikaans for 'Tree snake'.

The boomslang averages $4\frac{1}{2}$ ft (1·4 m) in length. It has a short head with very large eyes and a slender body and tail covered above with narrow, oblique, strongly keeled scales. It is common throughout the well-wooded parts of Africa south of the Sahara but is absent from the rain-forest and semi-desert regions.

Towards the end of the dry season the female boomslang lays 5–16 elongate eggs of

Boomslang *Dispholidus typus,* the dreaded large African Tree snake.

about 1 in (25 mm) in length. The newly hatched young are about 15 in (38 cm) in length.

The boomslang hunts by day and may stay in a tree or group of trees for several days if food is plentiful. Its diet consists largely of chamaeleons, but during the nesting season many fledgling birds and eggs are eaten; adult birds are rarely caught. Lizards, frogs and rats are also devoured but other snakes are rarely attacked.

If disturbed, the boomslang will always try to escape at speed, but when cornered it inflates its throat with air, giving the impression of an enormous head, then makes savage lunges at its aggressor with gaping jaws. Its venom is extremely toxic, destroying the fibrinogen in the blood and causing

Another 'boomslang', the mangrove tree snake.

extensive internal bleeding. Because the amount of venom produced by a boomslang is very small, the specific anti-venom is in short supply. FAMILY: Colubridae, ORDER: Squamata, CLASS: Reptilia.

BOX TURTLE *Terrapene,* an animal like a European garden tortoise living in the eastern United States, where it is native, from New England to Florida and Texas. Its peculiarity is that the shell on the underside is hinged across the middle and the two halves can be brought up in front and behind to completely close the shell after the head and legs have been withdrawn.

It is reported that some hounds used in deer hunting and gundogs used for quail become addicted to Box turtles. A hound may find a Box turtle and carry it around instead of tracking deer, or a gundog may 'point' a Box turtle instead of a bird. Some dogs will habitually seek out the turtles, bring them home and bury them, but without doing them harm. FAMILY: Emydidae, ORDER: Testudines, CLASS: Reptilia.

BRONTOSAURUS, well known and much figured gigantic dinosaur. Complete skeletons of *Brontosaurus* have been excavated from the Upper Jurassic of the western United States. This huge quadrupedal herbivore had a total length of some 68 ft (21 m) and a calculated live weight in excess of 35 tons (36 tons). Its head was disproportionately small, its vertebral column massive, for supporting the huge body, and the limbs pillar-like. Recent evidence suggests that *Brontosaurus* and its allies spent much of their life on dry land and were not the lagoon dwelling monsters so often figured. ORDER: Saurischia, CLASS: Reptilia.

BULLFROGS, large frogs the males of which have a call that has been likened to the bellowing of a bull. In different parts of the

world the name refers to a particular species: the American bullfrog is *Rana catesbeiana;* the African bullfrog is *Pyxicephalus adspersus* and the Indian bullfrog is *Rana tigrina.* These are only related to one another in that they all belong to the family Ranidae or true frogs. Small frogs have a highpitched call, large frogs have a lowpitched one which is also louder.

The American bullfrog grows to 8 in (20 cm) the females being larger than the males. It is robust and powerful, a greenish drab colour with small tubercles on the skin, strictly aquatic preferring still pools with shallows and plenty of driftwood or roots along the banks. The jumping ability of American bullfrogs is well-known and a contest is held every year in Calaveras to commemorate Mark Twain's famous tale "The Jumping Frog of Calaveras County". In fact the bullfrogs' jump, about 6 ft (2 m), is easily beaten by smaller, more athletic species of frogs from South Africa.

American bullfrogs emerge from hibernation in May and breeding lasts until July, the males calling from the edges of lakes and ponds. The tadpole reaches a length of 6 in (15 cm) and it is three years before it changes into a froglet. The adults eat anything of the right size, including mice, lizards, birds, fish, salamanders and other frogs, even those of the same species. Bullfrogs are easily caught by dangling a piece of cloth on a fish hook in front of them, and the meat of the large hindlimbs is considered a delicacy.

The African bullfrog is up to 9 in (22·5 cm), the male being larger than the female, which is unusual. It is plump and olivecoloured with many longitudinal folds in the skin. The mouth is enormous, reaching back to the shoulders and there are three tooth-like projections on the lower jaw. African bullfrogs burrow, shuffling backwards into the soil and remaining buried, with only the tip of the snout exposed. Like their American

counterpart they will eat anything and are well-known for their cannibalism. They are dormant during the dry season emerging to breed at the beginning of the rains when they congregate in shallow pools. The calling of the males and the laying of eggs occurs in the daytime and the frogs are not disturbed by intruders. In fact, they are aggressive and will jump at intruders with gaping jaws and bite viciously. The males are sometimes reported to remain with the developing tadpoles and protect them. It is more likely that they are in fact feeding on them and adults have often been found with their stomachs full of tadpoles. The tadpoles are small and gregarious swimming around in large swarms. The young frogs which are about 1 in (2·5 cm) long emerge after about seven weeks and there are often enormous numbers around pools. On such occasions the young bullfrogs immediately start to eat each other.

African bullfrogs are eaten by pelicans and Nile monitors and are also considered a great delicacy by the local people in many regions.

The Indian bullfrog is a similar olive colour and reaches a length of about 6 in (15 cm). It is shy and solitary and never found far from water, preferring ditches and marshes. In most areas it breeds at the beginning of the monsoon.

They are eaten in parts of their range but in Pakistan, at least, the idea of doing so is abhorrent. There the belief is that if a woman spits in the mouth of a bullfrog and puts it back where she found it she will not become pregnant.

In South America a large species of *Leptodactylus,* not a member of the Ranidae is sometimes referred to as the South American bullfrog. FAMILY: Ranidae, ORDER: Anura, CLASS: Amphibia.

BULL SNAKES *Pituophis,* common, nonpoisonous snakes of North and Central America commonly about 6 ft (2 m) long. Although commonest in rocky and semidesert country, they also frequent farming areas of states such as Iowa and Nebraska and may be encountered basking in the sun on roads. Bull snakes are attractively patterned with dark brownish diamond marks on a beige background. The Western bull snake *Pituophis catenifer* and its relative *P. sayi* are important destroyers of harmful rodents such as Pocket gophers, Ground squirrels, rats and mice which are killed by constriction or pressure. They also eat many eggs of groundnesting game birds including quail and duck. Bull snakes mimic rattlesnakes by vibrating the tail, at the same time making a whirring noise in the throat.

This mimetic display is only part of the

The bullfrog of North America, so named from its bellowing call and its heavy build.

The Indian common bullfrog serves as food for other animals as well as human beings. It is also used in biology classes and laboratories in southern Asia.

story. Bullsnakes have a special membrane, the epiglottis, in front of the glottis and, when air is forced past it, it vibrates like the reed in a wood-wind instrument. The note produced is staccato—a hiss amplified by the membranous flap. It has been compared with the bellowing of a bull, which is probably an exaggeration. The presence of an epiglottis is unusual in snakes. The 'bellow' is accompanied by a rapid vibration of the tip of the tail, a trick found in many snakes in moments of excitement. When the tail is near dry leaves or twigs this produces a rustling sound resembling to some degree the rattle of a rattlesnake. The effect on the human observer, if not on small animals, is enhanced by the bullsnake's habit of trying to look ferocious by blowing up its body, writhing and coiling and making sham strikes with the head.

A large number of snakes give audible warnings, as well as signalling displeasure by visual display. The commonest sound is the well-known hiss, which at times can be very penetrating, or loud as in the puff adder, said to make a noise like a horse blowing air through its lips. Yet snakes have no true voice and are deaf as well.

Instrumental music of a more remarkable kind is produced by two other North American snakes, the Sonoran coral snake *Micruroides euryxanthus* and the Western hook-nosed snake *Ficimia cana*. These draw air into the cloaca and expel it rhythmically at second-intervals, making a low popping sound. FAMILY: Colubridae, ORDER: Squamata, CLASS: Reptilia.

BUSHMASTER *Lachesis muta,* the longest of the New World venomous snakes inhabiting the northern portions of South America, Trinidad and ranging northward into Central America to Costa Rica. Although it does not attain the volume or weight of the largest rattlesnakes, the bushmaster can exceed 12 ft (3·6 m) in length. It is the only egg-laying (oviparous) species of the New World Pit vipers, and apparently the female incubates the eggs.

Large fangs inject considerable venom deep into prey which is usually held fast, whereas most viperine snakes, for reasons of safety, bite and then release their prey, to follow it to where it dies. The tail terminates in an incomplete, silent, small 'rattle.' The bushmaster may be locally plentiful throughout its patchy range but is seldom seen due to its retiring nature. It prefers to remain concealed but if unduly disturbed, it has a lengthy striking reach. This, plus its peculiar manner of striking, may bring it ever closer to the intruder rather than farther away. Bites are, however, not as common with this species as among the fer-de-lance of the same areas. In captivity, the bushmaster is keenly aware of its surroundings and its quiet, almost lethargic appearance is deceptive. FAMILY: Crotalidae, ORDER: Squamata, CLASS: Reptilia.

C

CAECILIANS, long-bodied, limbless amphibians without common names which superficially resemble large earthworms. They are invariably blind and the eyes are covered with opaque skin, or in some cases by the bones of the skull. There is a small sensory tentacle just in front of each eye, lying in a sac from which it can be protruded. The tentacle has two ducts which communicate with Jacobson's organ, a sensory area adjacent to the nasal cavity. There is no tympanic membrane and it is likely that caecilians 'hear' by picking up vibrations in the ground via their lower jaw. Caecilians move, like snakes, by sinuous lateral undulations of the body. Many are able to burrow quite rapidly and the majority spend most of their time below ground level. A number of species are, however, aquatic. Caecilians vary considerably in size. The largest *Caecilia thompsoni*, from Central Colombia, reaches a length of 55 in (139·7 cm), the smallest is *Hypogeophis brevis*, from the Seychelles in the Indian Ocean, $4\frac{1}{2}$ in (11·2 cm) long. The maximum diameter recorded for any caecilian is 1 in (2·5 cm).

The body of caecilians is divided by a number of folds in the skin which give a ringed appearance, as in an earthworm. Many species bear small scales in pockets just below the epidermis. The scales are small, rounded and composed of a large number of plates. The presence of scales in the caecilians is considered to be a primitive character since the ancestors of the modern amphibians had scales although all other living amphibians are scaleless.

In the majority of caecilians the hind end is short and rounded, but a few species have a small 'tail'. The vent may be a longitudinal, circular or transverse opening. Externally the sexes cannot be separated but the male has an intromittent organ, a modified portion of the gut which can be everted. Fertilization is therefore internal. Some species, such as *Ichthyophis*, lay eggs in cavities in the mud or among rocks close to water. The female usually coils around the developing eggs. The larvae develop within the egg capsule and although gills are present these are resorbed before hatching. Others lay eggs which develop into free-swimming larvae with external gills. In other species the eggs are retained and develop within the mother, some species producing live young which have developed outside the egg-capsule within the mother.

The left lung in caecilians is very small, the right one is large and long. Respiration is probably also through the skin which is well supplied with dermal glands that keep it moist. The skull, which is very hard and compact, consists of a few large bones, its structure related to the burrowing habit. The lower jaw has a large jaw muscle, and the jaw is opened by raising the skull rather than by dropping the lower jaw. Ribs are present but there is no trace of limbs or limb girdles.

Little is known of the biology of caecilians since they are often difficult to find and have only infrequently been kept in captivity. They are apparently carnivorous and feed on earthworms and small insects, especially termites. They need moist surroundings and are usually drab in colour although some have a little colour. *Rhinatrema*, for example, may have a vivid yellow strip along the side of the body.

The 158 species of caecilians are distributed throughout the warm-temperate regions of the Old and the New World from sea level to around 6,000 ft (2,000 m). They are virtually unknown as fossils.
ORDER: Apoda (or Gymnophiona), CLASS: Amphibia.

CAIMAN LIZARD *Dracaena guianensis*, 3–4 ft (90–120 cm) long, lives along both brackish and freshwater shorelines of Brazilian and Guiana waterways. Superficially it resembles the caiman of that area, its enlarged dorsal scales looking like the raised osteoderms on crocodilians. It feeds mainly on molluscs, crushing these between its powerful jaws armed with large, oval crushing rear teeth, the mollusc being held in place by the tongue and muscular gum-folds that enclose the teeth.

Although these lizards may locate and retrieve their prey underwater, unlike the crocodilians they devour their food on shore (in captivity, at least). FAMILY: Teiidae, ORDER: Squamata, CLASS: Reptilia.

A typical caecilian, legless amphibian.

CAIMANS, tropical cousins of the alligator, in the 100 million year old crocodilian order. Except in scientific publications the caiman is usually erroneously called an alligator. Few people would buy a caiman skin handbag, so hide dealers simply use the skin of the caiman and the name of the more widely known alligator. Live baby South American Spectacled caimans, *Caiman crocodylus crocodylus*, imported into the United States for the pet trade, are sold as alligators also.

Caimans as a group are smaller in size than the other crocodilians but possess the same general characteristics. The caiman's powerful tail, lashing from side to side, propels him through water at a rapid rate. The back has a tough hide reinforced by bony plates. The throat contains a fleshy flap that can be closed to permit breathing at the water's surface with only the tip of the nose showing. The nostrils have external valves and the eyes are doubly protected by eye lids and a movable, clear membrane. The teeth of the lower jaw fit into pits in the upper jaw when the jaws are closed.

The Smooth-fronted caiman, *Paleosuchus trigonatus*, and the Dwarf caiman *Paleosuchus palpebrosus*, from the Amazon, are the smallest of the caimans. To protect their bodies from rapids in the swift waters they inhabit, the bony plates in the armour of these small creatures extend down to the belly. As an adaptation for survival against modern man's destruction the armour of these caimans is more effective than the awesome jaws of a crocodile because it renders the skin useless for the world's hide industries.

Caimans occur only in the western hemisphere. South America contains most of the eight species of caiman. The huge Black caiman *Melanosuchus niger* reaches a length of 15 ft (4·6 m) in the Amazon basin and Guiana region. Central America is the home of the Dusky caiman, *Caiman crocodylus fuscus*.

The Spectacled caiman from the Amazon and Orinoco regions has been introduced into the swamps of the southern United States and has survived. Most people, after they have brought their exotic baby caiman, decide the animal is more than they can handle, and release it. Evidently the caiman colonies in the United States represent these released babies.

The potential life span of the caiman can approach 40 years. Most caimans reach sexual maturity at a length of 5 or 6 ft (1·5 – 1·8 m). It is rare if one caiman reaches adult size from an average hatch of two dozen young. There are many predators that

Black caiman, one of the eight species of crocodilian peculiar to South America.

A spectacled caiman.

Western red-backed salamander *Plethodon vehiculum*, of North America, up to 12 cm long, ranges from British Columbia southwards to western Oregon.

eat caiman eggs. Turtles, rodents, crocodilians and birds take a heavy toll of eggs and young.

Mating occurs with the male mounting the female in the water and twisting his tail beneath hers to accomplish a union. Approximately one month after conception the female builds a nest close to a stream, composed of decaying leaves and branches. The nest is shaped into a mound by the female using her feet to throw the rotting debris while gradually backing around the nest. The eggs are laid only a few inches deep in the mound. The female repairs any damage to the nest and keeps the rotting vegetation and eggs damp by constantly crawling from the water to the top of the mound. The heat from the decaying vegetation keeps the eggs at a constant 90°F (32°C). Observations made on the breeding habits of captive Spectacled caimans at the Atlanta Zoological Park, USA, indicate that the female protects the nest from small predators such as turtles, but not from man. If the female guarding the nest is killed the eggs will not survive in the wild.

When the young in the eggs are ready to hatch they respond to any activity on the mound by making 'croaking' sounds. The female caiman hears the young and digs down to them. The young usually hatch the moment the rotting vegetation is removed and rush for the nearest water.

Young caimans grow rapidly and eat huge quantities of crayfish, fish, insects, snails, snakes and small rodents. Within three years

Smooth-fronted caiman.

the 8 in (20 cm) hatchlings reach a length of 3 ft (90 cm). The same growth rate can be obtained in captivity if the caimans are kept at a temperature of 85°F (29°C) and fed a varied diet. Larger caimans occasionally catch land animals that come to the water to drink but they never prey on man.

Caimans and many other crocodilians are doomed to extinction because of man's quest for their skins. It would be one of the greatest tragedies in the earth's evolutionary history if an animal that has survived for millions of years was exterminated for a few handbags and shoes. FAMILY: Alligatoridae, ORDER: Crocodilia, CLASS: Reptilia.

CARNOSAURS, a group of large bipedal carnivorous dinosaurs belonging to the order Saurischia. They were the dominant predators of the Jurassic and Cretaceous periods and represent the largest land predators in the earth's history. They had a world-wide distribution but their numbers were small judging by the scarcity of their fossils. The main organ of predation was the massive head carried on the short and powerful neck. The jaws were set with a battery of dagger-like teeth. The carnosaur forelimb underwent progressive reduction and was all but vestigial in advanced forms like *Tyrannosaurus*.

CAUDATA, tailed amphibians, also known as Urodela, have a long body with a long tail which is retained in the adult, not lost during metamorphosis as in frogs and toads. Their limbs are largely unmodified, the fore and hindlimbs being of similar proportions. They have a wide geographical distribution and are

found in most tropical, sub-tropical and temperate regions. They are, however, absent from southern South America, most of Africa, Australia and the Malay Archipelago. Linnaeus in 1758 recognized a single genus with three species. Today, 54 genera and around 300 species are recognized, usually grouped into four suborders, the Cryptobranchoidea, Sirenoidea, Salamandroidea and Ambystomatoidea.

The earliest known fossil caudate, from the Upper Jurassic of Wyoming (140 million years old), is the limb bone known as *Comonecturoides*. There is abundant fossil material from the Cretaceous (62–130 million years old), largely of Sirenidae, but it gives little direct information on the ancestry of the modern caudates.

Caudate amphibians range from 2–60 in (5·0–150·0 cm) and occupy a variety of habitats. They may be aquatic, semi-terrestrial, terrestrial or even arboreal. As in other amphibian groups the skin is kept moist by secretions from dermal glands. These glands pour secretions onto the surface of the skin, so preventing the animal drying out, a moist skin being necessary for breathing. Although many caudates have lungs the skin is important for the uptake of oxygen and the giving out of carbon dioxide. Some caudates lack lungs entirely and breathe through the skin only. In many species the dermal glands also produce noxious secretions as a protection against predators. In some species the hindlimbs are reduced in size or even lost altogether and the number of toes on the forelimb is frequently reduced from four to three.

The Palmate newt *Triturus helveticus,* tailed amphibian of the order Candata.

The eyes are usually large and prominent but in some cave dwelling species they are very small and the animals are blind.

Breeding habits vary. Fully aquatic eggs may be laid or the eggs may be retained in the female and the young born as miniature adults. The young, or larvae, frequently have external gills used to extract oxygen from the water. These are generally lost in the adult, but in some species the larvae fail to develop into adults and retain their gills yet are able to breed. Such larvae are said to be neotenous.

Many of the caudates have the power to regenerate lost parts, such as a tail or a limb.

CENTROLENID FROGS, sometimes considered as a subfamily of the Tree frogs and like them have an additional element of cartilage in each finger and toe. They are distinguished from the Tree frogs, however, in having the end bone in each digit T-shaped and in having two of the long bones in the ankle region, the astragalus and calcaneum, fused into a single bone. There are thought to be about four genera, although very little is known about most of the species. They resemble the Tree frogs in their appearance and arboreal habits and are found from Mexico to Brazil.

Frogs of the genus *Cochranella* are green and about 1 in (2·5 cm) long. The skin of the underside lacks pigment and the bones and viscera can be seen through it. The head is broad and short and the eyes face forwards more than in most frogs. This gives them binocular vision which allows them to judge distances well, an important feature in an arboreal frog. Males of the genus *Centrolenella* have a bony, curved spike on the upper-arm which protrudes through the skin. Its function is completely unknown.

The breeding habits of this family are not well-known. The eggs are laid in disc-like masses on the undersides of leaves overhanging water and in some species the male has been reported to remain near the eggs. When the tadpoles hatch out they drop into the water where they continue their development. FAMILY: Hylidae, ORDER: Anura, CLASS: Amphibia.

CERATOPSIANS, a group of fossil reptiles belonging to the assemblage usually known as the dinosaurs. The ornithischian dinosaurs (order Ornithischia) are characterized by the possession of a pelvic girdle in which the pubic bone has an anterior prong. This type of pelvis is referred to as tetraradiate, to distinguish it from the triradiate type found in the other major dinosaur group, the order Saurischia, which lacks an anterior extension of the pubis.

The history of the ceratopsians is confined to the Upper Cretaceous and they were hence a thriving-group 100 million years ago. Ceratopsian fossils are mostly from North America, a small number have been found in Asia and it is possible that the group also extended into South America. Members of the suborder Ceratopsia have relatively large heads which usually bear large, bony horns. The skull is characterized by the presence of a large posterior bony 'frill' which extends over the neck region almost to the shoulders. This is an extension of two of the skull bones and in the more primitive ceratopsians it may have had large gaps or fenestrae, but in the more advanced forms it is quite solid. It was probably evolved to provide better accomodation for the muscles concerned in jaw movement, but it also provided protection for the vulnerable neck. The main variation in structure in the ceratopsians is in the size of the frill and also in the position and size of the horns. In *Triceratops,* of the Upper Cretaceous of North America, a pair of

Reconstruction of a scene in Cretaceous times a hundred million years ago showing a Ceratopsian.

Two colour patterns of the same chameleon *Chamaeleo lambertoni*.

horns are present just behind the eyes (brow horns) and a single median horn is found on the snout (nasal horn). *Centrosaurus,* also from the Upper Cretaceous of North America, lacks the brow horns but has a large nasal horn.

The jaws of ceratopsians are usually drawn out into a 'beak-like' structure due to the development of an extra bone, the rostral, in the upper jaw. A similar extension, the predentary, is found in the lower jaw. The ceratopsians were quadrupedal and the hind-limbs were always longer than the forelimbs. The foot had four short toes each with a small hoof and the hand had five digits.

The more advanced ceratopsians like *Triceratops* and *Centrosaurus* were probably evolved from more primitive forms which resembled *Protoceratops*. Numerous specimens of this form are found in the Upper Cretaceous of Mongolia. *Protoceratops* has a neck frill, but this is widely fenestrated, and it does not have horns. SUBORDER: Ceratopsia, ORDER: Ornithischia, CLASS: Reptilia.

CHAMELEONS, old world lizards especially noted for their adaptation to life in the branches of trees and shrubs. There are two genera with 90 species in the family; the genus *Chamaeleo* is by far the biggest with about 70 species. Some authors distribute the 20 species of the Stump-tailed chameleon amongst various genera, but here they are considered to belong to genus *Brookesia*.

Female chameleon *Chamaeleo pardalis*.

An unusually marked chameleon.

Most chameleon species are to be found in tropical Africa and Madagascar. Although the variety of species lessens southwards chameleons can also be found in the Cape Province in southern Africa. The Common chameleon *Chamaeleo chamaeleon* is the most northern representative of the family and can be found in North Africa, southern Spain and Portugal, Malta, Krete in the north of the Arabian peninsula and in India and Ceylon. Most chameleons are medium sized lizards of about 6–12 in (15–30 cm) length, but there are some tiny ones of just a few centimetres in length (e.g. species of the genus *Brookesia*) and some giants amongst the species of the genus *Chamaeleo* that reportedly reached a length of 32 in (80 cm) in some forms in Madagascar and Africa.

The chameleon's body is usually flattened from side to side; the head often has a showy crest, horns or skinfolds. The teeth are acrodont like those of the agamas. The eyelids are grown over to a circle of about the size of a pupil out of which the big eyeballs protrude on each side of the head. The eyes can be moved independently of each other which especially fascinates the human contemplator. The chameleon's tongue is not slit like that of most lizards. Instead it is built like a catapult with a club-like tip and can be shot out at high speed to a length greater than the chameleon's total body length. The prey is hit by the tip of the tongue, glued to it and drawn back to the mouth at the same speed. The shooting out of the tongue greatly increases the radius within which food can be caught. The size of the prey depends on the size of the chameleon itself: small to medium-sized ones will catch mainly insects; the large ones will also capture other lizards, small mammals and birds.

The tongue bone is well developed in all chameleons and plays an important part in the catapult mechanism of the tongue. While at rest the muscular tongue is curled around the tongue bone. Before shooting the circular muscles at the back end of the tongue contract violently and try to push the tongue down from the pointed continuation of the tongue bone. This, however, is only possible after the longitudinal muscles relax and thus become inefficient in their role as adversaries to the circular muscles. As this relaxation is very sudden the tongue shoots out of the mouth under the resulting pressure, rather as one would shoot an orange pip by squeezing it with the finger-tips. It is withdrawn together with the glued-on prey through the elasticity of the tissue and a repeated contraction of the longitudinal muscles.

The limbs of a chameleon are long, thin and carry the body rather high. The toes are united into two opposing bundles on each

foot: two toes on the outside and three on the inside on the front feet and three on the outside and two on the inside on the hind feet. This has changed each foot into a pair of clasping tongs that enable the chameleon to get a firm grip on a perch. In addition the species of the genus *Chamaeleo* have a prehensile tail which even on its own could support the weight of the body.

The chameleon's ability to change its colour is well known although the layman often has a greatly exaggerated idea of this. The physiological colour change in most chameleons is, however, a very noticeable and quick process. But the chameleon cannot always match its surroundings. The body colouration of the day-active arboreal chameleons is a good protection, for example, a green or bark-coloured skin according to environment. Very often, however, colouration and markings play a part in disputes with another member of the same species; sometimes they just mirror a specific physiological condition. A surprising number of chameleons have a pale whitish sleeping colouration and with the help of a torch can easily be found in the dark foliage where they would be completely protected by their colour during the day. Male and sometimes also female chameleons hold territories which they will defend jealously against others. But only very rarely do real fights take place although the horns and crests on the heads of a number of species would probably make good weapons. When the two rivals are at viewing distance they threaten each other by displaying their brilliant colours, always showing the side of the inflated body to the enemy in order to look more impressive. Characteristic swayings of the body emphasize the threat posture and sometimes the mouth is opened wide to show the contrasting colouration of the mucous membrane.

In the wild this psychological warfare is usually sufficient to force an opponent to retreat. Only under the restricted conditions in captivity do real fights occur and the bites can inflict serious wounds and sometimes even kill a rival. The defeated male will assume the unobtrusive colours of either a female or young one and retreat slowly. The victor will let him go without further interference: through the change in colour he has become uninteresting and is no longer a rival.

Because of their bizarre appearance and their interesting biology chameleons are favourites in terrariums. But the results of captivity are not very encouraging. Usually they die after a few months even if they took food initially. Only occasionally can specimens of a few species be kept and bred in a terrarium. One of the many reasons for this failure is the strict holding of territories which makes it impossible to keep one male within range of sight of another of the same species.

Most chameleons lay eggs which the

female deposits in holes in the ground which she has previously dug herself. Digging holes into the ground and laying eggs in them is a highly dangerous affair for the arboreal chameleon. Some species, mainly in the subtropical climate of southern Africa and in some higher parts of the highlands have become viviparous. The fully developed young ones are born in their egg membrane; they free themselves of this membrane immediately after birth and start an individual life. They need no guidance from their parents to become expert hunters. FAMILY: Chamaeleonidae, ORDER: Squamata, CLASS: Reptilia. (Ill. p. 49, 50.)

CHEECHAK *Hemidactylus frenatus,* or Common house gecko. It gets its name from the call it makes when prowling about at night for food. It prefers native huts and some city buildings as its habitat. Its origin was mainland Asia, but by hitching a ride on boats and in cargo, it has spread to most of the Pacific Islands. In the daytime, the cheechak is dark brown to nearly black as it hides in crevices. At night, when on the prowl, it becomes almost ghostly white. FAMILY: Gekkonidae, ORDER: Squamata, CLASS: Reptilia.

CHELONIA, name of the order which includes tortoises, turtles and terrapins, now replaced by the order *Testudines.

CHINESE SALAMANDER *Batrachuperus karlschmidti,* also known as the White dragon, a salamander of the family Hynobiidae, 6 in (15 cm) long, which occurs in the mountains of Szechwan and Sinkiang in China. Like other members of this primitive family this salamander is largely aquatic. Its name is derived from the White Dragon Pool, on Mount Omei, sacred to the worship of the salamander since the monks in this area believe the pool is the abode of the King of the White dragons. Superstition has it that if someone kills one of the salamanders a violent storm will occur. Nevertheless, it seems that local people often collect these salamanders which are killed and dried since they are supposed to provide relief from stomach troubles. FAMILY: Hynobiidae, ORDER: Caudata, CLASS: Amphibia.

CHUCKWALLA *Sauromalus obesus,* one of the iguanas, the New World equivalents of the Old World lizards (Lacertidae). The chuckwalla is a heavy-bodied reptile which attains a length of $1\frac{1}{2}$ ft (46 cm). Its robust head, powerful legs, coat of small scales and long tail are typical of many iguanas. Predominantly herbivorous, the chuckwalla feeds on the flowers and fruits of cacti living in desert areas of the southwestern United States, Northern Mexico and Lower California. It is notable for its ability to inflate its

The common chameleon of the southern half of Africa is *Chamaeleo dilepis* (opposite).

lungs so that the body becomes almost globular. When threatened, the chuckwalla runs into a rock crevice, inflates itself and is virtually impossible to remove by force. FAMILY: Iguanidae, ORDER: Squamata, CLASS: Reptilia.

COBRAS, snakes capable of spreading a 'hood' when alarmed: the long anterior ribs swing upward and forward, stretching the skin like the fabric of an umbrella.

When the Portuguese established themselves in India at the beginning of the 16th century, they encountered a snake that they called *Cobra de capello* (snake with a hood), and the English subsequently adopted the name 'cobra' for any African or Asian elapid snake which could spread a hood. The true cobras belong to the genus *Naja,* derived from the Sanskrit *naga*—snake. Africa, with five species, is the centre of distribution for the group, two more species occur in the Middle East and the Indian cobra is widespread in Southeast Asia.

The true cobras may reach 8–9 ft (c. 260 cm) in length. Their bodies are covered with smooth scales which may be dull as in the Egyptian cobra, or very shiny as in the Forest cobra. The head is broad and flat and the hollow fangs are set well forward in the upper jaw.

The Egyptian cobra *Naja haje* appears on ancient Egyptian royal headdresses, rearing up with hood spread. It has a wide distribution in Africa and Arabia, but is absent from rain-forest and desert regions. It reaches a length of over 8 ft (2·4 m) and is a relatively thick and heavy snake. It is usually brown to black, often with lighter speckling. In southeastern Africa a spectacular colour variety is banded in black and yellow. Juveniles are uniform yellow.

The Cape cobra *Naja nivea* is restricted to South Africa, the Kalahari and South West Africa. It may be bright yellow, golden-brown or speckled yellow and brown.

The Forest cobra *Naja melanoleuca* occurs in evergreen forests of West, central and southeastern Africa, reaching its southern limit in Zululand. It is probably the longest species of the genus, reaching 9 ft (2·7 m), but it is more slender than the Egyptian cobra. The Forest cobra may be black or yellow-brown, heavily speckled with black, while a banded variety is found in the Guinea savannah of West Africa.

The Black-necked spitting cobra *Naja nigricollis* occurs in the savannah regions bordering the rain-forests from West Africa south to Angola, Zambia, Malawi and Tanzania, with subspecies extending into the Western Cape Province. Young cobras are dark grey, but adults are usually uniform black above. There is a single broad black band on the throat. The Black-necked cobra reaches a length of 8 ft (2·4 m).

The Mozambique spitting cobra *Naja mossambica* is widespread in southeastern Africa. It rarely exceeds 5 ft (1·5 m) in length and is pale grey to olive above and salmon-pink below, with a series of irregular black bands and blotches on the throat. A subspecies *N. m. pallida* occurs from southern Egypt south to northern Kenya; it is pink with one or two black bands on the neck. Another subspecies *N. m. katiensis* occurs in West Africa.

Two poorly-known species occur in southwest Asia, these are *Naja morgani* of Iran and *Naja oxiana* in the region east of the Caspian Sea.

The Indian cobra *Naja naja* has a wide range from West Pakistan east to southern China and the Philippines. The body is usually brown, often with narrow light rings. On the back of the neck is often a dark-edged pale marking that may take the form of a pair of spectacles or a dark-centred ring.

Several other cobras are placed in separate genera; these include the *King cobra, the *ringhals and the Water cobras of the genus *Boulengerina,* which occur in central Africa.

Female cobras lay between eight and 25 eggs in a hole. The newly hatched young are about 10 in (25 cm) in length.

Cobras are active at night, when they do most of their hunting. During the day a cobra may often be found basking in the sun close to its refuge, which may be a termitarium, rodent burrow or a rock crevice. Cobras' diets include rodents, birds and their eggs, lizards, other snakes, amphibians, and fishes, even locusts are occasionally devoured. Cobras are notorious poultry raiders, taking eggs and young birds. The Forest cobra is the most accomplished catcher of fish, but the Black-necked cobra is known to be a 'fishing snake' in Victoria Nyanza.

A cobra will usually try to escape when disturbed by man, but if surprised or cornered, it will raise its head and neck, at the same time spreading the hood. If approached it will strike, or may even glide forward to attack. When a cobra bites successfully, it will often hang on and chew, injecting large quantities of venom. A full bite, if untreated, will cause death in man in about six hours through the action of the venom on the nervous system.

Four species of cobra have modified fangs which allow them to project a spray of venom into the eyes of an enemy, causing temporary blindness. The venom causes permanent damage to the eyes if not quickly washed out. The 'Spitting cobras' are the Black-necked cobra, Mozambique cobra and ringhals of Africa and the Southeast Asian populations of the Indian cobra. FAMILY: Elapidae, ORDER: Squamata, CLASS: Reptilia. (Ill. p. 49, 50.)

COELUROSAURS, small bipedal dinosaurs, delicately constructed, agile bipeds adapted for fast-running in open country. Their long and graceful hindlimb bones were thin-walled reducing the body weight. In advanced forms the long forelimb had a three fingered hand with opposable thumb for grasping. In the more primitive of them the dentition was carnivorous but in later and more specialized forms the jaws were toothless and an insect or egg diet has been suggested for these. All coelurosaurs were small for dinosaurs some being no larger than a chicken and the largest not exceeding 9 ft (3 m) in length. Coelurosaurs had a world-wide distribution in the Mesozoic. One group, the 'bird mimics' *Ornithomimus,* were extraordinarily similar in their skull and limb structure to the ostrich and no doubt lived a very similar life. See dinosaurs, ORDER: Saurischia, CLASS: Reptilia.

COLUBRIDS, a family of the higher snakes belonging to the group Caenophidia (see snakes) which also includes the families Elapidae and Viperidae. The classification of the higher snakes has been based largely on the venom apparatus. Those snakes with the two most elaborate types of apparatus have been separated into the Elapidae and Viperidae, while the remainder, comprising 1,800 species and 280 genera, have been placed in the family Colubridae. These 1,800 species share no real distinctive features and differ among themselves as much as they differ from the Elapidae and Viperidae. They show various degrees of development of the venom apparatus, from non-venomous to the poisonous boomslang, and they also have different kinds of teeth and upper jaw bones, which are the characters on which the higher snakes tend to be classified. As a result specialists tend to differ on how the family should be subdivided and altogether the Colubridae are difficult even for the specialist to disentangle. Many of the better known groups of species are dealt with under separate entries and these are listed at the end of this article. Here we are concerned with some of the general features to be found in the family.

Some species, including the Thirst snakes have uniform series of solid teeth—that is, solid as opposed to grooved or hollow teeth for discharging venom—used in swallowing the prey but they appear to play no part in subduing it apart from this. Some of these use constriction in overcoming their prey, the King snakes being an example. In others the teeth are graded in size or those in the back of the jaw may be abruptly enlarged forming fangs, sometimes separated from the teeth in front by a gap. Other species have enlarged teeth in the middle of the lower jaw below the eye which interlock with enlarged teeth in the lower jaw, an unusual feature that gives a firm grip on the small invertebrates on which they feed. Many colubrids have two or, more rarely, three teeth at the posterior end of the

Grass or ringed snake *Natrix natrix* of Europe, non-venomous, lives near water and feeds largely on amphibians.

upper jaw grooved for the conduction of venom. These are often referred to as the Rear-fanged snakes. They have to take a full bite and then 'chew' in order to engage the fangs, although some of them can tilt the upper jaw to some extent so as partly to erect and thus better engage the fangs.

The only colubrids known to have venom that can be dangerous to man all live in Africa and include the Mole vipers, the Twig snake and the boomslang. The Rear-fanged snakes generally eat small vertebrates in which they are able to engage their fangs without difficulty. Even when they bite a man, however, they rarely engage the fangs because they cannot open the mouth wide enough to take in a human limb, they can only engage a finger or a toe.

All colubrids are much alike in bodily proportions and appearance, differing in details such as the size of the eye and the shape of the pupil. They also differ widely in habitats, some living in trees, others on the ground, others burrowing. They differ widely, moreover, in their internal anatomy, in addition to the difference in the teeth and the jaws, in such things as the bones of the skull, the vertebrae and the positions of heart, liver and kidneys, as well as in the degree to which the left lung is reduced in size. The large scales of the head of colubrids are, however, surprisingly uniform, and one pattern is found in four-fifths of the species. It is usually in the burrowing snakes that the head scales are simplified and so depart from this general pattern.

Most colubrids when threatened make off rapidly and although they do not travel fast their ability to move through small crevices enables them to disappear with disconcerting rapidity. A few have colour patterns that mimic those of dangerously poisonous snakes, like those that mimic the Coral snakes of the American tropics. The African Herald snake *Crotaphopeltis* draws itself up and spreads the angles of its jaws giving a convincing imitation of a viper. The African Egg-eating snake imitates the Hissing viper. The American Bull snake makes an extremely loud hiss while the Twig snake inflates its throat when disturbed so displaying a prominent pattern which may have a deterrent effect also. The Hog-nosed snake and the European Grass snake both use the behaviour sometimes referred to as shamming dead. American snakes of the genus *Scaphiodontophis* are remarkable for being able to cast portions of the tail when this is held, somewhat in the manner of lizards, but they cannot regenerate these lost parts. See Aesculapian, Bull, Egg-eating, Fishing, Garter, Grass, Hog-nosed, King, Mangrove, Racer, Thirst, Tree and Twig snakes, and also the boomslang. FAMILY: Colubridae, ORDER: Squamata, CLASS: Reptilia.

CONSTRICTORS, the term often used to refer to the larger members of the snake family Boidae, well known for their ability to overpower their prey by constriction. It is less widely known that many smaller species of snake belonging to other families are also constrictors. The North American racers, genus *Coluber* and the European Smooth snake *Cornella austriaca* are good examples.

When feeding, a constrictor first seizes its prey in its mouth, holding on with its strongly recurved teeth. It then wraps its body around the victim and slowly tightens its coils until the victim is unable to breathe and dies from suffocation. During this process most constrictors will endeavour to use their prehensile tail to obtain a purchase on some convenient fixed projection such as a rock or tree trunk. Like all snakes, constrictors swallow their prey whole.

Although some of the larger constrictors are very powerful their strength is frequently exaggerated. Stories of constrictors crushing their victims to pulp and breaking every bone in their bodies are not borne out by scientific observation. In reality bones are rarely broken, the body of the victim showing little sign of mechanical damage other than that inflicted by the snake's teeth.

Not all constrictors kill their prey by constriction. Many, particularly the smaller species such as the European Smooth snake, use their coils only to subdue their prey while it is swallowed alive. ORDER: Squamata, CLASS: Reptilia. (Ill. p. 50.)

COPPERHEAD *Agkistrodon contortrix,* venomous snake related to the Water moccasin and rattlesnakes. Adult copperheads are generally less than 1 yd (91 cm) long and are named from the coppery or reddish-brown head. The body is brownish with 15–25 rather irregular and darker brown cross bands. Copperheads often superficially resemble the Common milk snake *Lampropeltis doliata* but may be distinguished from this harmless species by the vertical elliptical pupil and the facial pit. The four subspecies of the copperhead are distributed over much of the central and eastern United States.

Copperheads may be found in a variety of habitats, including woods, rocky country and semi-desert. In the early spring they are active during daylight, but during the hotter summer months become mainly nocturnal and spend the day resting under logs and in crevices. Copperheads have frequently been reported as hibernating in assemblies, sometimes with other species of snakes. Mating of copperheads occurs in April and May and two to ten young are born in August or September. Copperheads display a very catholic taste and have been reported as eating small mammals, birds, lizards, snakes, frogs, caterpillars and cicadas. A large fraction of the bites from venomous snakes in the eastern United States is due to copperhead attacks. Happily, human fatalities are uncommon, but this species must always be regarded as highly dangerous and respected as such. FAMILY: Crotalidae, ORDER: Squamata, CLASS: Reptilia. (Ill. p. 51.)

CORAL SNAKES, highly venomous snakes with hollow or grooved fangs fixed to the front of the upper jaw, related to the cobras, of Africa and Asia, the mambas of Africa and the kraits of Asia. They are characterized by the head being only slightly defined from the neck, the slender body having an oval cross-section and the eye having a vertical, elliptical pupil. The vertical pupil is associated with twilight or nocturnal activity and indicates that these snakes hunt their prey mostly at night.

Coral snakes are restricted to the New World, from the United States southwards into the tropical forests of South America. The Eastern coral snake *Micrurus fulvius,* renowned as a snake-eater and up to 3 ft (90 cm) long, is one of the few very dangerous snakes in the United States. It occurs southwards from North Carolina to Florida and westwards through the Gulf states to southern Texas and Mexico. The Arizona or Sonoran coral snake *Micruroides euryxanthus,* of southeastern Arizona, western New Mexico and Mexico, is about half the size but several other species, found in Mexico and the tropics of South America, may attain a length of 5 ft (150 cm).

Coral snakes usually have a striking colour pattern of broad, alternating orange or pink and black bands separated by narrow yellow rings. This is probably a warning colouration, indicating to other animals that the snake is dangerous and best left alone. Several harmless snakes, for example, the Milk snakes, *Lampropeltis doliata* and *Atractus latifrons,* which live in the same habitats as Coral snakes mimic their warning colouration and presumably derive some benefit from doing so. It has, however, been suggested that the banding on these various species is an example of disruptive colouration, where the pattern serves to break up the outline of the body, so rendering the animal less recognizable to enemies. In general, Coral snakes are secretive burrowers and spend the day hidden in grass tussocks or other dense vegetation or in runs under stones and rocks. They are, in fact, rarely seen above ground during daylight, but may become active in the day after rain. The jaws of Coral snakes are, unlike those of most snakes, only slightly distensible, so that they feed on small or slender prey such as other snakes and lizards. Coral snakes are very poisonous.
FAMILY: Elapidae, ORDER: Squamata, CLASS: Reptilia. (Ill. p. 52.)

CORDYLID LIZARDS,

members of the family Cordylidae, most of which have the body covered by bony plates underlying the scales, except for a granular lateral groove which allows for expansion.

The Plated lizards *Gerrhosaurus* are widespread in Africa south of the Sahara. The Rock plated lizard *G. validus* is the largest species, averaging 2 ft (60 cm) in length and about 2 in (5 cm) in width. It occurs in the warmer parts of southern Africa. The Tawny plated lizard *G. major* is slightly smaller, but has a wide range from Togo southeast to Zululand. The smallest species is the Yellow-throated plated lizard *G. flavigularis,* which occurs from the Sudan south to Cape Town. These lizards all have well-developed limbs, as have the Dwarf plated lizards *Cordylosaurus,* which are confined to southwestern Africa.

The Whip lizards *Tetradactylus* show an interesting transition from *T. seps* with five digits on each limb through to *T. ellenbergeri* which has no forelimbs and only minute vestiges of hindlimbs. This genus is restricted to South Africa, with the exception of *T. ellenbergeri* which ranges from Angola east to Tanzania.

The Girdled lizards *Zonosaurus* and the Keeled plated lizards *Tracheloptychus* are confined to Madagascar.

The Girdle-tailed lizards of the genus *Cordylus* are more robust than the Plated lizards and have rings of long spines covering the rather short tail. This is less readily shed than in most lizards and is curled round the head and body for protection when the lizard takes refuge in a crevice. Many species have spines on the back of the head, particularly the sungazer *Cordylus giganteus,* which reaches a length of 14 in (35 cm). The genus is confined to southern Africa, with the exception of *C. tropidosternum* which reaches Kenya.

The Crag lizards *Pseudocordylus* are 12 in (30 cm) in length and have flattened bodies covered with rather small scales. They are usually found in mountainous regions of South Africa from Table Mountain to the Drakensberg.

The flat-lizards *Platysaurus* have the body covered with smooth granules and look as if they have been run over by a steam-roller. The largest species, the Emperor flat-lizard *Platysaurus imperator* reaches a length of 15½ in (39 cm). The males are brightly coloured, but the females and juveniles are usually black above with three cream stripes. Flat-lizards are most abundant on granite and sandstone outcrops in Rhodesia, Transvaal and Mozambique.

The snake-lizards *Chamaesaura* are slender reptiles up to 2 ft (60 cm) in length, three-quarters of this being tail. The limbs are hardly used, although *C. aenea* retains five digits on each limb. At the other extreme *C. macrolepis* lacks forelimbs and has only vestigial monodactyl hindlimbs. The snake-lizards range from the Cape Province north to Uganda.

The Plated lizards, Whip lizards and flat-lizards lay eggs, whereas the Girdle-tailed lizards, Crag lizards and snake-lizards give birth to live young.

Most cordylid lizards feed on insects and millipedes, but large Plated lizards and the sungazer will eat small vertebrates, especially lizards. Some species like the Rock plated lizard are largely vegetarian.

Many species take refuge in rock crevices, the flat-lizards being adapted for squeezing into narrow cracks. Others, like most Plated lizards and the sungazer, live in holes in the ground.
FAMILY: Cordylidae, ORDER: Squamata, CLASS: Reptilia. (Ill. p. 51.)

CORROBOREE TOADLET

Pseudophryne corroboree, small 1 in (2·5 cm) amphibian living in moist areas up to 4,000 ft (1200 m) elevation in the Australian Alps. When winter temperatures reach near to freezing, the Corroboree toadlet burrows deep beneath the snow and hibernates. It breeds by depositing eggs singly among plant roots near a stream where plenty of moist soil is available all year. Unlike other amphibians, the Corroboree toadlet is unable to change its brilliant yellow and shiny black stripes, so it is compelled to be a secretive species. It walks clumsily on tips of toes instead of jumping as other frogs and toads do.
FAMILY: Bufonidae, ORDER: Anura, CLASS: Amphibia. (Ill. p. 52.)

COTTONMOUTH,

alternative name for the amphibious, venomous snake known as the moccasin or Water moccasin *Agkistrodon piscivorus.* Closely related to the copperhead *A. contortrix,* the cottonmouth is dark brownish-black with paler markings. It is noted for its habit of widely opening its white-lined mouth when threatened, thus giving rise to the name cottonmouth. It inhabits much of the southeastern United States, where it feeds on fish, frogs and small mammals. FAMILY: Crotalidae, ORDER: Squamata, CLASS: Reptilia.

CROCODILES,

13 species belonging to the order *Crocodylia, the others being known as alligators, caimans and gavials. They differ from alligators and caimans in that the large fourth tooth in the lower jaw which fits into a notch in the upper jaw remains visible even when the mouth is closed. Moreover, the teeth of the upper and lower jaw are more or less in line, those of the lower jaw engaging between the teeth of the upper jaw. The two ribs on the first cervical vertebra diverge considerably. Bony scutes are usually restricted on the underside to the front of the thorax.

The best known species of true crocodiles is the Nile crocodile *Crocodylus niloticus* which occurs all over Africa south of the Sahara, as well as Madagascar and the Seychelles Islands. Only a few decades ago it died out in southwest Asia (the River Zerka in Israel). At one time this species reached lengths of up to 33 ft (10 m) but nowadays it is hard to find specimens more than 20 ft (6 m) long. In western and central Africa, as well as in Ujiji on Lake Tanganyika, lives the 13 ft (4 m) Long-snouted crocodile *Crocodylus cataphractus,* the snout of which is up to 3½ times as long as it is wide at the base. In contrast, the Broad-nosed crocodile *Osteolaemus tetraspis,* of western and central Africa, has an extremely short snout and is rarely more than 6 ft (1·8 m) long. It has brown eyes and is said to spend more time in the jungle than in water. It feeds mainly on freshwater crabs and soft turtles using its comparatively blunt teeth.

In Asia lives the 13 ft (4 m) long mugger or Swamp crocodile *Crocodylus palustris,* mainly in India and Ceylon, perhaps also in Burma. It differs from the very similar Nile crocodile by its somewhat shorter snout and the less regular arrangement of the scutes on the back, the central longitudinal rows being somewhat broader than those at the sides. The Siam crocodile *C. siamensis,* which has somewhat the same length, is restricted to Thailand and Indo-China and the islands of Java and Borneo. It is characterized by a triangular raised portion in front of the eyes, with the apex of the triangle facing forward, and a longitudinally directed bony ridge between the eyes. Despite its name, the somewhat longer Sunda gavial *Tomistoma schlegeli* does not belong to the gavials (Gavialidae) but to the true crocodiles. Although its snout is extremely long, and up to five times as long as its width at the base, this does not stem from the main part of the skull in the manner of a beak but gradually merges with the skull. This species is found on the Malayan peninsula as well as on the islands of Sumatra and Borneo.

The Estuarine crocodile *Crocodylus porosus* is spread over a vast territory stretching from Ceylon to the Fiji Islands, including northern Australia. It lacks the large post occipital scutes, the scutes on the back overlie only small oval ossifications and on the snout there is a pair of scute-like bony ridges extending from the front corners of the eyes up to the nose. The Estuarine crocodile reaches 33 ft (10 m) in length and lives at the mouths of rivers and in salt water. It can be seen swimming many miles from the coast in the open seas.

Similar bone ridges on the snout, even though shorter and less pronounced, are found in the New Guinea crocodile *C. novaeguineae* and the Philippine crocodile *C. mindorensis,* which also occurs in the Sulu Archipelago. Both forms, which differ from the Estuarine crocodile by the well built post occipital scutes and the completely ossified scutes on the back, are perhaps only geographical races of a single species; their length is up to roughly 10 ft (3 m).

Apart from the Estuarine crocodile, in northern Australia we find the Australian crocodile *C. johnsoni* which is only 8 ft (2·5 m) long and is recognized by its long narrow snout.

True crocodiles are also at home in the New World. The most northern species is the light olive coloured American or Sharp-nosed crocodile *C. acutus* in the south of the Florida peninsula, on the islands of Cuba, Jamaica and Hispaniola, as well as from Mexico southwards over the whole of Central America to Venezuela, Colombia, Ecuador and Northern Peru. It is characterized by its

narrow and long snout having a bulbous dome in front of the eyes. The scutes on the back are somewhat irregular and form only four to six interconnected longitudinal rows. Whilst this species reaches almost 12 ft (3·5 m), the Bulbous crocodile *C. moreletii,* found in the east of British Honduras and in Guatemala, is only a little more than 8 ft (2·5 m) long and is almost black when aged. Here, too, the snout carries a lump in front of the eyes but has a much broader and shorter effect than in the previous species. Restricted to Cuba there is the barely 7 ft (2 m) long Cuba crocodile *C. rhombifer* which has a triangular raised portion in front of the eyes similar to that in the Siam crocodile. The older individuals are almost black and exhibit light yellow spots on the back legs. The only wholly South American species is found in the region of the Orinoco river, namely the Orinoco crocodile *C. intermedius* which reaches the stately length of up to 15 ft (4·5 m). It differs clearly from all other American species of crocodile by its extremely narrow and very elongated snout. FAMILY: Crocodylidae, ORDER: Crocodylia, CLASS: Reptilia. (Ill. p. 52, 53, 57.)

CROSSOPTERYGII, a group of fishes very important in evolutionary history because it is generally agreed that numbered amongst them are the ancestors of all amphibians, reptiles, birds and mammals, including ourselves. Strictly the Crossopterygii comprise two sub-groups, the Rhipidistia and Actinistia or coelacanths. One species of the latter is alive today but all the Rhipidistia are extinct. The rhipidistians were freshwater forms ranging in geological time from the Lower Devonian to the Lower Permian (390 million—260 million years ago). Like the living lungfishes (Dipnoi) they had lungs and their fins show a structure antecedent to that of the tetrapod limb. However, the closeness of their relationship to the Dipnoi is in dispute. SUBCLASS: Crossopterygii, CLASS: Pisces.

CRYPTOBRANCHIDAE, largest of living amphibians and known as Giant salamanders. Their origin dates back to the days of the dinosaurs and they are only distantly related to other living salamanders.

The family contains two genera: the Asiatic genus *Megalobatrachus* containing two equally large species, the Chinese giant salamander *M. davidianus* and the Japanese giant salamander *M. japonicus,* and the American genus *Cryptobranchus* with but one smaller species the hellbender *C. alleganiensis.*

The Asiatic forms reach a length of over 5½ ft (167 cm) and there are references in ancient writings to much larger sizes. The hellbender female grows to just under 2½ ft (74 cm), the male to only 22 in (56 cm).

The Giant salamanders have maintained their primitive characteristics and their size. All are exceptionally grotesque and ugly, robust creatures with a flattened head as wide or wider than the body. The nostrils and eyes are small, inconspicuous and in the Japanese species further obscured by numerous fair-sized tubercules found on the head and body. The legs are sturdy but short with five stubby toes on the hindfeet and four on the frontfeet. From behind the head an undulated skin fold extends on each side of the body to the base of the tail, which is laterally compressed into a broad oval fin. The skin is slimy, dark greyish brown with irregular darker or lighter mottlings. When injured, they secrete white irritating fluid from pores on the back. The Giant salamanders have small teeth in both upper and lower jaws. The hellbender has four internal gill arches on each side of the head, and retains a single pair of gill openings. In the Asiatic species the number of paired gill arches is reduced to two and the gill openings are absent. The Chinese species has small, bead-like barbels below the chin.

Fossil remains of Giant salamanders are found over an extended area, including Europe. A large skeleton of an extinct central European species *Andrias scheuchzeri* was originally described in the 18th century as belonging to an antediluvian human child under the name *homo diluvii testis* 'man a witness of the deluge'. Today the range is much reduced, the three remaining species living isolated, far from each other. The Chinese giant salamander is found in the waters descending from the Himalayan Mountains into the western Chinese provinces of Chinkiang and Tungkiang and also in northern Kwangtung.

The most popular Chinese name is *Nei-yü,* mentioned as long ago as 600 BC. Occasionally it is also referred to as *Wah-wah yü.* Western science suspected its existence from the study of ancient writings and in 1869–70 Abbé Armand David, a Jesuit priest and naturalist, collected the type specimen. It differs little from the previously discovered Japanese species and at first was regarded as only a geographical race. Its legs and toes are proportionately longer, the skin tubercules are smaller, and arranged in pairs in rows. The largest specimen on record was collected near Kweiyangfu in 1923. It measured 5 ft 9 in (175·3 cm).

More than 1,000 miles to the east on the islands of Japan lives the Japanese giant salamander popularly called the *Sancho-uo.* It was introduced to western science in 1829 when Phillipe François de Siebold brought a living specimen to Europe, which lived 50 years in captivity. Its dermal tubercules are larger, single, and irregularly placed.

The hellbender is found in the Appalachian mountain region of the eastern United States and in a couple of smaller areas in the Ozarks.

All Giant salamanders need cool, well oxygenated water. Their habitat is restricted to limpid mountain streams and rivers with moderate current. They are totally aquatic, spending their days in a hollow dug under logs or rocks, usually solitarily. During the late summer breeding season the males find an appropriate nesting area upstream and prepare the site before they are joined by the females. The females lay a long garland of connected grape-sized eggs, each with a pea-sized nucleus surrounded by clear jelly. Fertilization is external. 200–600 eggs are laid by the Asiatic salamanders; 300–450 by the hellbender. In the hellbender, the female pushes the eggs onto the bottom to which they adhere. Several females may lay in one nest. The male then chases the females away and guards the eggs for some time. The male *Sancho-uo* reputedly winds the egg garlands around his body and aggressively defends them against potential predators during incubation. When the larvae hatch, in two to three months or in the following spring, the male abandons them. Their rate of growth is very slow.

The Japanese giant salamander young, for instance, are only $1\frac{1}{4}$ in (3 cm) long in four months, 4 in (12 cm) in a year and a half, and less than 8 in (20 cm) in three years. They do not reach sexual maturity for at least five years, perhaps much later.

Giant salamanders feed mostly on crayfish, but will eat almost any aquatic animal they can capture and swallow. They leave their underwater shelter after dark, and presumably return to the same place at the end of the hunt. In cold well-aerated water they can extract enough oxygen to stay submerged indefinitely. However, if the demand increases because of their activity or the oxygen level of the water is insufficient, they come to the surface and gulp atmospheric air. Captive hellbenders occasionally engage in a peculiar rocking motion to bring fresh water to their surroundings.

With the growing human population and increasing water pollution, the survival prospects of the Giant salamanders is poor. Both the Asiatic species are caught for human food. Some Chinese salamanders find their way to the Hong Kong markets, but otherwise their status is unknown. In Japan, the Giant salamanders are growing scarcer and are now under government protection. The hellbenders are not generally eaten, but they are accidentally caught by fisherman which usually results in a fatal injury. Even more serious is the threat to their habitat.

It seems that the Giant salamanders, whose size, ancient origin and discontinuous distribution inspired Karel Capek's early science fiction classic *War with the newts* in which these salamanders, challenging man for the possession of the Earth, are rapidly losing the war. See Giant salamander and hellbender. SUBORDER: Cryptobranchoidea, ORDER: Caudata, CLASS: Amphibia.

CRYPTOCLEIDUS, one of the plesiosaur group of reptiles (see Sauropterygia) which first appears as fossils in rocks transitional in age between the Triassic and Jurassic periods and was extinct by the close of the Cretaceous. Every feature of the plesiosaur skeleton was perfectly adapted for free swimming marine life. *Cryptocleidus,* from the Upper Jurassic of Europe, exemplifies such features. The relatively small head with jaws beset with conical teeth, denoting a fish diet, was carried on the very long vertebral column. As in all plesiosaurs the limbs were modified as paddles with each digit lengthened, by the addition of accessory phalanges, so increasing the paddles' surface area. The powerful plate-like shoulder and hip girdles carried the extensive locomotive musculature. SUBORDER: Plesiosauria, ORDER: Sauropterygia, CLASS: Reptilia.

CRYPTODIRA, the most advanced group of the Testudines, able to retract the head within the exoskeleton by S-shaped bending of the neck in the vertical plane. The suborder includes all the tortoises and common turtles and terrapins. They are distributed throughout the tropical and subtropical regions and the warmer temperate areas.

CYNODONTS, advanced group of carnivorous mammal-like reptiles which flourished in the early Mesozoic and which lie close to, if not on, the direct line of evolution to the mammals. In nearly every feature of their anatomy the cynodonts show a close approach to the mammalian structure. The teeth were differentiated into incisors, canines and molars, and the latter in advanced forms were cusped for masticating food. In all a bony secondary palate separated the nasal passage from the mouth so that air could be breathed while food was being chewed. The limbs were underslung in mammalian fashion, a large departure from the sprawling gait of their immediate ancestors. Long ribs surrounded the thorax and a mammalian type diaphragm was no doubt present. Much evidence suggests that the cynodonts were in fact warm-blooded reptiles. ORDER: Cynodontia, CLASS: Reptilia.

DABOIA *Vipera russelii,* or Russel's viper, a very colourful adder found in India and southern Asia and on some Indonesian islands.

DEATH ADDER *Acantophis antarcticus*, a dangerous *elapid snake that looks like an adder because of its short body. It lives in Australia and New Guinea, where there are no adders or vipers.

DENDROBATIDAE, the Arrow-poison frogs of South America, characterized by having a pair of small plates at the tip of each digit. In other features they most closely resemble the true frogs (Ranidae) and are sometimes included as a subfamily of that group.

There are only three genera, *Dendrobates, Phyllobates* and *Prostherapis*, of small frogs with smooth skins, most of them brightly coloured and with a remarkable variation in the colours. *Phyllobates aurotaenia*, for example, is a vivid red with black markings. *Dendrobates trivittatus* may be either completely black or spotted with white or brown or may have a vivid pattern of black and yellow stripes along its body.

The poison from which these frogs get their name is produced by small glands in the skin. Most amphibians have such glands as a protection against predators but the strength of the poison varies. In these frogs it is particularly strong. It is usually considered that the vivid colouration is associated with their poisonous skin, serving to warn predators, but the most brightly coloured specimens are not necessarily the most poisonous. Individuals of *D. pumilio* which are dark blue, and difficult to see in the dark forest, have eight times more poison in their skin than those which are bright red and very conspicuous.

The poison from the skin of *Phyllobates aurotaenia* has been isolated and is given the name of batrachotoxin. It acts on the heart and nervous system and one millionth ounce (0·014 mg) is sufficient to kill an animal weighing 14 lb (7 kg). This means it is about 250 times more powerful than strychnine or curare. Arrow-poison frogs are used by the Indians of South America as a source of poison for their arrow tips. The frog is held over a fire and the heat causes the glands to eject poison which is scraped off the skin. The arrows are dipped in the poison and dried and birds and monkeys shot with such arrows are paralyzed almost immediately.

Many frogs in this family have an interesting method of caring for their tadpoles. In *Prostherapis trinitatis*, from the Andes, the 9–15 eggs are laid in moist places but not actually in water. The male remains by them and when the tadpoles hatch they climb onto his back where they stick to the skin and continue to develop. During the day the frog stays hidden on land but moves into pools at night. After about a week the tadpoles swim off and complete their development. Similar habits have been observed in the other genera of the family and in several other families of frogs as well.

Many Arrow-poison frogs have discs on the tips of their fingers and toes and are able to climb well but only a few have taken to a life in the trees. The majority live on the forest floor among the dead leaves and on the margins of streams and pools. FAMILY: Dendrobatidae, ORDER: Anura, CLASS: Amphibia.

DIMETRODON, or 'sail-lizard', famous North American Permian reptile that was an early member of the mammal-like reptiles. It was an active carnivore, some 12 ft (3·7 m) long, with large jaws set with shearing teeth. The most spectacular feature was the presence of enormous upright, bony spines on the backbone which in life supported a membrane of skin. This adaptation is seen in several early mammal-like reptiles and would seem to be concerned with stabilizing the body temperature, the large surface area of sail permitting both heat absorption and radiation depending on external conditions. Complete skeletons of *Dimetrodon* have been found in North America. ORDER: Pelycosauria, CLASS: Reptilia.

DINOSAURS. For 120 million years the land faunas of the world were dominated by two great orders of reptiles, the Saurischia and Ornithischia, which are commonly grouped together under the name Dinosauria (Gk *deinos*-terrible, *saurus*-lizard). The dinosaurs were a diverse group of reptiles for their habits were nearly as varied as those of the mammals today. There were, however, no marine or aerial forms. Many were fully terrestrial, adapted for fast running in the uplands, while others inhabited the lowlands and were semi-aquatic in habit. Although some were small and of delicate construction, among the dinosaurs we find the largest land herbivores and carnivores of all time.

The known record of dinosaurs extends from the Middle Triassic, some 190 million years ago, to the end of the Cretaceous, about 70 million years ago. The reasons for their final extinction are far from clear but the demise of so dramatic a group has overshadowed, in the mind of the layman, the fact that for an immense span of time they were highly successful. The popular impression that they were a group of cumbersome monsters with a low state of mental organization, ill suited to a changing environment, and trapped in an ever increasing spiral of gigantism is far from true. In their locomotory and feeding adaptations they outstripped all other land reptiles and it is even doubtful if the tiny and more highly adapted mammals which existed throughout the Mesozoic – the 'Age of Reptiles' – played any significant role in their decline.

History of discovery. The years 1824–25 mark the beginning of dinosaur discovery and studies. In 1824 William Buckland, Oxford cleric, geologist and eccentric, described the bones of a huge carnivore from the Jurassic rocks of Stonesfield outside Oxford. He gave the name *Megalosaurus* to these remains and suggested they belonged to a giant lizard. In the following year a Sussex geologist, but doctor by profession, Gideon Mantell, described the teeth of a massive herbivorous reptile from Sussex to which he gave the name *Iguanodon*. In fact, the first tooth of *Iguanodon* had been found by Mrs Mantell in 1822 but her husband delayed publication to search for more evidence to overcome the scepticism of his geological colleagues. This caution was understandable for the greatest anatomist in Europe, Baron Cuvier, on inspecting a tooth sent by Mantell had identified it as that of a rhinoceros.

The name Dinosauria for a new group of reptiles to include these and other discoveries was first used by Sir Richard Owen in 1842. This name was valid until 1887 when Seeley, another noted British expert on fossil reptiles, recognized that dinosaurs comprised two quite distinct orders of reptile, of equal importance, which evolved independently along with crocodiles, pterodactyls, and birds from an ancestral group called *thecodonts. To these two independent dinosaur orders Seeley gave the names Saurischia and Ornithischia and these names remain today. Although both orders evolved from a common group in the Triassic their relationship to one another is not especially close. The distinction between the Saurischia ('lizard-pelvis') and Ornithischia ('bird-pelvis') is primarily based upon the structure of the pelvic girdle which articulates the hindlimbs. In saurischians the pelvic girdle of each side is a three pronged structure somewhat similar to the pattern in lizards, and hence the name for this order. In all ornithischians, however, the pelvis is a four pronged structure a pattern strikingly similar to birds – so much so that for a long time birds were thought to have evolved from ornithischians. A feature unique to ornithischians is the presence of a median toothless bone, the predentary, at the front of the lower jaw. In habit, the Saurischia includes bipedal carnivores (e.g. *Tyrannosaurus*), and quadrupedal herbivores (e.g. *Brontosaurus*). The Ornithischia also includes both bipeds (e.g. *Iguanodon*) and quadrupeds (e.g. *Triceratops*) but all were herbivores. Both orders are found in the Triassic and both continued to evolve and diversify throughout the remainder of the Mesozoic.

The Saurischia was in many respects the more conservative of the two orders, its members preserving many of the anatomical features found in the thecodont ancestors. Two quite separate lines of saurischian evolution can be followed and the two groups which can be distinguished are called the Sauropoda and Theropoda. The sauropods, were all quadrupedal and plant-eaters and it is in this group of dinosaurs (the *Brontosaurus* belongs here) that we see gigantism taken to the limits. They were small-headed forms and the greater part of their enormous length was accounted for by the extensive neck and tail. That they were lowland forms spending their lives browsing on the soft marshland vegetation is certain but to what extent they were amphibious is debatable, and we shall return to this question. The theropods were strikingly different from sauropods in their adaptations for all were bipedal and were the dominant predators of the Mesozoic.

Sauropods, as we have seen, were without

exception plant eaters and in all but a few forms attained enormous size. From their skeletons it is possible to determine fairly accurately their live weight. *Brontosaurus*, for example, was just over 65 ft (20 m) long and in life would have weighed some 35 tons. In *Diplodocus* and *Brachiosaurus* the body length was 90 ft (28 m) but in the former where the body, judging by the skeleton, was slender and the tail very long the live weight was similar to *Brontosaurus*. In *Brachiosaurus* however the body was of massive construction and the tail short, and this dinosaur must have weighed 50 tons.

Problem of gigantism. This is a convenient time to discuss the problem of gigantism remembering that this phenomenom is not confined to the sauropods among the dinosaurs, and in fact is not confined to the reptiles. It has however been suggested by some experts that due to the excessive growth of the pituitary gland, which in part controls size, the dinosaurs were caught up in an inflationary spiral, unable to control their growth, and that this was one of the major factors causing their extinction. They became too big to move without an enormous expenditure of energy, and to nourish so large a body became increasingly difficult. As evidence it has been found that in some giant dinosaurs the bony recess in the braincase which housed the pituitary is large. One can, however, argue that without a large and active pituitary dinosaurs could not have become very big, and, furthermore, that in many respects it is efficient to be big. To understand the reason why, it is necessary to consider the physical relationship which exists between the surface area and volume of a three dimensional object. A mouse has an enormous surface area relative to its volume but a large dinosaur has a very small surface area relative to its volume. This ratio is physiologically important for the following reasons. The large dinosaur with its relatively small surface area of skin would absorb heat slowly in the daytime and lose heat slowly by radiation in the cool of the night. It seems likely therefore that the largest of the dinosaurs had the benefit of a fairly stable body temperature unlike the small reptiles of their time and today. In mammals special adaptations of the skin and other organs have been necessary to stabilize the body temperature. The ratio of surface area to volume also has a marked effect on an animal's food requirements and again we can see how large size can make for efficiency. The small animal loses much of its metabolic energy by radiation through its large area of skin and must feed continually to compensate for this extravagance. The larger dinosaurs however did not need to do so although when they did feed a prodigious bulk of food would be required. A massive herbivorous dinosaur would need to have cropped a large area for

its support. For this reason gigantism is never found in island species where pygmy races are often the rule.

It must be admitted that the advantages of gigantism are not obtained without some difficulty. With increased size great stresses are put on the body's internal scaffolding, the skeleton. When an animal increases in length its mass increases as a cube of the linear increase whereas the cross-sectional area of each supporting bone, and this determines their strength, increases by the square of the linear increase. In other words as an animal gets bigger its weight increases at a considerably faster rate than that of the strength of the supporting skeleton. This factor imparts a limit to size but the evidence suggests that the sauropods, and other giant dinosaurs, although approaching this limit, functioned successfully without hindrance. It has always been assumed that the sauropods of necessity spent most of their lives in water dependent on the buoyancy for additional support. That some of their structural features are adapted for amphibious life is not denied but recent evidence suggests that sauropods spent as much time out of the water as in.

The sauropods. Being plant eaters and not requiring large jaws for predation the sauropods had disproportionately small heads. With so small and light a head they could afford the luxury of a very long neck. This enabled the sauropod to crop vegetation over a large ground area while the body was stationary and thus energy was conserved.

The small jaws were set with simple rather peg-like teeth which suggests a diet of soft riverine vegetation. The eyes and nostrils were set high on the skull which might indicate a semi-aquatic life. In *Diplodocus* there is a single common nasal opening on top of the skull which might have functioned as a snorkel.

The sauropod backbone was of massive construction for support of the viscera but the sides of each vertebra were ingeniously hollowed out to reduce their weight without loss of strength. Along the top of the vertebral column ran large ligaments to winch up the head and neck. The limbs were of pillar-like construction for support of the enormous body weight and terminated in elephantine feet with the toes embedded in great pads of tissue.

The origin of the sauropods can be traced back to a group of Triassic dinosaurs of world-wide distribution called prosauropods. It is often said that the sauropods are secondarily quadrupedal having evolved from bipedal ancestors. The shortness of the forelimb compared to the hindlimb has been cited as evidence for this theory. This feature is however typical of all dinosaurs and was present in their thecodont ancestors, the majority of which walked on all four legs. The recent discovery of large Triassic quadrupedal prosauropods, and their trackways, in southern Africa further suggests that the sauropods never passed through a bipedal stage of locomotion.

The sauropods, in terms of variety and numbers, reached their peak of development in the Upper Jurassic and by the Cretaceous were already in decline. It should however be stressed that fossil land vertebrates are rarer in Lower Jurassic and Lower Cretaceous times because throughout the world marine deposits predominate.

The richest fossil localities for sauropods are the Upper Jurassic Morrison and Tendagaru strata, of the western United States and Tanzania respectively. Rich Cretaceous deposits are found in Patagonia and Mongolia. Sauropod remains are not uncommon in Europe but the combination of poor rock exposure, a low erosion rate, and a declining stone-quarrying industry reduces the chances of discovery today. However there is one remarkable site in France for on a mountain slope outside Aix large numbers of complete and fragmentary sauropod eggs are found.

The theropods. The second group of the Saurischia is the Theropoda. Without exception all theropods were bipedal and the great majority were flesh-eating. Two separate groups of theropods can be distinguished and these are called coelurosaurs and carnosaurs.

The coelurosaurs were small for dinosaurs, *Compsognathus* from the Jurassic lithographic limestone of Bavaria was turkey-sized and the largest known coelurosaur had a maximum length of about 15 ft (5 m). They were delicately constructed and probably adapted for fast running in open country.

The coelurosaur skull was light and bird-like in construction. In the more primitive forms the jaws were set with sharp pointed teeth but in some advanced Cretaceous forms teeth were absent. It is likely that the toothed species fed on small reptiles and mammals and that the others had turned to an insect diet. The head was carried on a long and slender, upright neck. All the bones of the skeleton were thin-walled to reduce weight. The forelimb was quite well developed and in some Cretaceous forms ended in a three fingered hand with the thumb opposable for grasping prey. In all coelurosaurs the long and slender hindlimbs were adapted to give fast action and a long stride.

Coelurosaurs had a world-wide distribution throughout the Mesozoic but, for reasons not yet clear, their fossils are far more abundant in rocks of northern latitudes. One group, the ornithomimids ('bird-mimics'), from the Cretaceous of North America and Mongolia, is of particular interest. The ornithomimid skull and skeleton were extraordinarily ostrich-like in structure and ornithomimids no doubt led a very similar life to the ostriches today being

adapted for fast running. When, as in this case, two quite unrelated groups of animals, by reason of their similar mode of life, develop the same kinds of anatomical features we call this phenomenom 'convergent evolution'. In some ornithomimids teeth were absent and these forms probably fed on insects. The skeleton of another ornithomimid, *Oviraptor,* was found in Mongolia beside a nest of dinosaur eggs. As the eggs belonged to a very different dinosaur, a ceratopsian, it is tempting to think that *Oviraptor* ('egg-robber') was an egg-eater and was trapped in the act.

Dinosaurs of Ghost Ranch. Of all regions where coelurosaurs have been found, none is more famous than Ghost Ranch in New Mexico. From a single site a number of perfectly articulated skeletons of the Triassic genus, *Coelophysis,* have been excavated. The skeletons of both young and old were tumbled together as witness to some local catastrophe. Cannibalism must have been rife for within the skeletons of the larger specimens are found the dismembered fragments of the young. The Ghost Ranch locality is an exception because coelurosaur skeletons are rather rare, no doubt because the fragile bones did not preserve well.

The carnosaurs, the other theropod group, include the largest land-dwelling predators of all time for here belong forms like *Tyrannosaurus* with a length of 50 ft (16 m) and a weight of 8 tons. The massive hindlimbs supported the weight of the body, the skull was 4 ft (1·2 m) in length and was carried some 20 ft (6·1 m) clear of the ground.

One of the main features of carnosaur evolution was the progressive increase in skull size which was accompanied by the progressive reduction in size of the forelimb. The relationship between these two trends is easily explained for in carnosaur evolution the head took over completely the function of predation and the arms became unimportant in the seizure and destruction of prey. In the Upper Cretaceous tyrannosaurs where these two related trends are taken to the limit, the skull reached enormous proportions, and the forelimb was almost vestigial.

When we described the sauropods we noted that because their heads were small and light they could afford the benefits of a long neck. In carnosaurs the situation is quite different for as the head increases in size for predation the neck must shorten for its carriage. In the tyrannosaurs the disproportionately large head was carried on a short neck of massive, compressed, and sometimes partly fused vertebrae. To offset in part the mechanical disadvantages of so large and heavy a head we find that in Cretaceous forms particularly the skull is a marvel of construction. Large openings were developed between the bones so that the whole structure of the skull is a system of columns and arches

allowing reduction in weight without sacrificing mechanical strength.

Both the upper and lower jaws of carnosaurs were armed with serrated dagger-like teeth. The lower jaws were loosely hung from the skull enabling a large gape to the jaws. As in snakes, the two halves of the lower jaw did not meet in a bony junction to form a chin. This condition allows a gape in the horizontal plane so that large objects can more easily be swallowed.

The carnosaur vertebral column was pivoted on the fulcrum of the pelvis and a heavy and powerful tail was necessary to counterbalance the weight forward of the pelvis. When at rest the tail and hindlimbs would form a tripod.

The carnosaur hindlimbs were ideally adapted for bipedal locomotion with the upper bones, the femora, massively strong to carry the main limb musculature, and the lower leg long to increase the stride.

Carnosaurs are very rare in the Triassic and their derivation is obscure. In the Upper Jurassic the fragmentary remains of the European form *Megalosaurus* and its allies are found, and in North America complete skeletons of *Allosaurus* have been excavated. The giant tyrannosaurs are all Cretaceous in age, noted genera being *Tyrannosaurus* in North America, *Gorgosaurus* in Canada, and *Tarbosaurus* in Asia.

The Ornithischia is the second order of dinosaurs. Apart from the diagnostic pelvic pattern, already mentioned, many other features set apart ornithischians from saurischians. All were plant-eaters and the teeth tended to be set on the back half of the jaws and were often crowded together to form a file-like grinding surface. It would seem that unlike their herbivorous saurischian cousins they favoured a hard plant diet. The toothless fronts of the jaws were probably covered in horny pads. Although many members developed a bipedal mode of locomotion, the forelimb in these remained well developed and the dinosaurs at rest dropped down onto all fours. In many respects ornithischians were a less conservative group than the saurischians and show many unusual features of skull and armour. Although many were large they never reached the gigantic dimensions of saurischians.

In the Mesozoic scene, particularly towards the end of the era, ornithischians made up the bulk of the dinosaur fauna and filled the same role as do the great herds of herbivorous mammals in Africa today. Moving in herds across the Mesozoic landscape they were alert for the approach of predators. Some forms with their horns or spiked armour were a match for all but the largest of carnosaurs, but others, without defensive armour, took to the water in times of danger.

Although common in Upper Jurassic deposits around the world, the order reached its peak of development in the Cretaceous. Only one or two skeletons have been found in rocks of Lower Jurassic age, a reflection of the predominance of marine deposits at this time, and only within the last few years have their remains been found in Triassic rocks.

Four groups of ornithischian dinosaurs can be recognized: the bipedal ornithopods, the quadrupedal stegosaurs with bony plates along the back, the quadrupedal and heavily armoured ankylosaurs, and the quadrupedal, horned ceratopsians.

The suborder Ornithopoda includes the earliest known ornithischians for their remains have been found recently in Triassic rocks in South Africa, South America, and China. All ornithopods were bipedal although the arm and hand structure shows that it could be used in locomotion. In the earliest members, like the Triassic genus *Heterodontosaurus* from South Africa, we find the primitive ornithischian tooth condition in which teeth are present on the front of the jaws. The next stage of dental evolution is found in Jurassic and Lower Cretaceous ornithopods like *Camptosaurus* and *Iguanodon* where leaf-like teeth are restricted to the back two-thirds of the jaws. The most specialized type of ornithopod dentition is found in the Cretaceous hadrosaurs, or Duck-billed dinosaurs, where the back halves of the jaws are set with parallel rows of teeth crowded together to form a pavement-like structure for grinding hard plant material.

Mass death of dinosaurs. Perhaps the most famous of all ornithopods is *Iguanodon,* originally described by Mantell. This dinosaur reached a length of 35 ft (10·6 m), the hindlimbs being very massive, with three splayed toes on the foot, for support of the heavy body. A complex lattice of tendons ran along the back which helped to support the body when rearing up on its hindlegs. The hand was five-fingered, the outer two digits being weak and the thumb bone in the form of a long bony spike for defence. Iguanodont bones and footprints have been found in Europe, Asia, and Africa. The most remarkable occurrence of all was discovered in Belgium in 1877 when coalminers at Bernissart opened up at a depth of 1046 ft (322 m) a Cretaceous deposit filling a gully in the old Carboniferous landscape. A herd of *Iguanodon* had fallen into this gully and were entombed. Despite difficulties of excavation at this depth some 30 skeletons, many complete, were successfully removed to Brussels.

Not all ornithopods were large and one small form of particular interest is *Hypsilophodon*. This Cretaceous form found in England has a delicate skeleton about 4 ft (1·2 m) long. The structure of its hands and feet suggests an arboreal life, and if this is so then *Hypsilophodon* is the only known dinosaur to occupy this niche.

The hadrosaurs, or Duck-billed dinosaurs,
were yet another ornithopod group and these were the most abundant ornithischians of the Upper Cretaceous, with a world-wide distribution. The Duck-bills take their name from the fact that the front of the skull and lower jaw was drawn out into a large flat beak. Although bipedal when moving at speed, the presence of hoof-like ends to the hand digits clearly indicates that the hadrosaurs could walk on four legs.

We have already mentioned the complex tooth series in hadrosaurs but another remarkable skull feature is the development in this group of bony crests on the forehead. The North American genus *Corythosaurus* shows this character well. In the related genus *Parasaurolophus* an even more bizarre development was the presence on the snout of a long backwardly directed spur of bone passing over the top of the skull. When sectioned it is found that the nasal passage is carried back inside this to the apex and then turns forward along it to reach the throat region. Many suggestions have been made to account for the U-shaped nasal passage but none is convincing. The bone has no opening at its apex so the early theory that it functioned as a snorkel is discounted. That the long nasal passage could be used as an air store when *Parasaurolophus* submerged is unlikely because the storage area is so minute when compared to the estimated lung volume. The most recent theory is that hadrosaurs were far more terrestrial than has been previously supposed and that enlarged nasal passages were only concerned with the sense of smell. Warned of the approach of a predator, the hadrosaur took to the water.

The Upper Cretaceous rocks of Canada have yielded some superbly preserved hadrosaurs and in a few cases even the skin and much of the musculature has been fossilized. The skin was covered with small scales and extended between the fingers and toes as webs supporting the idea that hadrosaurs were at least semi-aquatic. The deep and powerful tail was possibly adapted as a swimming organ.

The Stegosauria was an even more strange group of ornithischians, their main diagnostic feature being the armour on the back. The stegosaurs were quadrupeds although the limb structure indicates that they were derived from bipedal ornithopods. The forelimb was very short in proportion to the hindlimb, and the back strongly arched so that stegosaurs stood high at the rump but low at the shoulders. The digits of both hand and foot ended in hoof-like pads. The head was disproportionately small and the brain kitten-sized. In stegosaurs however the spinal cord swelled out in the pelvic region to form an accessory 'brain' controlling locomotion.

The most obvious and remarkable feature of the stegosaurs was their armour which was confined to the upper surface of the body. In the best known form, *Stegosaurus* from the
Upper Jurassic, the body was 20 ft (6·2 m) long and the neck, trunk, and tail carried a double row of vertical and triangular bony plates. The end of the tail was armed with four long, defensive spikes.

The earliest known stegosaur is a form found in England called *Scelidosaurus*. The remains come from a Lower Jurassic marine deposit, the carcasses having been carried to the sea by rivers at the time of death. Stegosaurs had a cosmopolitan distribution in the Upper Jurassic and Lower Cretaceous but none survived into the late Cretaceous.

Reptilian tanks. The third suborder of the Ornithischia is the Ankylosauria. These quadrupedal herbivores demonstrate the greatest degree of armour plating found in dinosaurs and with good reason have been called 'reptilian tanks'. Some reached a length of 20 ft (6·2 m) and in all the much flattened head and trunk was protected on its upper surface by a mosaic of bony plates. Typically the tail had a flexible armour of bony rings. In some the shoulder and tail regions carried long bony spines. With so heavy a body it is not surprising that the legs were very short and the feet broad.

The ankylosaurs were restricted to the Cretaceous, well known forms being *Polacanthus* from the European Lower Cretaceous and *Ankylosaurus* from the North American Upper Cretaceous.

The Ceratopsia is the remaining suborder of the Ornithischia and is the last dinosaur group to appear in the fossil record for no ceratopsian is known before the Upper Cretaceous. Here belong the rhinoceros-like horned dinosaurs with *Triceratops* the most famous genus.

Considering the group as a whole a number of evolutionary trends can be seen which continued throughout the Upper Cretaceous. The most important of these were: an increase in body size, enlargement of the head associated with increase in jaw length and the development on the skull of horns and a bony frill covering the neck, and a progressive reduction in limb length, particularly that of the back legs.

In the primitive ceratopsian, *Protoceratops* from Mongolia, the head relative to the body was of moderate size, and the skull carried an incipient facial horn but a well developed and fenestrated frill. A great deal is known about this little ceratopsian for their eggs and complete skeletons at all stages of growth have been collected. In *Triceratops* from North America the body reached a length of 25 ft (7·6 m) of which a third was accounted for by the head. In *Triceratops* there was a short nasal horn and a pair of long horns above the eyes. *Monoclonius* shows the reverse condition and in *Styracosaurus* there was a long nasal horn and at least eight horn-like processes on the margin of the collar frill.

The skull frill served both to protect the vulnerable neck region and also to provide a large surface area for the attachment of the powerful jaw muscles. The front of the ceratopsian's jaws formed narrow turtle-like beaks but behind these were batteries of shearing teeth. The whole structure of the jaw apparatus suggests an unusually tough and fibrous plant diet and it seems likely that the ceratopsians cropped the hard fronds of palms and cycads.

Despite more than a century's research many problems remain unanswered, not the least of which is the cause of the dinosaurs' final extinction.

Why did dinosaurs become extinct

It is often difficult to explain why a group of animals becomes extinct, but when we consider the dinosaurs, which for so long a span of time were both varied and successful, the mystery is greater and we can only speculate wildly on the causes. In attempting to do so it is important to appreciate from the start that extinction in any group of animals can result from two different factors. In the first case, species in a lineage become extinct because in their evolution they are replaced by newly evolved forms – the ancestor being unable to compete with its descendant. This pattern of extinction is certainly found in the dinosaurs for there was a wholesale extinction of dinosaurs at the end of the Triassic when new and more highly adapted groups appeared.

The second pattern of extinction is seen when a group disappears without issue. This may be related to internal factors, or to changes in the environment. The final extinction of the dinosaurs at the close of the Mesozoic was probably the result of a whole series of events in the Cretaceous. This was a time of great mountain building and as the earth's crust gradually heaved up and crumpled some regions would be subjected to uplift, and others to compensating downwarping. In the regions of uplift the lowland swamps and sluggish river systems would drain and its vegetation wither. In the regions of downwarping the seas would flood the lower ground. The lowland herbivores and in particular sauropods and hadrosaurs would be the first to suffer and as they declined the food chain would be broken, for now the predators were denied their prey. A second feature of the Cretaceous was the gradual replacement of the palm and cycad forests by modern types of plants, the gymnosperms. The traditional food of hadrosaurs and ceratopsians was in short supply by the end of the Cretaceous and this factor alone might account for their extinction.

These are only partial answers to the problem but what does seem certain is that neither gigantism nor competition from mammals played any significant role in their demise. A further question which remains

Midwife toad, a species in which the male alone cares for the offspring.

unanswered is why at the end of the Cretaceous not only the two orders of dinosaurs but the flying pterosaurs and both groups of quite unrelated marine reptiles, the plesiosaurs and ichthyosaurs, also became extinct. Perhaps we shall never know.

As Professor Colbert, our greatest living dinosaur expert, has said "when they died, they left their bones in the earth. Today one mammal, man, digs up these relics of the past and learns much from them and, at times, is confounded by them". (Ill. p. 52, 53, 54.)

DIPLASIOCOELA, a suborder of frogs. The term diplasiocoelous describes the structure of the vertebral column. In the first seven vertebrae the spool-shaped centra have the anterior face concave and the posterior face convex and in the eighth vertebra both faces are concave. The members of the suborder usually have, in addition, a shoulder girdle which is firmisternal, that is, the two halves are fused down the mid-line.

There are four families: Ranidae, true frogs; Rhacophoridae, Old World treefrogs; Microhylidae, the Narrow-mouthed toads; and Phrynomeridae, a small African family containing a single genus. ORDER: Anura, CLASS: Amphibia.

DISCOGLOSSIDAE, a family of frogs the members of which are characterized by having a round tongue completely attached to the floor of the mouth that cannot be flipped out to catch prey. They also have ribs throughout their life. The family is confined to the Old World and there are four genera.

Four species of *Bombina* are known as Fire-bellied toads and occur in Europe and western Asia. When seen from above the true Fire-bellied toad *B. bombina* is a dull little frog with a grey warty skin but underneath it is vividly patterned with red. Fire-bellies spend most of the time in water. The Yellow-bellied toad *B. variegata* is the least

discriminating and is found in any sort of pool or ditch throughout central and southern Europe. It hangs motionless in the water with only its snout and eyes above the surface and when disturbed can swim well, its toes being fully webbed.

The skin of Fire-bellied toads is poisonous, producing a white frothy liquid which irritates the mucous membranes. Just looking into a bag of freshly caught specimens causes fits of sneezing and watering of the eyes. The bright colouration of their undersides is a warning associated with this poisonous nature. Since the colours are not normally visible from above, however, a Fire-bellied toad, when disturbed and unable to escape, arches its back and folds its limbs up over its body, revealing its bright colours to its attacker.

Fire-bellied toads leave the water at the approach of winter and hibernate in burrows. The breeding season is long, beginning in April or May and lasting for two or three months. About 100 large eggs are laid in water and are attached to stones or plants.

The single species of *Barbourula, B. busuangensis*, is similar to the Fire-bellied toads except that it is even more aquatic in its habits. The fingers, as well as the toes, are webbed. It is found only in the Philippines.

The Painted frog *Discoglossus pictus* is a small, very active frog with a smooth skin which varies in its colouration, the olive-brown ground colour being marked with dark bands or patches while a yellowish stripe down the middle of the back and reddish ones along the sides may be present. It lives in or near water and like the Fire-bellied toads, but unlike most frogs, is able to swallow its food underwater. Its breeding follows the pattern typical of most frogs; 300–1,000 small eggs are laid in water where they lie in a mass on the bottom. The tadpoles are able to leave the water after two months.

Frogs of the other genus in this family,

Alytes, differ from the previous forms in that they live on land, either in burrows which they construct or in ones left by small mammals.

The Midwife toad *Alytes obstetricans* also has a very unusual method of breeding, the eggs being carried around attached to the hindlimbs of the male until the tadpoles hatch out. Pairing occurs on land and the female extends her hindlimbs to form a receptacle for the eggs. These are large and between one and five dozen are expelled in two long loops, each egg attached to the next by a tough elastic thread. The male fertilizes the eggs and then pushes his hindlimbs through the loops until the eggs are firmly wound round him. The female moves away and has nothing further to do with the development, while the male withdraws to his hole until the next night when he comes out to feed. He is not particularly hampered by his load and may repeat the procedure to add a second lot of eggs to the first. After about three weeks the tadpoles break through the egg capsules while the male is in water and swim off to complete their development. ORDER: Anura, CLASS: Amphibia.

E

EARLESS MONITOR *Lanthanotus borneensis,* or Earless lizard, the only genus and species of the family Lanthanotidae. It is a most unimpressive lizard 1½ ft (46 cm) long, with a dorso-ventrally flattened body, short limbs and tiny eyes. After its discovery in Sarawak in 1878 by the Austrian zoologist Franz Steindachner it was hardly ever found again and only a very few museums own a specimen. Even expeditions that set out especially to find this rare lizard had little success. It was only in the years after 1960 that the researchers Tom and Barbara Harrisson came across it by accident. With the aid of the local people they found many more after this in the wet soil, fields and forests of Sarawak and even in the irrigation ditches of the rice fields. *Lanthanotus borneensis* is excellently camouflaged: the elongated body is earthy brown, the small scales on head and body are interrupted by 6 to 10 longitudinal rows of larger cone-shaped scales that extend to the tail. The legs are very short, the movable lower lid of the tiny eyes has a transparent scale or window. The Earless monitor moves in a twisting manner, the short legs helping by pushing. Earless monitors avoid bright lights; apparently they are only active during the night and in their subterranean tunnels. They will lie motionless in their hide-outs or in shallow water for hours and days with only the nose protruding from time to time to breathe. If disturbed they flatten their already flat bodies even further and if taken in the hand they try to bite with their long pointed teeth. Nothing is known about their feeding or breeding habits in the wild; but some were kept alive in captivity for several years on small pieces of sole.

The Earless monitor has a special interest because it seems to be closely related to snakes. It is not a direct ancestor of snakes but gives a good impression of what the snake ancestor could have looked like as a subterranean reptile with degenerate limbs and eyes. The species is confined to Sarawak, Borneo, which suggests it is a relict species. FAMILY: Lanthanotidae, ORDER: Squamata, CLASS: Reptilia.

EFT. Old English name for a small lizard, it was later used for the Smooth newt and this persists locally for it in Britain, sometimes as effet or evet. In North America it is used for the terrestrial larvae of certain newts. In these the aquatic larval stage changes into the eft which leaves the water and lives on land for as much as three years. It then returns to the water, develops a tail fin and becomes a sexually mature adult. The eft differs from the adult in having a rougher skin and a tail which is not flattened from side to side, and in being a different colour.

In the Red-spotted newt *Diemictylus viridescens,* for example, the adult is olive-green with a few red spots and reaches a length of about 4 in (10 cm). The eft is called the Red eft, is brilliant orange or red and reaches a length of about 3½ in (8·8 cm). The adults live in ponds and ditches in the eastern half of North America while the efts are found sometimes on the forest floor, after rain, in large numbers, making no attempt to remain concealed.

The efts of other species of *Diemictylus* are also reddish in colour.

The eft stage is not always passed through. In some parts of its range a species may transform straight from the aquatic larva to the aquatic adult. None of the European newts has an eft stage. ORDER: Caudata, CLASS: Amphibia. (Ill. p. 54.)

EGG-EATING SNAKES. The true Egg-eating snakes are adapted to living on eggs that are at least twice the size of the snake's gape. The six species form a subfamily, Dasypeltinae, of the large snake family *Colubridae. Modifications in the structure of these snakes allowing them to engulf, swallow, pierce and crush eggs then regurgitate the shells are to be found in the extreme reduction of teeth, flexibility of the jaws, development of special neck muscles and of long, downward and forward directed spines on some of the vertebrae. These sharp spines, which are tipped with dense bone, penetrate the wall of the gut and form a mechanism for cracking eggs.

Five species occur in Africa south of the Sahara and in Arabia and belong to the genus *Dasypeltis.* One species, *Elachistodon westermanni,* found in northeast India is exceedingly rare; since it has grooved back fangs and a sensory nasal pit it may not feed exclusively on eggs. All true Egg-eaters lay eggs; there may be a dozen in a clutch. An adult 2 ft (61 cm) long *Dasypeltis* can eat a chicken's egg four times the diameter of its own head. Forcing the egg against a loop of its body the snake may take 20 minutes to engulf it. Once worked into the throat the egg is forced back, then as the snake arches its neck the shell is pierced by the spines on the backbone. As the snake moves its neck down again boss-like processes on the vertebrae in front of the spiny ones flatten the egg and by means of a valve in the oesophagus the contents are squeezed towards the stomach and the shell compressed into a neat package is regurgitated. Numerous species of snakes augment their diet with eggs but none is as highly specialized as the Dasypeltinae, although some Chinese rat snakes (*Elaphe*) are fairly similarly modified and one species at least has vertebral spines penetrating the oesophagus.

In pattern and proportions some species of *Dasypeltis* superficially resemble the venomous Night adder *Causus* and the Saw-scaled viper *Echis* and in West Africa and Sudan all three may occur together. In warning behaviour too *Dasypeltis* is similar to *Echis* for both employ their rough scales for stridulating. Generally the keels of the third to fifth row of scales along the sides of the body of the African Egg-eater are serrated and in its defence posture the snake coils up in a C-shaped curve, inflates itself and by rubbing the body coils against each other makes a loud rasping noise while simultaneously lunging with open mouth, although not biting the aggressor. FAMILY: Colubridae, ORDER: Squamata, CLASS: Reptilia. (Ill. p. 56.)

EGG-TOOTH, an organ on the snout of hatching embryo reptiles and on the bill of embryo birds used to cut open the eggshell. There are two kinds in reptiles. In turtles, crocodiles and the tuatara it is a small, pointed horny wart formed as a local thickening of the skin on the tip of the snout, and known as the egg caruncle. At hatching, the embryo slits open the flexible membrane lining the inside of the shell, then cracks the calcareous shell itself by stretching movements of the body and limbs. The caruncle is shed within a few weeks of hatching.

The 'egg-tooth' of lizards and snakes is a specialized type of real tooth at the tip of the upper jaw, stouter and longer than a normal tooth. And whereas the other teeth of the upper jaw point towards the lower jaw, the egg-tooth points forwards and outwards. In most species there is only a single egg-tooth, in the midline between right and left jaws. Geckos have a pair of egg-teeth, situated close together at the tip of the jaw, each resembling the typical single egg-tooth of other lizards. In all egg-laying snakes and most lizards the eggs have pliable shells and the embryo apparently slices right through it. After hatching, the egg-tooth (or egg-teeth, in geckos) is discarded, usually within a day or two. In the live-bearing lizards and snakes egg-teeth are reduced to a varying extent, but are usually not completely absent.

The egg-tooth in birds is scale-like and is shed soon after hatching. The American woodcock is exceptional in having a second egg-tooth on the lower mandible, also.

ELAPIDS, snakes belonging to the family Elapidae, one of two families of front-fanged snakes, the other being the Hydrophidae or Sea snakes. All are venomous. The family is most strongly represented in Australia. In Asia and Africa they account for only 10% of all snakes, there are only four in North America and none in Madagascar or Europe. Elapids include cobras, King cobra, Coral snakes, kraits, mambas, the taipan and bandy-bandy of Australia and Tiger snakes, all of which are dealt with under these names.

Elapids range from very large snakes, such as the King cobra, almost 20 ft (6 m) long to small Australian snakes less than 15 in (38 cm) long. The bite of the smallest elapids is little worse than a wasp sting. Some of the smaller snakes are sand-coloured but the large members of the family include the brilliant green of the mamba and the striking Coral snakes ringed in black, yellow and red.

The fangs of elapid snakes may be deeply grooved, for conducting venom, or in species such as cobras the edges of the grooves meet to form canals through which the venom flows. Apart from having venom-conducting fangs in the front of the mouth, a condition known as proteroglyphous, there is little to distinguish this family from other poisonous snakes. There is no easily seen external character or combination of characters to serve as a guide and recognition of these dangerous snakes depends on identifying the individual species. FAMILY: Elapidae, ORDER: Squamata, CLASS: Reptilia. (Ill. p. 55.)

ERYOPS, a representative of the extinct group of Amphibia known as the *Labyrinthodontia. It lived in the early part of the Permian period (about 260 million years ago) in Texas and the adjoining southwestern United States. It was about 6 ft (2 m) long with a massive skull about 18 in (46 cm) long. The skull in side view looks somewhat like that of an alligator, but is seen to be much broader in top view. There were 23 vertebrae forming the backbone of the trunk, a small number for a labyrinthodont. This, together with the massive legs, suggests that *Eryops* was more terrestrial than most labyrinthodonts. The shoulder girdle and hip girdle are like those of other large terrestrial, primitive amphibians and reptiles, and the limbs were held with the upper arm and the thigh parallel to the ground so that the animal must have had a slow, ponderous gait.

The structure of the vertebrae of *Eryops* is characteristic of the group of labyrinthodonts to which it belongs. The vertebrae, known as rhachitomous, each consist of four parts. Dorsally, as in all vertebrae, there is a neural arch bearing a neural spine and also processes to link it to the ones in front and behind. The arch surrounded and protected the nerve cord. Below this is the centrum accounting for the remaining three parts and corresponding to the single spool-shaped centrum of most terrestrial vertebrates. A crescentic wedge of bone, shaped like a slice of melon, known as the intercentrum is situated ventrally at the front. The other two structures are a pair of so-called pleurocentra, diamond-shaped in side view, situated behind and somewhat above the intercentrum. It has been suggested that this type of compound vertebra was to allow controlled torsion of the backbone, which could twist easily through a small angle, thus allowing the animal to lift its forefeet from the ground without having to raise the heavy head.

Eryops is one of the few fossil vertebrates in which large areas of skin have been preserved. These show a pattern of oval horny scales like those of reptiles, each about $\frac{1}{2}$ in (12 mm) diameter. Unlike those of most reptiles, however, these were underlain and supported by bone in the form of tiny bony plates, with many plates supporting one scale. It is unlikely therefore that *Eryops* could breath through its skin as do living Amphibia.

Although a large terrestrial animal *Eryops* is likely to have lived near lakes or swamps and to have bred in water, perhaps having a tadpole stage. It was certainly a carnivore judging from its numerous large crocodile-like teeth, and perhaps fed on the large clumsy herbivorous reptiles which were its contemporaries. ORDER: Rhachitomi, SUPERORDER: Labyrinthodontia, CLASS: Amphibia.

EURYAPSIDA, an assemblage of extinct and varied reptiles adapted for terrestrial, amphibious, or completely aquatic life. Apart from the presence in euryapsids of a single perforation on each side of the skull roof for the passage of jaw muscles, the member groups have little in common. The Permian protorosaurs were at the most semi-aquatic in habit, the Triassic placodonts were marine with an armoured turtle-like body and teeth for crushing shellfish, and the plesiosaurs were marine reptiles of the Jurassic and Cretaceous adapted in every feature of their body for life in the open seas. No euryapsid survived the close of the Mesozoic.

EYED LIZARD *Lacerta lepida,* also known as the Spanish or Ocellated lizard. It lives in southern France and the Iberian Peninsula and grows to 2 ft (60 cm), of which 16 in (40 cm) is tail. It is brownish green to reddish with black spots which sometimes form rosettes with black centres. On the flanks are bluish oval markings, the so-called 'eyes' or 'ocelli'.

FAMILY: Lacertidae, ORDER: Squamata, CLASS: Reptilia.

F

FER-DE-LANCE *Bothrops atrox*, a common, widely distributed venomous snake found in Mexico, Central and South America and nearby islands, especially Trinidad. It is sometimes called the tommygoff, a word derived from the Spanish and meaning simply 'snake'. This name was first applied specifically to the fer-de-lance during the construction of the Panama Canal, where it was an ever-present danger to the workmen. Depending on the area involved, the species is also known as 'Barba amarilla' (Yellow beard), 'fer-de-lance' (Iron lance), Terciopelo (Velvet snake), Jararaca, 'Cantil' and 'Labaria'. See Pit vipers, FAMILY: Crotalidae, ORDER: Squamata, CLASS: Reptilia.

FISHING SNAKE *Herpeton tentaculum*, one of the rear-fanged snakes of the subfamily Homalopsinae, members of which inhabit ponds, rivers and estuaries from China to New Guinea and northern Australia. They appear to be at home in both fresh and salt water. Their valvular nostrils are situated on top of the snout and a forward extension of the glottis plugs into the internal opening of the nostrils, thus preventing water entering the lungs via the mouth.

The Fishing snake, otherwise known as the Board snake, Tentacled snake or Siamese swamp snake is the most aquatic member of the subfamily and has much reduced, keeled ventral and subcaudal plates. It can readily be distinguished from its relatives by the presence of two leaf-like scaly tentacles on its snout. It attains a length of about $2\frac{1}{2}$ ft (77 cm) and is usually reddish-brown with white-edged dark cross-bars although lighter coloured individuals with longitudinal stripes are also encountered. It inhabits streams and swamps in Thailand, Cambodia and South Vietnam where its colour pattern forms an excellent camouflage against a background of aquatic vegetation. It has a remarkable habit of anchoring itself to some stem or root with its prehensile tail and adopting a rigid, board-like posture which greatly increases its plant-like appearance and consequently its concealment, not only from predators, but also from unwary fish and aquatic amphibians upon which it feeds. This rigid posture is maintained even when the snake is removed from the water. Although equipped with venom injecting apparatus it is not dangerous to man.

It has long been thought that the tentacles, which are muscular and movable, act as a lure to passing fish, but recent observations on captive Fishing snakes have shown that this is not the case. However, it is now believed that their only purpose is to enhance the snake's plant-like appearance.

The young are born alive, there being between seven and 13 in each brood. FAMILY: Colubridae, ORDER: Squamata, CLASS: Reptilia. (Ill. p. 55.)

FLYING DRAGONS, name commonly used for Flying lizards. They are among the most bizarre and gaudy members of the family Agamidae. 'Flying' is a misnomer, for unlike birds the 'wings' of these lizards are not supported by the forelimbs nor can they beat in flight. All four limbs are free for landing and for climbing on tree trunks but along the sides of the flattened body and between fore-and hindlegs are wings consisting of a thin membrane or skin stretched across greatly elongated and movable ribs. These ribs when extended provide the lizard with a taut patagium that can be opened and closed like a fan. When at rest on a tree the wings are closed; they open only when the lizard is displaying or when it is ready to launch itself from a trunk. As the lizard prepares to glide it turns, faces downwards, dives steeply, straightens out at an angle of about 22° and then as it is about to alight on another tree it banks so as to land in an upward position; the lizard then folds its wings. Although a few kinds of lizard can descend from the ground by parachuting, only the Flying dragon has the ability to glide and control the angle of descent.

Flying lizards have long dewlaps and wattles which in some species are vividly coloured, bright orange for instance in the large *Draco fimbriatus,* blue in the common *D. volans*. There is also sexual variation in the colour and length of these appendages. Over a dozen species are known, all restricted to the tropical forests of Southeast Asia and India and many feeding exclusively on ants. They reproduce throughout the year and one to four eggs, depending on species, are laid. None of the species attains a length of more than 12 in (30 cm). FAMILY: Agamidae, ORDER: Squamata, CLASS: Reptilia.

FLYING GECKO *Ptychozoon homalocephalum,* also known as Fringed gecko or Parachute gecko, of Southeast Asia, has flaps of skin on its legs, tail and sides, those on the flanks being half as wide as the trunk. It is usually assumed that these flaps help to conceal the animal when it flattens itself, at rest, on a tree. Within recent years, however, tests have shown that they act as planing surfaces enabling the gecko to parachute at a steep angle to the ground. FAMILY: Gekkonidae, ORDER: Squamata, CLASS: Reptilia.

FLYING SNAKES, four species of Southeast Asian snakes, one of which is the oriental Golden tree snake *Chrysopelea ornata*. They live in trees and have developed a capacity both to leap from branch to branch and to descend over considerable distances to ground level in an inclined glide. The leaping ability is achieved by the sudden straightening of the body from a strongly coiled position. When gliding the body is held straight with the broad undersurface concave to form a 'parachute' surface. It is unlikely that these snakes have any ability to control the direction of the glide. FAMILY: Colubridae, ORDER: Squamata, CLASS: Reptilia.

FRILLED LIZARD *Chlamydosaurus kingii*, an *agamid lizard whose name is derived from the large ruff or frill of skin around its neck. Although this frill normally lies in folds back along the body, when the lizard is alarmed or angered it opens its mouth wide and the frill is erected, supported by long extensions of the hyoid or tongue bone, which act like the ribs of an umbrella. The Frilled lizard grows to nearly 3 ft (1 m) in length, with rather spindly legs and a long tail. Its colour varies from grey or russet to almost black. Below it may be white to bright rusty red with a shiny black chest and throat.

A striking picture of the North American Green frog while leaping.

Horned frog.

It is found throughout the northern half of Australia except in desert areas, and also occurs in the drier open forests along the southern coast of New Guinea.

The Frilled lizard is partly arboreal, using a tree trunk as a vantage point from which it forages for the grasshoppers and other insects on which it largely feeds. The female lays about a dozen eggs in a shallow nesting chamber which she digs in soft earth. FAMILY: Agamidae, ORDER: Squamata, CLASS: Reptilia. (Ill. p. 57.)

FRINGE-TOED LIZARD, descriptive name applied to several groups of sand-dwelling lizards which possess fringes of pointed scales on their toes. These help them in moving over shifting sand.

FROGS, a name that should refer only to members of the family Ranidae, the true frogs. Since 'frog' and 'toad' are the only common names available for the many species of tailless amphibians, the term 'frog' is also used for many species not closely related to the Ranidae. They are described under the names of the various families while frogs and toads in general are dealt with under Anura.

The Ranidae are characterized by having a shoulder-girdle which is complete and is firmisternal, that is, the two halves are fused down the mid-line. There is a wide range of shapes and sizes found throughout the world except in the southern halves of South America and Australia.

Rana is the largest genus and is found all over the world except in southern South America, southern and central Australia, New Zealand and the eastern part of Polynesia. It is the only genus of true frogs to reach America or Europe. Its 200 species are 'typical frogs' and all are similar in shape, slim, agile frogs with a pointed head and protruding eyes. The hindlimbs are long and the toes are webbed. The skin is smooth and usually brown or green although there is considerable variation in the shades and patterns of this colouration.

The Indian cobra spreads its hood wide.

Forest cobra, or Black-and-white cobra,

Male of *Chamaeleo jacksoni* showing three horns. Other species may have one to five horns.

Chameleon shedding its skin. In contrast to snakes, which slough the skin in one piece, it is shed in large pieces.

The Egyptian cobra, also known as the Black cobra, is capable of swimming.

Boa constrictor *Constrictor constrictor* of the American tropics, rarely exceeds 10 ft (3 m) length.

Like lightning the tongue of the chameleon (*Chamaeleo*) shoots outwards. The prey is caught by the split tip of the tongue, not by a sticky slime on the tongue, as was formerly thought.

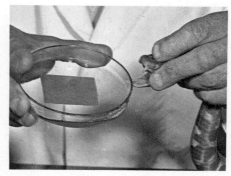

Inducing a copperhead to eject its venom into a glass dish, which will be used in the preparation of anti-venine.

The Rock plated lizard of Africa is the largest of the cordylid lizards.

The sungazer, one of the cordylid lizards, named for its persistent basking.

Crocodiles hatching.

Australian crocodile.

Conspicuously coloured Corroboree toadlet, remarkable for walking on the tips of its toes.

The strikingly patterned Arizona or Sonoran coral snake.

The Age of Reptiles, when dinosaurs were the dominant large animals, lasted 120 million years and ended 70 million years ago. With the aid of abundant

Diplodocus, one of the sauropods.

Crocodiles basking.

Reconstruction of *Ceratosaurus* (left) and *Stego-saurus* (right),

plant and animal fossils it is possible to reconstruct the landscape of those times together with its larger inhabitants.

Reconstruction of *Triceratops*, a three-horned extinct giant reptile.

Antrodemus and *Diplodocus*, contrasting types of extinct giant North American reptiles.

Newt from North America where the name eft is often used for the adult.

Restoration model showing head of a carnivorous dinosaur.

Restoration of *Anatosaurus*, Duckbilled dinosaurs.

Fishing snake *Herpeton tentaculatum*, of Thailand, has two blunt tentacles on its snout, which lure fish to its jaw.

Four-lined snake *Elaphe quatuorlineata*, of Europe, not aggressive but will bite if provoked.

Fishing snake of Asia and Australia.

Elapids are a family of snakes. One of the species is the Green mamba, which although arboreal and only occasionally coming to the ground, can sometimes be seen in water.

Four stages in the swallowing of an egg by an egg-eating snake.

A crocodile has in the lower jaw a large fourth tooth.

Frilled lizard of Australia showing alarm-threat display. It can grow up to 3 ft (0.9 m) and often uses a tree trunk to spot its food.

There are ten species of *Rana* in Europe, divisible into two fairly distinct groups: the 'brown' or 'land' frogs like the Common frog and the 'green' or 'water' frogs like the Edible frog. The Common frog *Rana temporaria* is about 4 in (10 cm) long and, although it varies greatly in colour, it is usually a shade of brown above with black-brown spots or patches. Largely terrestrial, it is usually found in damp grass. The Edible frog *Rana esculenta* by contrast, spends most of its time in water. These two species illustrate another difference common in the genus. In the male Common frog the vocal sacs which help amplify its call are situated under the skin of the throat and when the frog calls the throat swells up. In the Edible frog the vocal sacs are external and located at the sides of the mouth. During calling two small greyish balloons emerge behind the corners of the mouth.

In America a similar range of ecological niches to those in Europe are occupied by different species of frog. The Green frog *R. clamitans*, related to the Edible frog, is found in the eastern half of the USA. It is bright green on the head and shoulders and olive brown on the back. It lives in any kind of pond or swamp. The Leopard frog *R. pipiens* is found throughout North America except the Pacific Coast States and there are many subspecies. It is 3–5 in (7·5–12·5 cm) long and has a striking pattern of dark olive spots edged with yellow on a bronze-green background. It is remarkable that it is often found far from water in fields or orchards.

The hindlimbs of many species of frog are considered a delicacy in many parts of the world. In Europe the Edible frog is usually eaten although since it does not emerge from hibernation until late in spring the Common frog, which emerges earlier, is used in the early part of the year. In North America the large bullfrog *R. catesbeiana* is most commonly used but in areas where it does not occur other large frogs such as the Leopard frog or the Pig frog *R. grylio* are caught.

The brown and green colouration of most frogs helps to render them inconspicuous but in some the camouflage effect is more marked. The Striped rana *R. fasciata* of South Africa, for example, lives in marshes and has gold and brown stripes making it very difficult to see in the grass. Its toes are only slightly webbed and it is well adapted to climbing or diving into the dense mats of vegetation.

The Wood frog *R. sylvatica*, of northeastern USA and throughout Canada, lives among the dead leaves in oak woods where it is very difficult to find since its back is a plain light brown or buff, the colour of dead leaves. It is related to the Common frog of Europe and like it has a 'robbers mask', a dark band either side of the head from the tip of the snout through the nostrils and eyes to the shoulders.

Most frogs, because of their moist, permeable skin, can only live in damp places or in fresh water. Some species of *Rana* however are adapted to live in more unusual habitats. The Skittering frog *R. cyanophlyctis* ranges from Thailand to Southern Arabia, and is found in any kind of pool. It can tolerate considerable salinity and has been found in brackish pools near the coast. It has also been found near sulphur springs. The Crab-eating frog *R. crancrivora* of the Philippines can also tolerate brackish conditions and has even been reported to jump into the sea and swim out again without harm.

The Indian Burrowing frog *R. breviceps* is

Clawed frog, well known but not a true frog.

The Australian Burrowing frog, can burrow rapidly into loose soil and enters the water only to breed. The above animal was dug out from 1.5 m in a roadside bank.

North American Wood frog.

found in most parts of India and is short and squat and a mottled olive brown or tan. It lives in semi-desert and grassland and can burrow rapidly into loose soil using the spadelike tubercles on the hindfeet. It enters the water only to breed.

R. everetti from the Philippines has been collected from the leaves of shrubs on the banks of streams.

The breeding pattern is similar throughout the genus *Rana*. In the Common rana *R. angolensis* of Africa, for example, the males call from the banks of rivers or pools and attract the females to them. The male clasps the female behind the arms and fertilizes the eggs as they are ejected. Several thousand eggs are laid in water 1–2 in (2·5–5 cm) deep and each is enclosed in a spherical capsule of jelly. They sink to the bottom and debris sticks to the jelly, making them inconspicuous. The tadpole breaks out of the egg after about seven days and develops slowly reaching a size of about 3 in (7·5 cm). It metamorphoses after about one to two years depending on the food supply.

In other species of *Rana* the number of eggs laid and the sizes and times of development of the eggs and tadpoles vary, but the basic pattern is similar.

The Spotted rana *R. grayi* of South Africa, however, sometimes deposits its eggs on land. About 200 are laid in depressions in mud or vegetation about 1 ft (30 cm) from water. The tadpoles develop inside the egg capsules and break out after about five days. If the weather is dry, however, the tadpoles remain inside,

perhaps for weeks, until rain softens the capsules and the tadpoles can break out. They drop into the water where they continue their development, changing into frogs after three or four months.

Some species of *Rana* grow to a considerable size and are known as bullfrogs, but the largest known frog, another member of the Ranidae, is the Goliath frog *Conrana goliath*. This lives in rapids and waterfalls in Cameroun and Guinea, grows to 12 in (30 cm) in length and reaches a weight of nearly 8 pounds (3.6 kg). The tadpoles, however, are not particularly large, their maximum length being about 2 in (5 cm).

Although the genus *Rana* has spread throughout the world the family is almost certainly African in origin and the other genera of the family have a local distribution.

The many species of *Ptychadena* of Africa, known as Ridged frogs, are similar to *Rana* and are sometimes included in that genus, but they have several folds or ridges of skin along the back and have a pointed snout. The hindlimbs are long and they are good jumpers.

Several species of *Pyxicephalus* are found in tropical and South Africa including the African bullfrog *P. adspersus*. They are short and squat with rough skins. When disturbed they inflate their bodies. They are burrowing frogs and have a conspicuous spade-like tubercle on each foot with which they push the soil to either side as they shuffle backwards into the ground.

The Puddle frog *Phrynobatrachus natalensis*, of Africa, also of the Ranidae, is a small frog up to 1½ in (3·8 cm) in length with a pointed head and a fat body, the back covered with small warts. It is very common and lives by the edges of small ponds and rain pools. It can jump well despite its short legs and can also burrow rapidly into loose soil.

The chirping frogs *Arthroleptella* of South Africa are about 1 in (2·5 cm) long and are usually found beside mountain streams and waterfalls. Their breeding shows an interesting adaptation to this habitat. The Cape Chirping frog *A. lightfooti* instead of laying its eggs in the fast-flowing water lays them in moist patches of moss. The tadpoles develop inside the egg capsule, breaking out when the hind limbs develop. They stay in the moss and if placed in water are unable to swim and sink to the bottom. They metamorphose into tiny frogs after about a week.

Frogs of another South African genus *Arthroleptis* are known as 'squeakers' and in them the entire tadpole stage is passed in the egg capsule. The Bush squeaker *A. wahlbergi* lays batches of about 20 eggs in wet, decaying leaves. The young frog, about ¼ in (6 mm)

European Tree frogs, of the family Hylidae, not the Ranidae, therefore not true frogs, illustrating the divergence between common and scientific nomenclature.

Gaudy *Rana malabaricus* of West Africa.

long, emerges after about four weeks. In many species of this genus there is an unusual difference between the sexes. The third finger in the male is considerably longer than in the female. In the Nyika squeaker *A. xeno-dactyloides nyikae* it is nearly half as long as the body. This character is also found in two other genera of Ranidae, *Schoutedenella* and *Cardioglossa*.

Some species of *Platymantis* from the Philippines are adapted for an arboreal life. *P. guentheri*, for example, lives in aerial ferns and trees and the tips of the toes are expanded into adhesive discs similar to those in Tree frogs (Hylidae) while in *P. meyeri*, which lives mainly on the forest floor, the toes are not modified. Frogs of this genus also lay their eggs out of water. Those of *P. hazelae* are laid in groups of five to nine eggs in ferns. The complete development occurs inside the egg capsule and a small frog hatches after about seven weeks. During its development in the egg the larva does not develop gills but has two sacs in the abdominal wall richly supplied with blood vessels for respiration.

The Kloof frog *Natalobatrachus bonebergi* is so named because it is found in cool, shaded valleys or kloofs in South Africa. It has adhesive discs on the tips of its fingers and toes but those on the fingers are larger. This is explained by its unusual egg-laying habits. A mass of eggs is attached to a vertical rock face or leaf overhanging a stream; the female frog holds on with her hands, while her hindlimbs manoeuvre the eggs. After about six days the tadpoles wriggle out of the egg mass and drop into the water.

Frogs of the genus *Ooeidozyga* are found in South Asia and the Philippines. They are aquatic and rarely found out of the water. *O. laevis* is active at night when it may leave the pond but during the day it floats in the water with only its eyes and snout above the surface. If disturbed it dives to the bottom and

The confusion caused by the use of the word 'frog' is even better exemplified by the tomatofrog *Dyscophus antongilii* of Madagascar which belongs to the family Microhylidae or Narrow-mouthed toads.

Bullfrog of North America.

burrows into the sediment. During dry weather it is able to survive by burying itself in moist soil.

Members of the African genus *Hemisus* have adopted a more permanent burrowing habit. The Mottled burrowing frog *H. marmoratum* is a very strange little frog reaching a length of $1\frac{1}{2}$ in (3·8 cm). It has a fat, round body with short legs and a small head. The tip of the snout is hard and pointed and unlike most other Burrowing frogs this one burrows head-first. The spade-like snout is worked up and down while the frog pushes into the ground. In association with this habit the shoulder girdle is robust and fits up against the back of the skull so that the thrust from the legs is better transmitted to the snout. These frogs have a very unusual method of breeding in which the eggs are looked after by the female. At breeding time the male clings onto the female's back while she digs a small underground chamber about 3 ft (1 m) from a pond. The eggs are laid and fertilized in this chamber and the male then leaves. The female remains on top of the eggs while they develop. When the tadpoles hatch out she digs a tunnel to the pool and the tadpoles wriggle

along this and into the water where they complete their development.

Rattray's frog *Anhydrophryne rattrayi* also lays its eggs in a nest, probably made by the male, but the female does not stay with the eggs. The tadpoles remain in the nest in the liquified jelly from the eggs until they develop into frogs. The adults grow to only about $\frac{7}{8}$ in (2·1 cm) in length and the nest is a spherical chamber about 1 in (2·5 cm) in diameter in the mud underneath fallen leaves. The newly metamorphosed frogs, which are about $\frac{1}{6}$ in (4 mm) long, leave the nest after about four weeks.

The Hairy frog *Astylosternus robustus* is another member of the Ranidae. The 'hairs' which give it its name occur only on the male and look like fur on the sides of his body and on the thighs. They are not true hairs and are in fact projections of the skin richly supplied with blood vessels like the branches of gills. They provide an additional surface for respiration to supplement the lungs which, in this frog, are very small. They develop during the breeding season when the male frog is most active. FAMILY: Ranidae, ORDER: Anura, CLASS: Amphibia.

The edible frog, of Europe.

Golden tree frog *Hyla aurea*, family Hylidae, would pass for a true frog so long as its feet are hidden.

Tree frog *Hyperolius* sp, calling at night and showing the enormous vocal sac. Family Hylidae, so not a true frog.

Female edible frog among water crowfoot.

G

GABOON VIPER *Bitis gabonica,* of Africa south of the Sahara, the largest Puff adder, up to 6 ft (2 m) long. It has unusually long fangs, up to 2 in (5 cm) long, and is gaudily coloured yellow, purple and brown in a geometrical pattern. FAMILY: Viperidae, ORDER: Squamata, CLASS: Reptilia.

GALLIWASPS, lizards related to the Glass snake and slowworm, which resemble typical lizards except for their somewhat elongate bodies. Except that some of the species bear live young, such as *Celestus plei* of Puerto Rico and *C. montanus* of Honduras, practically no information is available about their habits or habitats. They are of interest because within the subfamily to which they belong there is a complete sequence from species with five toes on each foot to those with four, two or even one toe per limb. Finally, in the South American genus *Ophiodes* the front limbs are absent and the hindlimbs consist of only very small single-toed flaps. FAMILY: Anguidae, ORDER: Squamata, CLASS: Reptilia.

GARTER SNAKES, harmless snakes of the genus *Thamnophis.* They are the most common, and among the more colourful, snakes of North America. The majority are dark with two or three vivid yellow or orange stripes. All but one of the 20 species are limited to 20–30 in (50–75 cm) in length. The exception, *Thamnophis gigas* of California, is a comparative giant, reaching 5 ft (150 cm). All Garter snakes give birth to living young, with 14–40 in a brood. They subsist mainly on frogs or salamanders, are semi-aquatic and frequent heavily populated areas. Garter snakes make excellent pets and thrive in captivity. FAMILY: Colubridae, ORDER: Squamata, CLASS: Reptilia.

GAVIAL *Gavialis gangeticus,* a crocodile differing from all other living crocodiles in its extremely long snout which resembles a beak. It may be up to six times longer than broad. Adult gavials may be up to 20 ft (6 m) long. There are 29 teeth on each side of the upper jaw and 26 on each side of the lower jaw, all of approximately the same size, even the fourth

Wandering garter snake *Thamnophis elegans vagrans,* of North America, on floating algae with a speckled dace it has just caught.

lower jaw tooth being not noticeably bigger, as is the case in alligators and the true crocodiles. This fourth tooth also does not fit into any gap or hollow in the upper jaw. When the gavial's mouth is closed the teeth are locked between each other and point outwards at an angle.

The end of the snout broadens into an octagonal where during the breeding season the male develops a shell-like hump. This is the only known secondary sexual characteristic in crocodiles. The Indians compare this hump to an earthenware pot called 'ghara' and this is why gavials are often called gharials in English-speaking regions. When first mentioned in the scientific literature this crocodile was described as *Gavialis,* and the name has persisted.

The rear portion of the skull shows several differences to that of true crocodiles. The gavial's two upper temporal openings are round and the same size as the eye socket. Because of these and other characteristics some scientists are inclined to assume that the gavial is related to the now extinct sea-crocodiles of the family Teleosauridae from the Jurassic period.

Other scientists, however, consider the gavial's long snout to be the extreme of a development that had already been initiated in the family of the true crocodiles. The biological advantage of this particularly long

Gavial, the crocodilian of southern Asia with the long narrow snout associated with a fish-eating habit.

snout is presumably the considerable increase of the radius over which food can be caught; this is done by a sideways slash of the head.

The rest of the gavial's body is not very different from that of other crocodiles. The nuchal scutes are not separated but connected with the dorsal scutes, a feature also found in the so-called Sunda gharial, which is, however, a true crocodile.

The Indian gavial lives in southern Asia in the rivers Indus, Ganges, Mahanadi and Brahmaputra; a few also live in the Irrawadi and its tributaries. Gavials are also found in Lake Chilka which sometimes contains river water mixed with sea water.

Not much is known of the life-history of the gavial but it apparently does not differ significantly from that of the true crocodiles. The food consists mainly of fish but waterfowl and small mammals are also eaten. The gavial is also said to attack men or eat human corpses. On a few occasions jewellery has been found in a gavial's stomach. Nevertheless, this reptile has been considered a holy animal in India.

During the breeding season the female lays about 40 eggs with chalky shells in a cavity in a sandy river bank. The eggs are about $3\frac{1}{2}$ in (9 cm) long. The young on hatching are about 15 in (38 cm) long but the snout is still relatively short, only $1\frac{1}{2}$ in (3·8 cm) long. FAMILY: Gavialidae, ORDER: Crocodylia, CLASS: Reptilia.

GECKOS, a mainly primitive group of lizards with 675 species, and nearly 200 subspecies, distributed worldwide mainly in the tropics. They are famous for their nocturnal habits and, more especially, for their climbing abilities due largely to the structure of their feet. A few retain the conventional claw and toe, but many have retractile claws and 'snowshoe' pads for dashing across sand, but most geckos have developed 'friction' pads which enable them not only to climb a vertical wall or a pane of glass, but also to continue scampering across a ceiling upside down.

Geckos live in forests, swamps and deserts, on mountains, and on islands as long as the nights do not get too cold. They range from 2 in (5 cm) total length, to over 1 ft (30 cm), the majority being 3–6 in (7·5–15 cm) long. Roughly half the length is tail.

Their bodies are covered by a soft skin with minute scales, among which, in many species, are larger scales. A few species have fish-like imbricating scales on all or some parts of the body. In most species some of the scales on the underside of each toe are specialized as broad pads, at the base, the tip or throughout the toe. Each pad resembles a miniature densely packed pincushion; every microscopic bristle is split into delicate

Wall gecko (*Tarentola mauritanica*).

branches, each terminating in a disk-like thickening, the free face of which is slightly concave. Zoologists have long sought to unravel how the pads, with their pile of bristles, cling to smooth surfaces. Recent studies show that the multitudinous tiny terminal disks adhere by suction, but on surfaces where this is not possible, the bristles act like so many miniature hooks. The peculiar wriggling gait of the gecko is due to the fact that in order to lift its foot from the wall surface, it must curl each toe upward from the front to disengage the fringes without damaging them.

The sensory organs also have some marked peculiarities. The internal ear is different from that of other lizards, except for the Snake lizards; among other things the sound-sensitive cells are relatively numerous in many species, giving geckos good hearing, in some species apparently better than in man. This is linked with the widespread use of the voice.

The eyes attract attention because in almost all species they are lidless and usually large, often beautifully coloured. The closed lid, fused firmly in place, is entirely transparent and acts as a protective eyecap. This protects the eye from dust and other foreign particles. In fact, if the 'contact lens' becomes dusty, most geckos can use their long tongues as a windshield wiper and lick them clean again! One group of geckos possesses true eyelids but surprisingly some of them have been observed to lick the eye and the lids, which is something that is never done by 'normal' lizards possessing eyelids.

Being nocturnal, most geckos have elliptical pupils. This permits a more complete closure of the iris in daylight, and thus allows the eye to be more sensitive, and enables sight in feeble light at night. However, since in the daylight the elliptical slit is so tightly closed, the gecko's eyesight is greatly impaired. This is solved by an arrangement of scallops along the edge of each half of the iris so that when the pupil is narrowed down to a slit, the scallops match up to produce a series of 'pinholes' in the iris 'curtain' through which the gecko may peer at his world in bright daylight without risking injury to his very light-sensitive cornea. The pinhole system gives the gecko additional focusing advantages over the single, round pupil arrangement of diurnal animals.

The everyday life of geckos depends on whether they live in the tropics, in a temperate region, or in a desert. In tropical and temperate habitats most are climbers in bushes and trees or on rocks, whether equipped with toe pads or with claws only. Those in sandy deserts are ground-dwelling. The majority of geckos are nocturnal, and this is particularly true of the desert species, but several, mostly arboreal, are diurnal. Some species hunt insect prey by night, but

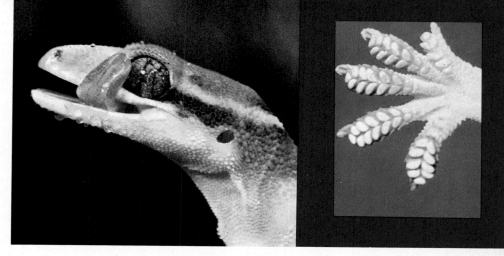

Left: a Gecko using its tongue as a windshield wiper cleaning its closed eye. Right: the underside of the front foot of Brook's house gecko showing friction pads enabling it to climb.

also bask in the sun. Indeed, many geckos forage on even cool nights, at substrate temperatures around 59°F (15°C). Presumably they require more warmth to digest their food properly, and some species obtain this through actually basking, but many others 'bask indirectly' under a thin cover, such as loose bark or a layer of sand.

Some species live singly or in pairs, with no two males tolerating each other; others occur in 'colonies'. As a result of fighting among themselves, part of the tail is frequently lost, especially in males. In a number of species the percentage of animals with broken (missing or regrown) tails was found to be higher among males than among females. The more slowly a reptile can run, the more he must rely on escape systems. In this case the tail of most geckos has undergone some changes. Not only does it break away easily when snatched by a predator, but some have tails that closely resemble succulent caterpillars to distract predators from the more important head end. Others have elaborate tails that resemble

Typical geckos *Gymnodactylus deccanensis*, of the Bombay area of India.

The geckos of the genus *Phelsuma* live on Madagascar.

leaves or lichen, or are bulb-shaped or fringed. Only one genus *Agamura* possesses a permanent type tail. At least a few have extra large tails from which reserve noúrishment can be drawn in lean times.

Geckos communicate among themselves in various ways. They are the only lizards that regularly vocalize. Crocodilians may grunt and roar, and snakes may hiss, but it is the gecko that has developed a real vocalizing technique in the reptile world. In many, usually the nocturnal species, the males utter special calls, something like 'tsak-tsak' or 'tik-tik', repeated a few times in succession. These masculine calls are different from the squeaking of either sex when seized. The social function of the male calls is not really known. The tokay *Gekko gecko* of south-

Pads of the tokay.

Phelsuma laticauda.

eastern Asia has a vocabulary of three different calls, all frighteningly loud. One is uttered in distress, another during aggression, but the function of the third, spontaneous, call, is again unknown. However, some geckos are mute, the distress squeak excepted, especially among Australian species, including several diurnal forms that apparently communicate by visual signals. The diurnal forms are often very colourful, many showing marked sexual dichromatism, and they employ various postures and gestures to broadcast their moods. Geckos will also wave their tails in cat-like fashion on various occasions, and some will announce their irritation by rattling the tail against the ground. The Plate-tailed gecko *Teratoscincus* of Asian deserts has the upperside of its tail covered with a series of enlarged imbricating scales; when the tail wriggles rapidly, these grate upon each other, and a buzzing warning sound emanates.

The female gecko usually lays two eggs, the few records of three eggs having been deposited are doubtful. Some of the smaller geckos lay only one egg, and some of these have been reported to lay only a single clutch each year. In other species three clutches have been reported and in *Teratolepis fasciata* of West Pakistan up to 12 clutches have been

Phelsuma madagascariensis.

Banded gecko (*Coleonyx variegatus*).

accelerate development of the embryo. The eggs of several unrelated species have hatched at 50–70 days at a fixed temperature of 86°F (30°C). Gecko eggs are relatively large and by the time the embryo curled within hatches, its length is between a third and a half that of its

Wall gecko.

parent. For example, adults of *Ptyodactylus hasselquistii* are some 6 in (150 mm) long, their nearly spherical eggs are over ½ in (13–15 mm) in diameter, and the hatchlings are over 2 in (55 mm). Adult *Teratolepis* average 3 in (75 mm), the oval eggs are about

noted in captivity during March and September. Although some geckos lay soft-shelled eggs, others lay hard-shelled, nearly spherical, eggs. The parchment-shelled eggs when dry shrink and may die; if moistened again before it is too late, they imbibe water, swell up and thrive. Accordingly, such parchment-shelled eggs are laid in damp situations, under stones or under bark or in the ground and the tokay will lay one or two eggs on a vertical surface which will adhere to it and harden to such an extent that it is impossible to remove the eggs without damaging them. Incubation time varies from species to species, and the higher temperatures usually

The largest gecko, the tokay (Gekko gecko).

$\frac{2}{5} \times \frac{1}{3}$ in (10×8 mm), and the hatchlings average $1\frac{1}{3}$ in (32 mm). The adult *Gehyra variegata* measures 4 in (100 mm), lays a single egg of just under $\frac{1}{2}$ in (11×10 mm), and the hatchling measures some $1\frac{4}{5}$ in (45 mm). The tiny *Tropiocolotes steudneri* of $2\frac{3}{8}$ in (60 mm) lays an egg of $\frac{1}{4}$ in (7×5·5 mm), and the hatchling measures about an inch (25 mm). Geckos of three New Zealand genera are ovoviviparous, the females giving birth to two, sometimes one or three, babies, which again, measure between a third and a half of the parent's length.

Young geckos grow rapidly and apparently almost all species breed before they are fully one year, or at the most two years, old. They subsequently continue to grow at a slower rate, and apparently are quite long-lived. One captive *Phyllodactylus europaeus* reached the age of 27 years. Many other captive geckos became 7–9 years old, and there are indications that natural longevity of some species approaches the latter-figure.

The relationship of geckos to other lizards has long been in dispute as they show primitive as well as highly specialized characters. One group closely related to them are the Australian *Snake lizards, despite superficial differences. The earliest fossils date from the Upper Jurassic. All geckos have a relatively thin-boned skull which lacks several bones commonly present in other lizards. Neither the post-orbital nor the temporal bony arches occur at the sides of the skull. The numerous, equal, slender teeth are attached to the inner aspect of upper and lower jaws. The skull is usually lower and broader than in most other lizards, in accordance with the geckos' usually flattened shape. The vertebral column resembles that of the *tuatara in many details. Thus a small bony intercentrum is attached below each joint, between successive vertebrae, throughout the body and tail. Practically every tail

vertebra is divided into anterior and posterior halves by an autotomy plane, evident also in the surrounding tissues. In certain species this autotomy system has been restricted to a few vertebrae at the base of the tail, or lost altogether. The limbs and their skeleton are always well developed, usually with five nearly equal toes. Indeed, the muscular system lacks some of the longitudinal abdominal muscles which assist in the snake-like locomotion of lizards with reduced limbs. FAMILY: Gekkonidae, ORDER: Squamata, CLASS: Reptilia.

GEPHYROSTEGUS, a fossil amphibian included in the *Labyrinthodontia. It lived in the late Carboniferous period (about 290 million years ago) in the region of the freshwater swamps which were later to become the seams of gas coal near Prague and Pilsen in Czechoslovakia. Forms which may be related are also known from a similar period in the eastern United States.

Specimens of *Gephyrostegus* are rare and often fragmentary, and are usually preserved as natural moulds impressed in a coal shale from which the bone has rotted away. They are thus frequently very difficult to interpret anatomically, but *Gephyrostegus* is very important to our understanding of vertebrate evolution. Within the labyrinthodonts it is grouped with the Coal measure anthracosaurs and with *Seymouria from the Lower Permian. For many years *Seymouria*, although much too late in time, was considered to represent the sort of animal which must have been intermediate between Amphibia and reptiles in the origin of the latter. However, *Seymouria* has a number of specialized features in the anatomy of the skull and *Gephyrostegus* is a much better candidate for a relict reptile ancestor, although still at least 20 million years too late.

The head and trunk together were about 8

in (20 cm) long and although the tail is not completely known it is likely to have been as long as the rest of the body. The limbs were comparatively large for a labyrinthodont amphibian and sufficiently strongly developed to suggest that *Gephyrostegus* was an active terrestrial animal. However, the head was comparatively larger than that of its primitive reptile contemporaries and anatomically close to that of an anthracosaur labyrinthodont.

The vertebrae are just those that would be expected in a relict reptile ancestor. Nearly all labyrinthodonts have the lower (centrum) part of the vertebra divided into two regions an anterior intercentrum and a posterior pleurocentrum. In reptiles the intercentrum is reduced to a tiny crescent, wedge-shaped in side view, or lost altogether while the pleurocentrum forms the main body of the vertebra on which the neural arch above it rests. In *Gephyrostegus* the pleurocentrum is like that of reptiles and the intercentrum is reduced as though on the way to the reptile condition.

However, *Gephyrostegus* was certainly an amphibian, living in or near the Bohemian coal swamps, probably breeding in water and possibly having a tadpole stage. SUPER-ORDER: Labyrinthodontia, CLASS: Amphibia.

GHARIAL, alternative name for an Indian species of crocodilian more correctly called *gavial.

GHOST FROGS, four species of rare South African frogs, so called because one of them, *Heleophryne rosei*, was found in Skeleton Gorge, near Cape Town. They are strange-looking frogs, flat with bulging eyes. The tips of the fingers and toes are expanded into discs. The adults are sometimes found under rocks and debris some distance from water or in burrows in the banks of cold, fast-flowing mountain streams. The breeding habits are not known and eggs have never been found. The tadpoles, however, are frequently seen clinging to the rocks in the mountain streams with their large suctorial mouths. In the cold water development is slow and it takes two years for the tadpole to develop into the adult. FAMILY: Heleophrynidae, ORDER: Anura, CLASS: Amphibia.

GIANT SALAMANDER *Megalobatrachus japonicus*, of Japan, is the largest living amphibian, reaching a length of 5 ft (1·5 m). A smaller relative *M. davidianus* lives in China, and a more distant relative, the hellbender *Cryptobranchus alleganiensis*, in the United States. The first Giant salamander was brought to Europe in 1829 by de Siebold and lived over 50 years.

The head and body are flattened and skin folds are present along the sides of the body. The tail is laterally flattened and the paired limbs are small in proportion to the body.

A gecko after using the familiar lizard trick of autotomy, throwing off part of the tail.

Being aquatic, and lacking external gills, the Giant salamander has to surface at intervals to breathe. Lungs are quite well developed and internal gills are lacking. The skin probably assists gas exchange.

Breeding takes place in late summer and the eggs, 6 by 4 mm, form a string as they emerge to become externally fertilized. The larvae have three pairs of external gills.

As it is carnivorous the Giant salamander can be captured by fishing, using fish, frogs or large worms as bait. The bait has to be brought near to the animal for a bite to take place. The point of a baited hook is forced into the end of a wooden rod and then, using the rod, the baited hook is directed to the spot where the salamander may be lurking. See Cryptobranchidae. FAMILY: Cryptobranchidae, ORDER: Caudata, CLASS: Amphibia.

GILA MONSTER *Heloderma suspectum*, one of the only two known venomous lizards. This species and its only near relative, the *Mexican beaded lizard, are the sole members of the family Helodermatidae. They are restricted to the New World and there is no fossil record indicating a previous range extending greatly beyond that of the present. Its closest relatives outside this family are the monitor lizards, especially the Bornean *Earless monitor *Lanthonotus* (which was once suspected of being venomous). Unlike most lizards, there has been little apparent specialization of the legs or feet. These appendages have not been reduced in favour of an undulatory mode of travel, or lengthened for increased speed and agility. The Gila (pronounced Hee-la) is a relatively stocky reptile, with a thick short tail, head and body. This bulging body, giving a large surface area in relation to volume, serves to inhibit moisture loss and over-heating in the event of prolonged exposure to desert heat and dryness.

This species, first mentioned by Baird in 1859, was called *Heloderma suspectum* because it was suspected of being a species of venomous lizard different from the already well-known Mexican beaded lizard. Subsequently, the Gila monster has been divided into two subspecies: the Reticulate Gila monster, mottled with pink and black, ranging throughout Sonora, Mexico into southern Arizona and into extreme southwestern New Mexico, and the Banded Gila monster with a more clearly defined banded pattern, living in central western Arizona, southern Nevada and over the border into southwestern Utah. The brilliant banded pattern of the hatchlings gradually becomes mottled and diffused with maturity.

The primitive venom-conducting apparatus consists of a number of grooved teeth in the front portion of the lower jaw. When a Gila chews its victim, venom flows through ducts from glands in the lower jaw, into the

When young the head region bears three pairs of gills but a partial metamorphosis takes place and the external gills are absorbed. All gill-slits close, whereas in *Cryptobranchus* one pair of gill-slits remain open throughout life. The eyes of the Giant salamander lack eyelids and larval teeth are retained. This retention of some larval characters is an example of neoteny.

The Giant salamander lives in cool swift streams. It is carnivorous but instead of pursuing its prey it waits till the prey is within reach and seizes it with a swift lateral movement of the head. Prey consists of fish, smaller salamanders, crayfish and other vertebrates. The senses of smell and touch are probably more important than sight in food capture.

Giant salamander, largest living amphibian, which may be 5 ft. (1.5 m) long.

The Gila monster, although venomous, feeds mainly on small defenceless animals and eggs.

contains no fracture plane, unlike other related lizards in which the tail is readily thrown off when the animal is suddenly disturbed or held. In some species, minute, scale-like vestigial hindlimbs are still discernible in the cloacal region and both pectoral and pelvic girdles are present. The body is covered by squarish-rhomboidal scales, arranged in straight longitudinal and transverse series. The jaws are armed with strong teeth. The scales are provided with separate, dermal bony plates or osteoderms. The tongue, indented in front, can be protruded and then retracted into a fleshy sheath. Most Glass snakes are brown, some have a striped pattern. In *Ophisaurus harti,* of southern China, the sides are ornated with blue spots. The length varies between 15 in (37 cm) in *O. gracilis,* of India and Burma, and 4 ft (125 cm) in *O. apodus* of southern Europe and Asia Minor. In *O. ventralis,* of the eastern United States, the tail is two-thirds of the total length.

The typical habitat of Glass snakes is wet or dry grasslands, such as wet meadows, coastal areas and rocky slopes. The lizards are oviparous, the female laying a clutch of 4–17 eggs and in two species, *O. harti* and *O. ventralis,* the female stays coiled around the eggs until they hatch. Their food is insects and other small arthropods, snails, small lizards and mice, which they hunt by day, more especially at dawn and sunset. Glass snakes do not move quickly and when caught make no use of their strong teeth in defence, but they do emit an evil-smelling substance from the cloaca. FAMILY: Anguidae, ORDER: Squamata, CLASS: Reptilia.

GRASS SNAKE *Natrix natrix,* a well known harmless snake. It is active and slender with a long tapering tail and grows to 3 ft (1 m) normally, although 6 ft (2 m) specimens

mouth between the teeth and lips, then by capillary action it follows the tooth-grooves into the victim's wound. Although unable to dash about like most other lizards, it can quickly snap its head sideways. The short teeth help retain the rodent or lizard prey, while chewing tends to inject venom which may serve to immobilize the prey more quickly. It is still not clear, however, just what purpose the venom serves in the daily life of the *Heloderma.* Humans are rarely, if ever, bitten unless they pick up this reptile in a careless manner. Such injuries have seldom resulted in death, but the venom has produced serious illness and is quite toxic.

The State of Arizona protects this rather inoffensive reptile, which is the animal emblem of the State. Nevertheless, the intrusion of mankind into the rural areas of Arizona has definitely reduced its numbers.

The Gila monster, in captivity, becomes lethargic in contrast to when in the wild when, although it spends a large share of its life in seclusion, is alert and active at certain seasons. In captivity it seems addicted to water and will soak for hours, which indicates that the wild Gila may retire to burrows that retain a significant level of moisture or humidity. FAMILY: Helodermatidae, ORDER: Squamata, CLASS: Reptilia.

GLASS SNAKES, sometimes called Glass lizards. They are slender and elongate, legless lizards, snake-like in appearance but with moveable eyelids and external ear openings, which are sometimes concealed under a fold of skin. The tail is very long but in at least two species it is not fragile and it

European Glass snake, a legless lizard.

European Grass snake protruding its tongue.

basis of such variations ten subspecies are currently recognized.

In England, after mating in April and June, about 8–40 eggs (according to the size of the female) are laid in June and July in manure or decomposing vegetation. The higher temperatures in such sites assist in incubating the eggs. In 6–10 weeks the hatchlings which are 6–7½ in (16–19 cm) long escape from the parchment-like egg-shell by rupturing it in several places with the egg tooth.

The Grass snake is basically terrestrial but its diet being fish and amphibians it is often associated with water. It relies on speed for catching its prey and for escape. Its defensive behaviour includes hissing, striking and playing dead, like the *Hognosed snake, as well as emitting the foul-smelling contents of the cloacal gland. FAMILY: Colubridae, ORDER: Squamata, CLASS: Reptilia.

occur. Females are larger than the males. The colour pattern varies considerably with the locality, age and individual. There is often a yellow, orange, white or even pink crescent on the neck with dark patches in front and behind this. There are several rows of dark markings down the body on a ground colour which can be green, grey, brown, bluish and even black. Partial albinos are found but they are not as common as black specimens.

This snake has an extensive distribution from North Africa, Britain and Scandinavia in the west, to the Caspian Sea and Lake Baikal in the USSR. Over its range the Grass snake varies not only in colour pattern but in bodily proportions and scalation and on the

GREEN TURTLE *Chelonia mydas,* also known as the Edible turtle, being the one used for soup, is peculiar for its greenish tinged fat. See turtles, marine.

GYMNOPHIONA, alternative name for the Apoda, an order of Amphibia containing the small, legless burrowing caecilians.

H

HAMADRYAD *Ophiophagus hannah,* alternative name for the *King cobra, the largest cobra and a snake-eater.

HAWKSBILL TURTLE *Eretmochelys imbricata,* the second smallest marine turtle long persecuted by man as the source of 'tortoiseshell'. All but very old hawksbills can be distinguished from other Sea turtles by their strongly overlapping scutes on the carapace. Restricted to tropical and subtropical seas, stragglers sometimes are found far north of the usual range. Females nest on sandy beaches, depositing 100–200 eggs per clutch. The beautifully coloured scutes of the adult carapace provide 'tortoiseshell', widely used in making ornate combs, brooches and similar jewellery. A cruel procedure of toasting the live turtle to peel the shell is often practised, in the mistaken belief that the turtle will re-grow the scutes when released. The shell of a large hawksbill reaches about 2 ft (60 cm). Fortunately, man-made plastics have largely replaced the use of natural shell. FAMILY: Testudinidae, ORDER: Testudines, CLASS: Reptilia.

HELEOPHRYNIDAE, a family of frogs established to include the single genus *Heleophryne* with four species, all from South Africa, which do not closely resemble any other frogs. The genus has been placed in turn in the families Leptodactylidae, Ranidae and Bufonidae but the tendency now is to place it in its own family, Heleophrynidae. See Ghost frogs.

HELLBENDER *Cryptobranchus alleganiensis,* largest salamander in North America is 18 in (45 cm) long, seldom seen, nocturnal and lives strictly under the water in the eastern United States. By day, it hides in cracks and crannies found around submerged rocks and logs. Its food consists of any smaller aquatic animals. Although possessing lungs and gills, it breathes mainly through the skin. Its fat, wrinkled, slimy, olive-coloured body is more repulsive than pretty. It reproduces by external fertilization of eggs placed in a scooped-out hole at the bottom of the pond. The male stands guard until the eggs hatch. FAMILY: Cryptobranchidae, ORDER: Caudata, CLASS: Amphibia.

HOG-NOSED SNAKES, generalized and adaptable snakes which lack poison glands and mostly eat their prey alive The Eastern hog-nosed snake *Heterodon platyrhinos* and the Western hog-nosed snake *H. nasicus* are common, harmless snakes of North America. The Eastern hog-nosed snake is thick bodied, rather sluggish and superficially viper-like, patterned with large blotches. It attains a length of 2–3 ft (61–91 cm). It is believed that the upturned snout, from which these snakes get their commom name, is associated with their burrowing habit. If molested they strike vigorously, writhe, hiss and flatten the neck into a cobra-like hood in an attempt to discourage potential enemies. However, they always strike with the mouth closed and never bite people. If this lively performance fails to frighten the attacker, the Hog-nosed snake exhibits thanatosis—that is death feign-

Western hognosed snake on the Great Plains.

ing—by turning onto its back with the mouth open and the tongue lolling. Moreover, if it is turned over so that it is belly downwards, in the normal way, it immediately turns over onto its back once more and resumes an attitude of death. The prey of the Hog-nosed snake is mostly amphibians, including toads. FAMILY: Colubridae, ORDER: Squamata, CLASS: Reptilia.

Horned frog *Megophrys nasuta* lives in India and belongs to the family Pelobatidae.

Horned frog.

A Horned frog *Ceratophrys dorsata*, of South America, looking more like a toad.

HORNED FROGS, very distinct and bizarre frogs of the genus *Ceratophrys,* found in most of South America, east of the Andes, from Colombia to Argentina. Once seen, they are easily remembered and identified. They resemble toads (Bufonidae) and are very stocky, almost round when sitting with their legs tucked in. The legs, particularly the forelegs, are short and powerful. The most characteristic feature, however, is the large head with a blunt snout and very wide jaws. In most other tailless amphibians the head is dorso-ventrally compressed, leaving only a narrow space between the eye and the margin of the jaw. This space usually equals the diameter of the eye and is frequently much less in big-eyed frogs. In Horned frogs the head arches high. Although the eye is moderate in relation to the overall size, the distance between the eye and the jaw may equal two and a half to three times the diameter of the eye. It is this and the horizontal pupil that gives these frogs their peculiar facial expression and their unique appearance. The 'horns', for which the Horned frogs are named, are not present

The Horned toad, really a lizard of the genus *Phrynosoma*.

in all members of the genus nor are they found only within it. Similar structures are found in other species in unrelated families, usually in fairly large species. In some Horned frogs these soft extensions of the upper eyelid are well developed, pointed, and may even curve slightly from their own weight. In other species they are rounder, little more than a heavy brow, while in some they may be absent altogether. Horns or no horns, however, there is no mistaking a Horned frog.

The function of the horns and their advantage to the bearer is a matter for speculation. They are soft, therefore useless for defence. They may shade the eye or camouflage it by breaking the circular outline, or afford some protection from injury to the eyeball. They may be purely decorative and enhance the bearer's appearance to the opposite sex, although this is doubtful, or they may make the individual look larger and more formidable to an aggressor, including other Horned frogs. Horned frogs are cannibalistic so discouraging predation by a fellow Horned frog may have definite survival value.

Different species of Horned frogs vary greatly in adult size. The smallest are little larger than a bottle cap; the largest would nicely fill a large soup bowl. They have a toad-like warty skin. Many species have a bold pattern of blotches or bars and some are vividly coloured. There are anatomical features that are apparent only when the skeleton is examined. Some species have a bony shield under the skin which protects the head and back. They also have teeth in the upper jaw.

Horned frogs live well in captivity. Be-cause of their colourful patterns and peculiar expression, they are impressive and the larger species in particular are desirable amphibian exhibits. Usually they sit partially buried in the earth in their terrarium. Unlike many other frogs, they are unlikely to damage their noses by leaping against the walls. They are unafraid; instead, when annoyed, they may attack and bite ferociously and can inflict a painful wound with their long teeth. This aggressiveness is well known in their native lands and inspires the belief that the bite is venomous. This is not so, however, and after some time in captivity they become tame and can be handled safely. They feed readily on frogs and mice which they easily subdue and stuff into their capacious mouths with their stout forelimbs.

Reproduction takes place in the typical frog manner, with the male grasping the female from behind with his forelegs. Several hundred eggs in a clear jelly-like mass are deposited. FAMILY: Leptodactylidae, ORDER: Anura, CLASS: Amphibia.

HORNED TOAD, the confusing common name of the iguanid lizard genus *Phrynosoma*, which is preferably known as the Horned lizard. Horned 'toads', which are very widespread in North America and Mexico, have short, flattened bodies armed with spines.

Typical species are small, about 3–4 in (7·5–10 cm), with a very short tail and have long hard spines on the head. The general appearance is somewhat toad-like. They have the odd habit of squirting thin jets of blood from the eyes, which is believed to constitute a passive defence mechanism. This behaviour is, however, sporadic and some people who know these reptiles well have never seen it happen. FAMILY: Iguanidae, ORDER: Squamata, CLASS: Reptilia.

HYLIDAE, a large family of frogs. Most are arboreal and are dealt with under treefrogs.

HYNOBIIDS, among the most primitive of living salamanders, they are confined to Asia, most species having a restricted distribution, often in high mountains. See White dragon. FAMILY: Hynobiidae, ORDER: Caudata, CLASS: Amphibia.

I

ICHTHYOPTERYGIA, subclass of extinct marine reptiles sometimes known as fish-lizards but better known as *ichthyosaurs. They were shaped like fishes and like them were fully aquatic but they breathed by lungs, so were surface swimmers, and their skin was without scales. All four limbs were modified to form flattened turtle-like flippers, by a big increase in the numbers of finger and toe bones. CLASS: Reptilia.

ICHTHYOSAURS, extinct marine reptiles that lived in the Jurassic and Cretaceous periods, 180–70 million years ago. They were fish-shaped or, better still, porpoise-shaped, the head having a beak-like snout, the body tapering to a fish-like tailfin and with a triangular dorsal fin, unsupported by bone, which can be clearly seen in those specimens in which the outline of the body is preserved as an impression in the rock. The jaws were armed with numerous conical teeth, striated on the surface and set in a groove in each jaw. The skin was brownish and without scales. The limbs were flippers, those in front larger than the rear flippers. The limb-bones were short and broad, the bones of the digits pentagonal or hexagonal and set in a mosaic. Ichthyosaurs were 1–30 ft (0.5–9.9 m) long or more. They swam near the surface, using the tail for propulsion and the flippers as balancers or for changing direction. They were worldwide, and small skeletons inside the larger skeletons in some specimens leave little doubt they bore living young (ovoviviparous). ORDER: Ichthyosauria, CLASS: Reptilia.

ICHTHYOSTEGA, the best known of three genera of fossil amphibians from East Greenland. They are the earliest tetrapods known, coming from a geological horizon which is either Upper Devonian or basal Lower Carboniferous (about 350 million years ago).

Ichthyostega had well-developed legs and limb girdles. In most details of its anatomy it was typically amphibian: it had a well developed vertebral column and strong tetrapod-type ribs. However, some structures show that it was not far removed from its fish ancestry. Among these are a tail bearing a fin

supported by fin spines and a skull still carrying vestigial bones behind the jaw articulation which are remnants of those which in fish support the gill covers. ORDER: Ichthyostegalia, SUPERORDER: Labyrinthodontia, CLASS: Amphibia.

ICTIDOSAURS, an extinct group of highly advanced mammal-like reptiles found in rocks of uppermost Triassic age in southern Africa. They are only known from fragmentary skull and jaw material but their characteristics are of great interest for their close approach to the mammalian structure. *Diarthrognathus* is the best known genus. Ictidosaurs are best considered as a lateral and sterile offshoot of the mammalian line.

IGUANAS, the largest and most elaborately marked group of lizards in the New World. The family is almost totally restricted to that area, except for two genera in Madagascar and one genus in Polynesia. Iguanids range from species 3 in (7.5 cm) long to those 6 ft (2 m) in length. Their diets may be insectivorous, carnivorous, herbivorous or omnivorous. Many forms are territorial. All are oviparous except for the Swift lizards

Sceloporus and Horned lizards *Phrynosoma* some of which are ovoviparous. The eggs are soft-shelled and buried underground.

The Common iguana *Iguana iguana* ranges from the lowlands of central Mexico south into southern South America. It lives in the vicinity of ponds or rivers at altitudes from sea-level to the mountains. Iguanas bask on branches of trees during the day, usually over water so that if danger appears the reptile can drop (sometimes for a considerable distance) into the river or pool, dive, and remain submerged on the bottom for many minutes. These reptiles are fast runners, good climbers, swimmers and divers. Although well equipped for survival, this species has a reputation as a dietary delicacy. To hunt the iguana, young boys will follow a river, then while one of them climbs a tree to frighten the reptile into the water, two or three others dive in to catch the iguana where it is concealed in the rocks or debris on the bottom. This method is very effective, and in many regions this lizard is now very scarce or extinct.

This species has been sold in market-places in the tropics by stringing the animals together alive by the tendons of their hind

Ichthyosaur remains from the Lower Jurassic rocks of Germany, so perfectly preserved that the skin and other soft parts can be studied.

The Common iguana is one of the Green iguanas.
The Common iguana is widespread throughout tropical America.

limbs on poles for sale to the public. Because of this inhumane practice and their increased scarcity, the department of conservation of Mexico strictly protects this species, and it is now hoped that in many areas the iguana will begin to re-appear in numbers.

A number of species of large Ground iguanas *Ctenosaura* occur throughout Mexico and range farther north than the Common iguana. They are also found south into Central America. Although they do ascend trees, they prefer to hunt for food on the ground as they are mainly carnivorous. One form, the Black-and-white ground iguana *Ctenosaura similis* has large muscular jaws enabling it to prey on small rodents, other lizards and an occasional bird. These iguanas are also used as food by the local people.

In the Caribbean area, island forms of the Ground iguanas of the genus *Cyclura* have remained isolated from one another for long enough to evolve into several distinct forms. All of these primitive forms have a similar body build, are mainly ground-dwellers, and feed both on vegetation and small animal life. However, on the Lesser Antilles and the Virgin Islands near northern South America, the Ground iguanas are extinct and are known only from fossils found in caves. These islands are occupied by the Common iguana, and it is possible that some overlap in competition resulted in the eventual extinction of the cyclurids in these areas.

One of the largest of these insular iguanas, is the Rhinoceros iguana of Haiti and neighbouring areas, which attains perhaps the greatest weight (although not the greatest length) of the iguanids. This reptile has heavier jaws than other members of this group. This, plus a grotesque pattern of enlarged scales on the head, including three prominent pointed scales on the snout, accounts for its popular name. Despite its formidable appearance, it is quick to run from man, and is hunted with trained dogs, which may result in the capture of one lizard in a day after hours of hunting. However, when cornered it can strike out with its tail with considerable force, and can bite hard when handled. It is becoming extremely rare because of extensive hunting for use as food and for zoological gardens. *Cyclura macleayi*, the Cuban Ground iguana, is another lizard rapidly becoming depleted in numbers. Current economic difficulties in Cuba and the Isle of Pines have resulted in increased pressure on populations of this lizard which will no doubt continue.

Island forms of these iguanas or, indeed, any other reptile can be depleted far more rapidly and with much less effort than mainland forms. Each island species is distinct and if it becomes depleted, there is no other source from which its numbers can be rebuilt. On the mainland, however, while local predation on a species may dent an overall population, if protection is introduced members of the species will often return to fill the gap. For this reason, it is doubtful if many insular forms of iguanas will long survive within the limited confines of islands that are being increasingly heavily populated.

One island form of iguana in the Pacific, the Marine iguana *Amblyrhynchus cristatus* has evolved on a number of the Galapagos Islands. A lack of natural enemies has resulted in a reptile that is apparently unafraid of man, but an inhospitable environment has produced some alterations in the basic iguana pattern resulting in a unique reptile. The Marine iguana, although possessing a very workable and strong (but little understood) territorial attitude, occurs in large herds, sometimes piled many deep on coastal lava rocks. It is vegetarian, but feeds mainly on various seaweeds growing at the bases of cliffs and in vast underwater 'fields'. These lizards submerge to graze on these beds of seaweed and are the only ones that have become adapted to a marine environment. Until Brookfield Zoo, Chicago, succeeded in maintaining a colony of these reptiles for more than three years, these intriguing reptiles had never before been successfully maintained in any number as an exhibit in a zoological park.

All iguanas have conventional legs and feet, and there appears to be no evidence that

A Common iguana, climbing a manchioneal tree, strikes an aggressive attitude.

Marine iguana of the Galapagos is remarkable in that it is the only lizard that habitually enters the sea,

these are being lost, as is the case with many other lizard groups.

The tail of the Common iguana is edged with a row of sharp, serrated dorsal scales resembling a 'saw tooth'. When the long, slender, whip-like tail is swung toward an enemy, the blow can cause pain, and the sharp edge can cut through a cloth shirt. The iguana can shed its tail as a defence measure as can many lizards but the regenerated tail may not develop the 'saw tooth' characteristic.

Iguanas are voiceless, as are most reptiles, but a cornered iguana (particularly the

cyclurids) can emit very audible gurgling hisses.

The ornamental scalation, enlarged and erectile throat fan, and dorsal fringe of the Common iguana produces a most fearsome appearance and is used by the males to indicate that territories are occupied without the need to resort to fighting. In the more primitive cyclurids which lack such conspicuous ornamentation, battles are rather commonplace. In fact, the startling ornamentation of the Common iguana has resulted in its being employed in film-making to play the role of 'dinosaur' in many

science-fiction movies by magnifying the size of the beast on the screen to many times that of the humans it encounters.

Although the dark-coloured Ground iguanas are not capable of changing colour to any detectable degree, the Green iguanas can alter their shades of green or red considerably. In captivity, and even under artificial light, these lizards remain a dull green or shade of grey or brown. However, in the tropics and in their natural environment, these lizards are often a brilliant, almost fluorescent green or bright orange. Unfortunately, these colours begin to fade over a period of days after they have been captured. FAMILY: Iguanidae, ORDER: Squamata, CLASS: Reptilia.

IGUANODON, ornithischian *dinosaur of the Upper Jurassic to Lower Cretaceous. It was a large bipedal herbivore with a maximum length of about 35 ft (10·5 m). The hindlimbs were powerful and the thumb bore a bony spike used in defence. The fossil skeletons and footprints have been found widely in Europe, and in North Africa and Asia. *Iguanodon* is of great historical interest as it was one of the first dinosaurs found, the original description by Mantell being based on teeth and bones from southern England. A remarkable collection of close on 30 skeletons was recovered in the 1870's from a subterranean deposit discovered in a coalmine at Bernissart in Belgium. ORDER: Ornithischia, CLASS: Reptilia.

K

KING COBRA *Ophiophagus hannah,* the largest species of *cobra, reaching a length of 18 ft (5½ m) and remarkable for its diet, which consists entirely of other snakes. The female builds a nest of leaves and coils herself above the incubating eggs. FAMILY: Elapidae, ORDER: Squamata, CLASS: Reptilia.

KING SNAKES, North American nonvenomous snakes of the genus *Lampropeltis,* that range from a little over 2 ft (60 cm) to 6 ft (180 cm). The Eastern king snake *Lampropeltis getulus* is one of the largest and has a wide distribution over much of the eastern United States. It occurs in several races or subspecies which may be recognized by minor differences in the colour pattern and the numbers of scales on the underside. It is strikingly coloured, usually black with numerous small yellow spots. King snakes are constrictors and their food includes a wide variety of small mammals and lizards, but it is commonly smaller snakes, including rattlesnakes, to whose venom they are immune. FAMILY: Colubridae, ORDER: Squamata, CLASS: Reptilia. (Ill. p. 97.)

KOMODO DRAGON *Varanus komodoensis,* of the small island of Komodo, to the east of Java, is usually regarded as the largest living lizard. It reaches at least 10 ft (3 m) long and weighs 360 lb (163 kg). However, Salvador's monitor *V. salvadorii,* although of more slender build, is believed to reach 15 ft (4·6 m) long. See monitors.

KRAITS, highly venomous southeast Asian snakes. The widely distributed Banded krait *Bungarus fasciatus* and the Indian krait *B. coeruleus* of India and Ceylon are probably the most common. The Banded krait has a warning colouration of pale yellow with glossy black bands, and grows to about 4 ft (120 cm). Kraits are generally inoffensive and prefer to feed on other snakes, but they can be exceedingly poisonous to man. Numerous fatal cases of bites from kraits have been recorded and death may occur in as little as three hours. FAMILY: Elapidae, ORDER: Squamata, CLASS: Reptilia.

L

LABYRINTHODONTIA, a group of fossil Amphibia all of which are now extinct. They ranged in geological time from the Devonian–Carboniferous boundary, some 350 million years ago, to the end of the Triassic, 180 million years ago. They comprise one of the three major groups into which the Class Amphibia is divided, the others being the *Lepospondyli, also all extinct, and the Lissamphibia, the present-day frogs, toads and salamanders.

Although technically Amphibia, the labyrinthodonts were very different from the living Lissamphibia. Many were very large, up to about 15 ft (5 m) long. The skull was massive and the outer, dermal layer of bones formed a complete covering not only for the bony braincase but for the jaw-closing and other cranial muscles as well. This 'dermal roof' was perforated only for the external nostrils, eyes, and the median pineal eye. The surface of the skull was ornamented with a raised pattern of bumps and ridges, typically giving a honeycomb appearance.

The name labyrinthodont refers to the structure of the teeth as seen in microscopic cross-section. These have the usual central pulp cavity, an outer layer of enamel and an intermediate layer of a substance called dentine. The dentine, however, gives the labyrinthodont tooth its distinctive appearance in section, with wavy radial lines of primary dentine extending inwards towards the pulp cavity. This type of tooth is shared by the labyrinthodonts with the group of fishes which probably included their ancestors. Labyrinthodonts had a row of conical teeth along the upper and lower jaws, like most vertebrate animals, but also had a parallel internal row of larger tusks of similar structure on the surface of the palate.

The form of the body in labyrinthodonts varied a great deal. All had four legs, which, like those of the earliest reptiles, were held with the upper arm or thigh more or less parallel to the ground, at least on land. However, the relative size of the legs and the length of the trunk varied very greatly, although all possessed a long tail. Labyrinthodonts differed from the living amphibians in having well-developed bony ribs

forming a strong rib cage. It is also probable that all had scaly skins and bony scales are preserved with some of them: thus it is improbable that they were able to breathe in part through the skin as do the modern Amphibia.

The fossil labyrinthodonts we know from the Carboniferous period, representing the first 60 million years of their history, seem mostly to have been aquatic, living in the vast stagnant swamps which were to form the coal seams of Europe and North America. Typical of them are the Anthracosauria, large long-bodied forms which must have looked like very elongated crocodiles with tiny legs and must have swum like an eel or a snake. The largest anthracosaurs were the longest labyrinthodonts known.

In the early part of the Permian period which followed the labyrinthodonts evolved a number of terrestrial forms with stout limbs and comparatively short bodies. By this time, however, the labyrinthodonts were clearly divisible into two groups, both with land living representatives. One group, related to the anthracosaurs, is of interest because of its structural resemblance to the earliest reptiles, but it died out at the end of the Permian. The other, of which *Eryops* is typical, survived until the end of the Triassic. However, the Upper Permian and Triassic forms were secondarily aquatic, again with small limbs, but this time with short, very flattened bodies.

The labyrinthodonts look much more like reptiles than like the living amphibians. However, they are classified as Amphibia for one overriding reason. It is assumed that they did not lay the terrestrial amniote egg which characterizes higher vertebrates and affords protection, food and water to the developing young. In other words, they probably developed as tadpoles and in fact some labyrinthodont tadpoles are preserved as fossils. Also, all aquatic labyrinthodonts have grooves in the skull marking the course of the lateral line sense organs, which detect pressure changes under water and are present in all fish and some Amphibia, but never in reptiles. It is assumed, however, by most vertebrate zoologists that the ancestry of reptiles, and thus of birds and mammals,

including man, can be traced back to labyrinthodont stock. CLASS: Amphibia.

LACERTID LIZARDS, an Old World family of lizards distinguished by the presence of bony plates (osteoderms) on the surface of the skull and also by having in most cases a central aperture in the skull roof through which the pineal 'eye' projects to appear as a pale spot on the head surface. Lacertids lack osteoderms in the skin of the body. They also lack the very smooth, usually regular scaling typical of skinks, to which they are closely related.

Present-day lacertids are small to moderately sized, from about 4 in (10 cm) to 2½ ft (76 cm) but a Pleistocene species existed in the Canary Islands which was probably twice this length. The body of a typical lacertid is subcylindrical and usually somewhat flattened. The head is somewhat elongated and the snout is obtusely or sharply pointed. Males have a relatively larger head than females. All have well developed limbs which are never much reduced in size. The tail is typically whip-like and about twice the length of the head and body. However, in some species it may be less than the head-body length and in others it is up to five times this measurement. The head is covered with large plate-like scales and the ear aperture is always well developed and clearly visible. Most lacertids have normal, more or less opaque eyelids but in a number of species the lower one has a transparent 'window' which allows the lizard to see with its lids shut. In one group, the Snake-eyed lacertids, *Ophisops,* the eyelids are fused so that these species must always look through the 'window' which in this case is very large. The belly-scales of lacertids are relatively big and typically arranged in regular longitudinal and transverse rows. Just in front of the shoulders most species have a well developed and permanent fold in the ventral skin—the collar. The dorsal scaling is very variable, a majority of species have small granules on the back but a substantial minority possess large keeled scales and a number of species have a narrow central area of large plates combined with granular flanks. Unlike members of some other related families, lacertids cannot change their colour pattern rapidly, although it may vary somewhat with age and with certain environmental factors. The patterns encountered are very variable within a species but frequently the colouring of the back blends well with the lizard's typical environment, thus sand-dwelling species are often pale and reticulated while grass dwelling species are greenish or brown with prominent stripes. The ventral surface, in contrast, is often conspicuously coloured, especially in males, where it may be red, yellow, green or blue. Some species also have bright spots on the flanks.

There are about 180 species and some twenty genera of lacertid lizards distributed over Europe, Asia (as far south as Borneo) and Africa, but not Madagascar. Africa has the greatest diversity of forms. Lacertids occur from the tropics to well within the Arctic Circle (the Viviparous lizard *Lacerta vivipara*) and from sea-level up to 12,000 ft (3,700 m) (Allen's lizard *Algyroides alleni,* in Kenya). The majority of forms are wholly or mainly ground dwelling but some are habitual climbers either on trees or rocks.

The various genera are adapted to a wide range of environments and a large number of forms are found in dry or even desert conditions. The most specialized of these live on wind-blown sand and show modifications related to this habitat. Thus the toes have series of flattened, pointed scales along their sides which prevent the lizard sinking into the soft sand. Many species have valvular nostrils which keep the sand out and pointed snouts with which they probe their substrate for food in the same way that wading birds probe mud; some species are able to bury themselves rapidly. These sometimes have a broad shovel-shaped snout and modifications of the skeleton which allow them to breathe easily below the surface of the sand. Some or all these features are found in three separate regions: the Sahara and Southwest Asia (*Acanthodactylus*), Southwest Africa (*Meroles*) and Central Asia (*Eremias*).

The East Asian Grass lizards *Takydromus* and their West African parallel, Ford's lacertid *Poromera fordii,* are adapted to life in dense herbage and are capable of running over the top of tall grass. They have spiny belly scales, which help to maintain the lizards' precarious grip on yielding grass blades, and long tails, up to 5 times the length of their body, which help spread their weight.

A number of African species live almost entirely in the tropical forest where they climb among the trees. The most peculiar of these is the Spiny-tailed lacertid *Holaspis guentheri,* which is extremely flattened, even its tail and legs. It hides in the narrow crevices on tree trunks and is unique among lacertids in being able to glide from tree to tree. Its very flattened body makes a reasonably satis-

factory aerofoil the area of which is covered by rows of flattened interlocking scales along the sides of the tail and hindlimbs.

In Europe most lacertids belong to a single genus *Lacerta,* the typical lacertids. This group includes the most familiar members of the family such as the Viviparous lizard and the Sand lizard, *Lacerta agilis,* the Common wall lizard *Lacerta muralis* and the Green lizard *Lacerta viridis.* The genus has undergone considerable radiation, some species being almost entirely ground dwelling while others climb a great deal. A number of forms inhabit various inhospitable rocks and islands in the Mediterranean. These lizards are often black and sometimes have swollen tails in which fat is stored.

Like the majority of lizards, most lacertids eat whatever small animals they can overpower. Usually these are invertebrates but large species like the Eyed lizard *Lacerta lepida* will, on occasion, eat small vertebrates such as other lizards, mice and young birds. Not all lacertids are exclusively carnivorous and a number of species will occasionally eat plant material especially when other food is unavailable. Indeed, two species living in the Canary Islands, Scimony's lizard *Lacerta scimony* and Gallot's lizard *Lacerta galloti* are mainly vegetarian and have peculiarly flattened and serrated teeth to cope with this diet.

Many lacertids confine their activities to a limited area which they defend against other members of their sex and species. Males have a characteristic threat gesture to warn off intruders: the body is laterally compressed, the head flexed downwards and the throat expanded. These movements expose the brightly coloured ventral surface to the rival. If he is not intimidated fighting often occurs and G. Kitzler states that this is often ritualized. Thus, in the Sand lizard each of the combatants bites in turn at the heavily armoured head of his rival, while in the Great green lizard *Lacerta trilineata* the fighters stand head to tail and grasp the hindleg of their opponent.

Nearly all lacertids lay soft-shelled eggs, usually in warm, moist earth or sand. But there is an exception, the Viviparous lizard, which delivers its young fully formed and enclosed only in a thin membrane from which they escape, in a few hours or days. Some lacertids in the Caucasus are peculiar in being parthenogenetic, usually only females are found and these are capable of reproducing without mating with males.

Young lacertids are essentially like their parents in form when they hatch but it is not uncommon for them to differ in colour, for instance the adult of an African species, *Eremias lugubris,* is usually buff coloured with indistinct stripes but the babies are jet black with irregular bright yellow blotches. The time lacertids take to reach maturity

varies. In the Spanish Sand lizard *Psammodromus hispanicus* and in the African Sand lizards, *Ichnotropis,* it is only a matter of months but in colder areas it may take three years or more. Very little information is available on the age lacertids reach in the wild. Some fast-maturing forms perhaps only occasionally enter a second year of life but most species generally live longer. Indeed the Eyed lizard has been kept for twenty years in captivity.

All the predators that usually attack small lizards, including various birds, snakes and less commonly carnivorous mammals, will eat lacertids. Although lacertids bite when grasped, most are too small to inflict damage on an attacker and they must depend on other anti-predator mechanisms, the commonest being flight to a secure refuge. The sorts of refuge available varies with habitat and it is common for lizards to be modified to allow entry into the types available. For instance, a number of species of *Lacerta* are flattened so that they can slide into the narrow crevices of the rocks among which they live. Like many other lizards, lacertids can shed their tail so providing a distraction for a predator, under cover of which the lizard escapes. The brightly coloured tails of many young lizards may be a device to attract attention to this expendable area of the body at a time when inexperience makes life particularly dangerous. Tail loss is less frequent in fast running species possibly because these use the tail to stabilize the body when moving at speed and its unnecessary loss would place the lizard at a great disadvantage.

A curious anti-predator device is recorded for Delalande's lacertid *Nueras delalandei* which, when attacked by a snake is said to grasp its own hind leg to form a ring with its body which is too broad for the snake to swallow. It has been suggested that the curious dorsal pattern of young *Eremias lugubris* mimics the appearance of a distasteful Tiger beetle.

Lacertids are of little obvious economic importance to man although Duge's wall lizard *Caderta dugesis* is said to be a nuisance on Madeira where it steals grapes from vineyards. However it probably balances this by eating large numbers of insects as well. The indigenous inhabitants of the Canary Islands, the Guarches, used to eat the large lacertids occurring there, although it is doubtful if they were a very important item of diet. In Europe a group of small typical lizards, commonly known as Wall lizards, for example, the Common wall lizard *Lacerta muralis,* are often frequently associated with human habitation and enter towns. This association with human activity has occasionally resulted in inadvertent transport of some species to new localities. Thus, the Italian wall lizard, *Lacerta sicula* has several isolated colonies in the Mediterranean distant from its original range. FAMILY: Lacertidae, ORDER: Squamata. CLASS: Reptilia. (Ill. p. 99.)

LACERTILIA, the name formerly used for the suborder comprising all lizards, now tending to be replaced by the name Sauria. Lizards first appear in the fossil record in Triassic times and have evolved along many different lines, some like the Triassic form *Kuehneosaurus* and the present day 'Flying lizard' being adapted for gliding flight, others like the Cretaceous mosasaurs and the modern salt-water iguanas for marine life, the limbless *amphisbaenids as burrowers, and the chameleons for arboreal life. In size lizards range from tiny forms measured in centimetres to species like the East Indian monitor which is 12 ft (3·7 m) long with some extinct members twice as large. From some ancestral type of lizard the snakes evolved in the Triassic. ORDER: Squamata, CLASS: Reptilia.

LEATHERY TURTLE *Dermochelys coriacea,* also known as the leatherback, the largest of the marine *turtles. Its occasional appearance in northern waters, off the west coast of Scotland, has given rise to stories of the Soay Beast. See legendary animals.

LEIOPELMIDAE, a family of frogs, the only one in the suborder *Amphicoela. It contains two genera, *Leiopelma* and *Ascaphus.*

LEPIDOSAURIA, a subclass of scaled reptiles including two living orders: the *Rhynchocephalia to contain the tuatara, and the *Squamata comprising all lizards and snakes.

A feature common to all primitive lepidosaurs is the presence of two lateral openings on each side of the skull for the passage of jaw muscles. In this they resemble the dinosaurs, crocodiles, and other *archosaurs and it is possible that the lepidosaurs and archosaurs diverged from a common stem. In lepidosaurs however the teeth are fused to the jaw bones and are not set in sockets. The most obvious lepidosaur feature is the scaly skin which is shed from time to time and which, in the snakes, has a locomotory function.

The oldest known lepidosaurs, the eosuchians, date back to the Lower Permian. They were of general lizard-like appearance and from them evolved all later groups: the Rhynchocephalia representing one line of evolution and first appearing in the Triassic, the lizards another dating from the Triassic; and from a lizard ancestry the snakes diverged in the Cretaceous. CLASS: Reptilia.

LEPOSPONDYLI, fossil amphibians with vertebrae which have spool-shaped centra, as in all modern amphibians. They were small-bodied measuring a few inches in length, with a maximum of 1–2 ft (30–60 cm). They are

known from rocks of the Carboniferous and Permian periods, spanning 110 million years. The oldest members of the group were the aistopods (order Aistopoda) which had long snake-like bodies and small limbs. In some cases the limbs are completely absent. A second group, the nectridians, (order Nectridia) were either elongate eel-like forms, or flattened with bizarre skulls with long posterior projections. The eyes were on the top of the head and the animals were probably bottom dwelling aquatic forms which never ventured onto land. The remaining lepospondyli are the microsaurs (order Microsauria) which were once thought to be the ancestors of the reptiles and hence were given the rather misleading name of microsaur which means 'little reptile'. They tended to have rather reduced limbs and probably lived in or around small pools. There is some evidence that they were gill breathers and hence could only make short trips onto the land. SUBCLASS: Lepospondyli, CLASS: Amphibia.

LEPTODACTYLIDAE, a large family of frogs which, in their internal structure, differ from the *treefrogs only in not having an additional bone in each finger and toe as treefrogs do. Externally, however, they present a wide range of shapes and sizes. They live in South and Central America (with a few species reaching North America), in Australia and in Africa.

The genus *Leptodactylus* comprises about 60 species ranging from southern Texas to Argentina. In general appearance they are very similar to typical frogs but the fingers and toes are not webbed. They vary in size from about 1 in (25 mm) to 8 in (200 mm). One of the largest is the South American bullfrog *L. pentadactylus* while another large species *L. fallax* is known as the *Mountain chicken.

All the species in the genus have similar breeding habits, the eggs being laid in a frothy mass either on or near the water. In the Mexican White-lipped frog *L. labialis,* the only species of *Leptodactylus* to reach the USA, the male digs a cup-shaped hollow about two in (50 mm) across under grass hummocks on the banks of streams or ditches. It calls from this hollow and the eggs are laid there. The jelly of the eggs is beaten into a froth and the eggs remain suspended in this while they develop. The tadpoles hatch out and remain in the moist hollow until they are washed into the water by rain. They change into adults after about 30 days.

The genus *Eleutherodactylus* comprises about 350 species, most in Central and South America with a few in North America. Almost all of them have the tips of the fingers and toes expanded into adhesive discs as in the treefrogs. The frogs of this genus lay their eggs out of water and the whole development

takes place inside the egg. In *E. martinicensis,* from the West Indies, about 25 large eggs are laid in a mass attached to the leaves of trees. During the development the tadpole does not develop gills but has a large tail well supplied with blood with which it breathes. A small frog ¼ in (6 mm) long breaks out of the egg after about 21 days.

The Greenhouse frog *E. ricordi planirostris* from the West Indies has been introduced into Florida. It is a small frog, ½–1¼ in (12–30 mm) long, and is terrestrial in habit, being found under leaves and other debris in gardens and other moist places.

At least eight other genera of Leptodactylidae also pass the complete development in the egg and lack the free-living tadpole stage. One of them includes the world's smallest frog *Sminthillus limbatus* from Cuba. The adults are less than ½ in (12 mm) long and the female lays only one egg.

Darwin's frog *Rhinoderma darwinii* was discovered by Charles Darwin during his voyage on the *Beagle.* It occurs in the forests of Argentina and Chile and is remarkable both in appearance and breeding habits. It is a small, lively frog about 1 in (25 mm) long and the tip of the snout is elongated into a pointed 'false-nose'. During the breeding season the developing tadpoles are carried round in the vocal sacs of the male. The female lays about 30 eggs on land and several males stay near them for about ten days until the tadpoles are nearly ready to hatch. Each male then picks up several eggs in its mouth and works them into his vocal sacs. These are enormously enlarged at this time reaching back, under the skin, almost to the hindlimbs. There may be as many as 15 tadpoles in the sacs and they remain there until they change into small frogs, when they are about ½ in (12 mm) long.

Other leptodactylids from South America which have an unusual appearance are the *Horned frogs *Ceratophrys.*

The other country in which the Leptodactylidae are common is Australia and here the family is represented by many genera. Several of them, like many of the genera in South America, undergo part or all of their development out of water. Some species of *Crinia* develop completely on land while in other genera such as *Pseudophryne* the egg develops on land but the tadpole lives in water. This habit of withdrawing part of the development from a watery environment, which is common in the Leptodactylidae (and in several other families of frogs), is probably an adaptation to avoid predators. In several genera of Australian Leptodactylidae in which frothy egg masses are laid these are hidden in burrows, as in *Kyarranus* and *Heleioporus.*

The five species of *Heleioporus* are all squat toad-like frogs and in all of them the breeding habits are similar. At the beginning of the winter rains the male constructs a burrow about 16 in (40 cm) long in the bed of a dried-up stream or marsh. The eggs are laid at the end of the tunnel where they remain until the burrow is flooded. The tadpoles then hatch and continue their development in the newly-formed stream or pool.

Another toad-like leptodactylid *Pseudophryne corroboree* is known as the *Corroboree toadlet.

Many of the Australian leptodactylids live in arid regions and are adapted to this in several ways, especially in the way they store water. All frogs can store water in the bladder and can later reabsorb and use it. In the Water-holding frog *Cyclorana platycephalus* the bladder is large and can hold a volume of water half the weight of the whole animal. During dry seasons these frogs are dug up by the Aborigines to eat, but they also drink the water from them. ORDER: Anura, CLASS: Amphibia. (Ill. p. 98.)

LIZARDS, one of three groups of reptiles making up the order Squamata, the other two being the snakes and the amphisbaenids. The lizards constitute the most primitive of these and are largely distinguished by the possession of well-developed limbs, although there are some lizards in which the legs are reduced in size or absent altogether so that they are snake-like in appearance. Additional features distinguishing lizards from the other two suborders are that in the skull the upper temporal arch is usually fully ossified and the parietal aperture in the roof of the skull is usually distinct. There is only a moderate amount of movement in the jaw bones as compared with the extreme movement in those of snakes. An outer ear opening or eardrum is usually visible. The vertebral column is either mainly or wholly procoelous, which means that the anterior face of the vertebra is concave. There are typically five toes on each foot, with well-developed claws, and even where the toes and the limbs are reduced in size or missing altogether at least some trace of the pectoral and pelvic girdles still remains. The skin is scaly and the scales are often supported by bony plates or osteoderms. The belly scales are usually larger than the scales on the back and the sides and they are arranged in regular longitudinal rows. The male copulatory organ is a pair of hemipenes, only one of which is inserted into the transverse cloacal opening of the female. In the resting position the hemipenes are withdrawn into pockets at the base of the tail. In some families of lizards some of the tail vertebrae have a predetermined plane of weakness across which a fracture can readily be made to cast off part of the tail. The lost portion of the tail is regenerated, an unsegmented rod of cartilage replacing the original bony axial skeleton.

There are 3,000 actual species of lizards which fall into the following suborders and families:

suborder Sauria

infraorder Gekkota

    family Gekkonidae—geckos
    family Pygopodidae—Snake lizards
    family Dibamidae

infraorder Iguania

    family Iguanidae—New World lizards
    family Agamidae—agamas

infraorder Rhiptoglossa

    family Chamaeleonidae—chameleons

infraorder Scincomorpha

    family Scincidae—skinks
    family Anelytropsidae
    family Feyliniidae
    family Cordylidae—Plated lizards
    family Lacertidae—True lizards
    family Teiidae—Teid lizards
    family Xantusiidae—Night lizards

infraorder Anguinomorpha

    family Anguidae—Slow worms
    family Anniellidae—Legless lizards
    family Xenosauridae

infraorder Platynota

    family Helodermatidae—Gila monster
    family Lanthanotidae—Bornean earless lizards
    family Varanidae—Monitor lizards.
(Ill. p. 97-99, 105, 106.)

LOXOCEMUS PYTHON *Loxocemus bicolor*, of the Pacific coast of Mexico between Sinaloa and Chiapas, has long been a controversial reptile. This two-foot (60 cm). rather stout, burrowing reptile has been classified by some as a Sunbeam snake and by others as a python. Latest investigations indicate the latter to be true, based on skull characters. This reptile constricts its food (small rodents and birds) and will attempt to hide its head in its coils if disturbed. If this is indeed a diminutive 'python', it would be the only member in the New World.

LUNGLESS SALAMANDERS, far the most successful group of modern salamanders; they include approximately 200 of the 300 species of Caudata or tailed amphibians. They are characterized by the complete absence of lungs and the presence of a naso-labial groove, a depression in the skin which runs from the external nostril to the upper lip. It is frequently glandular and probably drains fluids away from the nostril.

The more primitive and generalized species occur in North America and especially in Appalachia, whereas the more specialized forms have spread into western North America and Europe. Other genera have invaded northern South America: *Bolitoglossa, Oedipina, Pseudoeurycea, Chiropterotriton, Lineatriton, Thorius* and *Parvimolge*, making up 123 species collectively known as the neotropical salamanders. The more primitive forms such as *Leurognathus* are fully aquatic and have an extended aquatic larval phase. The Dusky salamander *Desmognathus fuscus* lays its eggs in small clusters in shallow excavations on land in the earth or beneath stones or logs. These excavations or 'nests' may be sited some distance away from water. The eggs have short twisted stalks and the whole batch resembles a bunch of grapes. The larvae are able to move about on land and after two weeks find their way to the water to spend 7–9 months as aquatic larvae after which they metamorphose into terrestrial adults. The life-history of the Red-backed salamander, *Plethonion cinereus* is typical of the fully terrestrial forms in which the female lays her eggs on land. The embryos develop rapidly and soon show well developed external gills, which are lost on hatching and the young resemble miniature adults.

Many of the Lungless salamanders are brightly coloured. The Red salamander *Pseudotriton ruber* is a bright red or orange with irregular black spots on the back, and yellow eyes, the colouration tending to become duller and more brown with age. The Long-tailed salamander *Eurycea longicauda* is yellow with conspicuous black markings and *Plethodon dorsalis* is often known as the Zig-zag salamander because it carries a wavy red or yellowish dorsal strip. The related *P. jordani* which has red patches on the side of the face and front part of the body is known as the Red-cheeked salamander. Some species are, however, drab, almost uniformly grey or black brown.

Some cave-dwelling species are uniformly white and are blind. In the Grotto salamander *Typhlotriton spelaeus* from southwestern Missouri the eyes can barely be seen between the lids which are largely fused together. Nothing is known of its life-history or breeding habits. The Texas blind salamander *Typhlomolge rathbuni* is a bizarre creature with external gills, a flattened elongate snout and long slender limbs. It is also uniformly white, but the Georgia blind salamander *Haideotriton walacei* has red plume-like gills. An interesting anatomical modification is seen in the Arboreal salamander *Aneides lugubris* in which the tips of the toes are enlarged and extensively supplied with blood. It is thought these may provide accessory areas for respiration.

Many salamanders, including the plethodontids, have the ability to shed and regenerate the tail. A large number of plethodontids have a constriction at the base of the tail which marks the place at which the tail breaks off. See also Salamanders. FAMILY: Plethodontidae, ORDER: Caudata, CLASS: Amphibia.

M

MAMBAS, large elapid snakes belonging to the genus *Dendroaspis*. They have a short maxillary bone on each side in the upper jaw which carries a long hollow fang with no small solid teeth following it, while there are a pair of elongate teeth at the front of the lower jaw. Mamba venom is a nerve poison and bites from the Black mamba *D. polylepis* are particularly dangerous. This is the largest of the mambas, reaching a length of 14 ft (4·3 m). It has a nervous disposition and secretes the most potent venom. When disturbed, it will rear up, spreading a narrow hood and gaping the jaws to show the blackish interior of the mouth. Any sudden movement will provoke a strike, which tends to be delivered on the head or body and will, therefore, prove fatal in a short time unless mamba serum is immediately available.

The Black mamba is a relatively slender snake with a long coffin-shaped head, oblique smooth scales on the body and a long tail. Despite its name, this snake is pale grey, olive or dark grey-brown, never a true black. Just after sloughing its skin it may be olive green with a bluish 'bloom' like that on the skin of a plum.

Jameson's mamba *D. jamesonii*, a slightly smaller species, is olive green and blackish posteriorly in the eastern part of its range, which extends from West Africa to western Kenya.

The Eastern green mamba *D. angusticeps* rarely exceeds 7 ft (2·1 m) in length. It is brilliant emerald green to yellow-green above, greenish white below, and extends along the East African coastal plain from Kenya south to Natal.

The Western green mamba *D. viridis* is restricted to West Africa and is usually speckled green and yellow.

Mambas lay 9–14 elongate eggs at the beginning of the rains, a termitarium being a favourite nesting site.

The two Green mambas and Jameson's mamba are arboreal and are usually found in forested regions. The Black mamba inhabits dry savannah and, although frequently found in big trees along rivers, it is equally at home on the ground and is particularly common on rocky hills covered with thick bush.

It seems to feed largely on small mammals, especially rats, squirrels and young dassies, but birds and reptiles are occasionally taken. The other three species feed on birds and their eggs, together with chameleons and other arboreal lizards. FAMILY: Elapidae, ORDER: Squamata, CLASS: Reptilia. (Ill. p. 100.)

MAMMAL-LIKE REPTILES, two extinct orders of *synapsid reptiles: the Pelycosauria and Therapsida, the latter having evolved from and replaced the former. The earliest of their fossils are found in Carboniferous rocks and the last in the Jurassic. Mammal-like reptiles gave rise to the mammals in the Triassic; and their abundant fossil remains illustrate all the structural, and by implication the physiological, stages involved in the transition from the reptilian to the mammalian condition. The typical mammal is a warm-blooded vertebrate capable of stabilizing its body temperature despite fluctuations in the ambient temperature. For this, it has evolved a complex of structural adaptations of which the most important are a hairy and glandular skin for thermal insulation and radiation respectively, an efficient jaw apparatus and digestive system for the extraction of the maximum energy from food, to allow a high metabolic rate, a double circulation to separate arterial and venous blood, a highly efficient respiratory system depending on rib and diaphragm movement for lung ventilation, and an improved locomotory apparatus. To co-ordinate all these activities the mammalian brain is both larger and more complex than the reptilian pattern.

MANGROVE SNAKE *Boiga dendrophila*, a rear-fanged snake of the coastal areas of Malaysia and Indo-China. It subdues its prey with venom, although its venom-potency is not known. An egg-layer, this attractive reptile is shiny black with wide-spaced narrow yellow bands. It prefers to lie on a tree-branch, loosely draped in a coil drooping on both sides of the limb. Normally quiet and inoffensive, an aroused Mangrove snake will flatten a vertical hood, open its mouth wide, and strike forward at least half its length to bite or frighten its tormentor. FAMILY: Colu-bridae, ORDER: Squamata, CLASS: Reptilia. (Ill. p. 100.)

MARSUPIAL FROG, several species of *treefrog in which the female carries her eggs in a large pouch on her back.

MASSASAUGA *Sistrurus catenatus*, the largest and most northerly of the pigmy rattlesnakes. Adults attain a length of 2–3 ft (60–100 cm). They range from Ontario and Pennsylvania in the east to Nebraska in the west, then south to New Mexico and Texas. Six to ten live young are born annually. Massasaugas are venomous, but bites are rare and fatalities almost unheard of. This species frequent margins of marshes or swamps bordered by hillsides or high ground. Although they feed on frogs and may be seen basking in depressions of swamp-grass, they are rarely found in water. FAMILY: Crotalidae, ORDER: Squamata, CLASS: Reptilia.

MASTIGURES, species of *Uromastix*, belonging to the *agamid lizards. They live in northern Africa and southwest Asia, in burrows. When resting their particularly spiny tails block the entrance to the burrow.

The 12 species of mastigures are about 1 ft (30 cm) long and distinguished from other agamids by their stout spiny tails, the short snout and the broad head the cheeks of which house strong jaw muscles, enabling the reptiles to reduce even hard food to small pieces with their small, acrodont teeth. The young animals feed mainly on insects but later eat seeds, fruits and dry vegetation. Mastigures are active by day and around 10 am they leave their burrows or shelters in rock crevices to bask. The adults then take up position on the higher points of the rocks where they have a good view of approaching predators.

When the mastigure leaves its shelter it is dark in colour but changes as it warms up. In the North African *U. acanthinurus* the body changes to a light green grey with a reddish head and tail as the lizard reaches an optimum temperature in the sun.

These lizards are sometimes eaten, but more often their dried and blown-up skins are sold as curiosities to tourists. In captivity the live animal readily takes unnatural foods and can become a likeable pet. FAMILY: Agamidae, ORDER: Squamata, CLASS: Reptilia.

MATAMATA *Chelys fimbriata,* one of the South American side-neck turtles, is most bizarre and weird looking, as its broad, flattened head and neck is covered with fringes of skin giving it a 'mossy' appearance. A fish wandering too close to its jaws may be engulfed by a sudden forward lunge of the head and inrush of water down the turtle's throat. Narrow, hard-rimmed jaws can snap open to a circumference equal to the wide, tubular throat. An elaborate hydraulic-action by use of a powerful hyoid apparatus not only pulls water into the throat but snaps the head forward to engulf the prey. Forward movement of the head is apparently stabilized somewhat by horizontal skin-flaps over the huge tympanum. FAMILY: Chelidae, ORDER: Testudines, CLASS: Reptilia. (Ill. p. 100, 101.)

MESOSAURS, a small and early offshoot of reptilian evolution adapted for aquatic life in fresh waters. The body was long and slender with an extensive snout set with needle-like teeth at one end and a well developed tail for locomotion at the other. The teeth would suggest a diet of fish.

Although their ancestry is uncertain and but a single genus *Mesosaurus* is known, mesosaurs are of considerable interest. The genus was geologically short-lived being restricted to the lowermost Permian and its interest lies in the fact that it has a discontinuous distribution, being found only in rocks of equivalent age in South Africa and Brazil. As the mesosaurs were freshwater reptiles such a distribution provided evidence for the theory of Continental Drift which argues a connexion in the past between eastern South America and western South Africa. This theory is today strongly supported by a volume of evidence, faunal, geological, and paleomagnetic.

MEXICAN BEADED LIZARD *Heloderma horridum,* one of the only two known venomous lizards, in the family Helodermatidae, restricted to North America. This lizard was known to the Indians of pre-Columbian times, and was described first by Hernandez in 1651. Even at that time, although the lizard was known to be venomous, it was described as seldom producing a fatal bite. It attains a length of nearly 3 ft (1 m), a third longer than its closest relative, the *Gila monster. There are at least three subspecies ranging from northern Mexico to beyond the Guatemalan border. It is mottled with yellow on a black ground.

This species appears to be more agile in

climbing rocks than the Gila monster, and the heavily tuberculated skin of the rear portion of the tail gives added assistance when this reptile ascends a vertical rough surface. Although it preys on eggs and young of birds, mainly of ground-nesting species, it also feeds readily on rodents (preferably the young) and lizards. Unless conditions in captivity are favourable, most individuals can be encouraged to consume only egg and meat mixtures. They seem to have an affinity for water in captivity.

Up to ten eggs may be laid and there is some indication that a mating taking place in a given year may not result in eggs being laid until the following year. This would explain the occurrence of eggs in two widely different stages of development in bodies of examined females.

The helodermids cannot readily discard the tail to escape enemies as can many other lizards. Rather, the tail serves as a storage for fat-bodies so that in times of drought the lizard can subsist by converting fat to energy as needed. Some little water is produced as a by-product of this exchange, which may help maintain hydration.

Although the eyesight of these lizards is adequate to detect moving objects, they track down their food by use of their broad, slightly-forked tongue which laps at the ground and air periodically. They do not taste the objects, but instead (like snakes) accumulate scent particles on the moist tongue surface and transfer these to a pair of Jacobson's organs in the roof of the mouth to identify their prey by scent.

The most recently named subspecies *H. horridum alvarezi,* discovered in the Chiapas highlands, is unusual in being nearly entirely black. It is slender and may be found basking on limbs of small trees. FAMILY: Helodermatidae, ORDER: Squamata, CLASS: Reptilia. (Ill. p. 99.)

MICROHYLIDAE, a family of frogs known as Narrow-mouthed toads. They are placed in the same suborder, Diplasiocoela, as the true frogs (Ranidae) but differ from them in having a reduced shoulder girdle. While some members of this family have a typical frog-like appearance many of them are specialized, either for an arboreal life or for burrowing. The family contains about 43 genera in Southeast Asia, Africa and the Americas.

Frogs of the genus *Dyscophus* are thought to represent the primitive stock from which the family has evolved. They are found in Madagascar and the shoulder girdle is less reduced than in other members of the family. *D. antongili* is a stout frog about 3 in (7·5 cm) long with short legs. Its back is bright magenta-red, an unusual colour in frogs.

Platyhyla grandis, another microhylid from Madagascar, is arboreal and resembles

a large treefrog (Hylidae). It is about 4 in (10 cm) long with a wide, flattened head and the tips of its fingers and toes are expanded into triangular pads, those of the fingers being particularly large.

Most of the Microhylidae are, however, burrowing and have small pointed heads and short legs.

The Sheep frog *Hypopachus cuneus* is found in southern Texas and Mexico and its common name refers to the call of the male which is like the bleating of a sheep. It is small and plump, about 1½ in (3·7 cm) long and spends most of the year in burrows, coming out to breed in the periods of heavy rain from March to September.

The other Narrow-mouthed toads found in North America belong to the genus *Microhyla.* They are similar in appearance and habits to the Sheep frog and are rarely seen except during the breeding season. The Great Plains narrow-mouthed toad *M. olivacea* is sometimes found in the burrows of the so-called tarantula spiders. It is apparently unharmed by the spiders and probably obtains protection from other predators.

Other species of *Microhyla* occur in South America and in Asia. In all of them the eggs are laid in water and develop into free-swimming tadpoles. These differ from those of most other frogs in that they do not develop horny beaks or rows of teeth around the mouth. Instead of scraping food off water plants they draw in water through the mouth and filter food particles from it. The tadpoles of *M. achatina* and *M. heymonsi* from Southeast Asia have the lips produced into a large funnel which is probably used in collecting food particles from the surface of water.

The genus *Breviceps,* of South Africa, is the largest microhylid genus, its 16 species and subspecies being known as blaasops or Rain frogs. The first name is Afrikaans and refers to the animal's behaviour when disturbed: it blows itself up into a hard round ball. Its other common name comes from its habits. It spends most of the year underground in burrows.

The Africans believe it is the frogs which cause the rain and are careful not to harm them. If one is accidentally dug up it is carefully replaced in its burrow and covered over. Rain frogs are all similar in shape, having a short bloated body about 1½ in (3·7 cm) long with short legs. ORDER: Anura, CLASS: Amphibia. (Ill. p. 103.)

MIDWIFE TOAD *Alytes obstetricans,* of western Europe in which the male collects the eggs, as they are laid in strings by the female, around his legs. Thereafter he takes care of them, visiting water periodically to keep the eggs moist and finally entering water as the tadpoles hatch. FAMILY: Discoglossidae, ORDER: Anura, CLASS: Amphibia.(Ill. p.103.)

Komodo dragon

MOCCASIN, *Agkistrodon piscivorus,* also known as the Water moccasin or *Cottonmouth, is an American venomous snake of the family Crotalidae.

MOLE SALAMANDER, common name for tailed amphibians more usually referred to as *ambystomatids (family Ambystomatidae).

MOLOCH *Moloch horridus,* the 'Thorny devil' of the arid regions of Australia is a lone genus in the large family Agamidae. Slow-moving, introverted and harmless, this lizard forms a complete antithesis of its name. About 8 in (20 cm) long, coloured orange and brown and covered with spines it feeds almost exclusively on ants. Another lizard, the Horned lizard or 'Horned toad' of the American southwestern deserts, although of an entirely different family, has evolved along parallel lines both in diet and in its spiny appearance.

There is no ready explanation why the moloch is spined although this would provide ample defence against a number of would-be predators. Molochs are egg-layers. FAMILY: Agamidae, ORDER: Squamata, CLASS: Reptilia. (Ill. p. 103.)

MONITORS, lizards belonging to the genus *Varanus,* of which 25 species are known. They range from small to very large, the biggest being the Komodo dragon *V. komodoensis* which may reach a length of 9 ft (3 m) and a weight of 165 lb (75 kg). Monitors are very snakelike with slender bodies and long necks and tails, and a forked tongue which can be extended well beyond the mouth. On the other hand, no monitor has degenerate legs. There are similarities, moreover, in the structure of the skull between the monitors and the earliest known snakes, and often monitors are referred to as ancestors of snakes, but recent research shows there is no direct line between these lizards and the

present day snakes. At best, monitors are related to the ancestors of snakes. It can only be coincidence that the Desert monitor *V. griseus* is called the 'King of the snakes' by the Arabs of North Africa.

Other characteristics in which monitors resemble snakes include their ability to swallow large prey and with this a solid bony sheath around the brain protecting the brain itself from pressure as the large prey is being engulfed. The bones of the jaws are movable on each other and give a wide gape to the mouth, the temporal arch is completely ossified and the two halves of the lower jaw are joined by a ligament, much as in snakes. On the other hand, no monitor has poison fangs and the teeth are relatively long, single-pointed, slightly curved and sometimes serrated on the rear edge enabling the lizards to grasp and seize their prey and also, in some species tear it to pieces for swallowing. In the more primitive monitors the rounded nostrils are on the end of the snout but in the more specialized species they form slits lying back near the eyes. The forked tongue can be stretched far forward and it carries back into the mouth odorous particles to be tested in the *Jacobson's organ in the roof of the mouth. The body scales are without underlying bony bases, or if these are present, they are only slightly developed. Each of the four strong legs bears five toes armed with strong claws. The tail is muscular and long and can be used to beat off enemies, and as there are no fracture points in the tail vertebrae no part of the tail can be discarded and regrown as in true lizards.

Monitors are found in Africa, southern Asia and, more especially, the islands of the East Indies and Australia. Although the various species are very similar in form they occupy very different habitats. *V. griseus* lives in the deserts of North Africa, whereas *V. niloticus* readily takes to the rivers in its search for food, while *V. prasinus* is at home

in the treetops in the tropical rain-forests of New Guinea. Monitors may either dig their own burrows or use the abandoned burrows of mammals or they may sleep in crevices in rocks or in hollow trees. The arboreal species rest on the branches of trees, and the larger species rest in thick undergrowth. Arboreal species like *V. prasinus* can cling to the bark of trees with their sharp claws.

All monitors are predators on any animals they can overpower. The smaller kinds eat mainly insects, the larger species catch lizards, small mammals and birds. Some are egg-eaters and the Nile monitor is famous for its ability to find the nests of crocodiles and gorge itself on the eggs (see ichneumon). The Komodo dragon also eats carrion and *V. exanthematicus* and the Nile monitor are remarkable because of the change in feeding habits as they grow, the older individuals eating hard-shelled food such as large snails and crabs, and the form of their teeth changes to thick.

The female deposits her eggs in a pit and covers them with sand and vegetable material which, warmed by the sun, act as an incubator. Sometimes a monitor will lay its eggs in a termite mound, the termites repairing the wall so sealing the eggs in. The young ones on hatching must find their own way out, and their exit is usually timed with the rainy season when the wall of the termitarium is softened. FAMILY: Varanidae, ORDER: Squamata, CLASS: Reptilia.
(Ill. p. 90, 104, 106.)

MOUNTAIN CHICKEN *Leptodactylus fallax,* a large frog of the family Leptodactylidae which includes many of the smaller frogs of the New World. Native to the West Indies, where it lives on the mountainsides, it is large and an important item of diet to the peoples of that region, hence the name 'Mountain chicken'. All frogs of this family reproduce by laying eggs in frothy nests built close to water but not in water as in most frogs. FAMILY: Leptodactylidae, ORDER: Anura, CLASS: Amphibia.

MUD DIVER, or Mud toad *Pelodytes* of which there are probably two species: *P. caucasicus,* the mountain form from Transcaucasia, and *P. punctatus,* from the lowlands of southern and western Europe. There is some doubt whether these are separate species or a single species with two subspecies. The Mud diver belongs to the family Pelobatidae, which includes the Spade-foot toads. The Mud diver is, however, smaller than the spade-foots and measures around $1\frac{1}{2}$ in (3·8 cm) in length. It lacks the spade and is characterized by its habit of diving into the water at the first sign of danger. The body is rather warty and individuals are especially adept at changing colour. FAMILY: Pelobatidae, ORDER: Anura, CLASS: Amphibia.

MUDPUPPY, a name correctly applied to *Necturus maculosus* and by extension to other salamanders of the genus *Necturus*. In the southern United States, however, these salamanders are known as waterdogs and the name mudpuppy is reserved for the adults of the Mole salamanders (Ambystomidae). In the North, the name waterdog is commonly used for the *hellbender *Cryptobranchus alleganiensis*. Some authorities, to compromise with the folk usage, call the southern forms of *Necturus* waterdogs. However, since there is no biological distinction it is just as well to call all of them mudpuppies.

There are four species of mudpuppies with some regional variations that make a total of eight recognizable forms or subspecies. Their only near relative is the degenerate, cave dwelling olm *Proteus anguinus* of Yugoslavia.

Mudpuppies are long-bodied salamanders the largest a little over 19 in (48 cm), but the usual length is less. They have an oblong head with a rounded snout. The four legs are short and each has only four toes. The tail is about $\frac{1}{3}$ the total length and is flattened laterally into either a broad oval or a tapering blunt point, according to species. Eyes are small and without eyelids. The most prominent feature are the external gills, the three branches on each side of the neck dark stubby when the mudpuppy is in well oxygenated water, but developing into large dark red plumes in warm or stagnant water. Mudpuppies retain throughout life the external gills, normally found only in salamander larvae, and reproduce technically in their larval form, a condition known as *neoteny. In contrast to other salamanders, such as the axolotl, they cannot be induced under any condition or treatment to assume any other form. They do, however, mature partially and when adult develop lungs, in addition to gills, and an adult tooth structure.

The colour varies considerably even within a species. When the group is taken as a whole, it can be anything from yellowish-brown to dark greyish-brown usually with varied arrangement of spots, small blotches or mottlings. There often is a dark bar through the eye.

Mudpuppies are found throughout the eastern half of the United States except the state of Maine, peninsular Florida and the ridge of the Appalachian mountains, and in southeastern Canada. They live in sluggish low gradient streams of the lowlands and in small lakes and ponds, preferring clear water with aquatic vegetation.

Mating takes place in late autumn. The male is reported to court the female actively and deposits a spermatophore. The female remains passive, but picks up the spermatophore. Fertilization is internal and egg laying does not begin until the spring of the following year. The female finds an appropriate site under a rock, or she may excavate a small nest usually with the entrance facing down stream. The eggs are attached singly to the underside of the nest's roof. The eggs are globular, $\frac{1}{4}$ in (5 mm) in diameter and surrounded by a layer of jelly. The female guards the eggs during incubation which may take a month or two depending on the water temperature (longer in cold water) and may stay with the larvae until they leave the nest. At this point they are less than an inch long. The young begin to feed on small aquatic animals, worms, insect larvae and small crustaceans. Later, crayfish form the bulk of mudpuppy diet but they will take other animal food, even fish eggs, sometimes accidentally ingesting vegetable matter in the process. Growth is slow. They do not reach maturity until the fifth year.

Mudpuppies do not adapt readily to captivity. They often refuse to feed and slowly starve. When in this condition they are also susceptible to a variety of infections. They are nocturnal, spending their days among rockwork of the aquarium into which they blend so well that they are difficult to see. If the oxygen level in the water is low, they will wave their feathery gills and this movement gives them away. An occasional specimen acclimatizes well and may then survive for a few years.

The name mudpuppy supposedly originates from the salamander's reported ability to emit yelping or barking noises, a fact that many authorities dispute, pointing out the lack of voice-producing mechanism. Some experienced amphibian watchers claim, however, that mudpuppies on rare occasion may emit audible sounds. All mudpuppies in my personal experience have remained silent. FAMILY: Proteidae, ORDER: Caudata, CLASS: Amphibia. (Ill. p. 102.)

NEWTS. Considerable confusion exists about the use of the terms, salamander and newt. *Salamandra* means 'lizard-like animal' and is the generic name for the terrestrial salamanders of Europe. The noun 'salamander', however, is frequently applied to all caudate amphibians and more especially to the more terrestrial forms. The term newt originated in the Old World, and in Europe has a precise meaning. It refers only to the European newts of the genus *Triturus*. In the New World the use of the name newt is less specific and it includes other genera such as *Salamandra, Pleurodeles, Diemictylus* and *Taricha* as well as *Triturus*. It seems advisable to use the term 'newt' for those forms which constitute the family Salamandridae, and the term salamander for those tailed amphibians not in this family. The major objection to this is that the Fire salamander *Salamandra salamandra*, the species for which the name 'salamander' was first used belongs to the family Salamandridae and should logically be called the 'Fire newt'. However, in view of the largely terrestrial habits of this form, the antiquity and familiarity of the name, the term Fire salamander is usually retained.

Newts such as the Smooth newt *Triturus vulgaris* and the Warty newt, *T. cristatus* are terrestrial during the greater part of the year and become aquatic during the breeding season when the male develops a prominent crest on back and tail. The crest is non-muscular, sensory and is usually brightly coloured. It is used to attract the female during the elaborate courtship displays by the male prior to breeding. The male's sperm are deposited in the water in a structure called a spermatophore produced by special glands in the wall of the cloaca. This is picked up by the female with her cloaca and the sperm then leave the spermatophore and swim to a specialized portion of the female reproductive system, the spermatheca or receptaculum seminis, and are stored there. The female generally lays 200–450 eggs which are fertilized inside her by the sperm. Laying usually starts three to ten days after the spermatophore is picked up and the female will not accept further spermatophores until the eggs are laid. These may be deposited singly or in small clusters and they are usually attached to the stem or leaf of a water plant or to a small rock. Laying usually takes place in the spring and metamorphosis is usually complete by the end of the summer when the young adults leave the water. They then remain on land until they become sexually mature three or four years later when they return to water to breed for the first time. Hibernation during the cold months of the year also takes place on land.

The Fire salamander, or Spotted salamander also extends into North Africa and was the first caudate amphibian to be described as such by Linnaeus in 1758. In ancient times it was thought this salamander was able to live in fire. The myth probably arose from people seeing the animal emerging from a log, in which it had sheltered, when this was put on the fire. The Fire salamander mates on land usually in July and about ten months later the female enters the water to bear live young. Each litter contains 10–15 young about 1 in (2·5 cm) long and possessing external gills which are lost during metamorphosis when the animals become terrestrial and acquire the orange-yellow patches characteristic of this species. The skin of the adult is kept moist by secretions of the dermal glands which also produce poisonous substances which afford some protection from predators. In laboratories the Fire salamander has been known to survive for at least 12 years.

Newts of the genus *Pleurodeles* occur in Spain, Portugal and northern Africa and have long pointed ribs which may even pierce the skin. The Waltl newt *Pleurodeles waltl* is said to live for 20 years in captivity.

The Red spotted newt *Diemictylus viridescens* of the eastern United States has a terrestrial stage the 'red eft' which lasts two to three years. After this individuals re-enter the water and become permanantly aquatic. They lose their bright red colour and assume a dull green appearance.

The California newt *Taricha torosa* lives in the coastal mountain ranges of California, is usually aquatic and develops a crest during the breeding season. Newts also occur in China and Japan and the Japanese newt *Cynops pyrrhogaster* is commonly kept as a pet.

Development in newts often involves *neoteny. This is especially well documented in the Alpine newt *Triturus alpestris*. Members of those species which inhabit freshwater areas in the low-lying plains of France and Italy metamorphose in the normal way and are not neotenous. In the cold lakes at higher altitudes development is retarded and neoteny is common.

Neoteny should not be confused with overwintering which also occurs in newts, when there is an early winter or a late spawning and the larvae, unable to metamorphose in time, are forced to hibernate as larvae. These tend to grow unduly large, so resembling the partially neotenic forms, but will metamorphose in the normal way the following spring or summer.

Newts are voracious feeders and will eat worms, slugs, snails and insects when on land, and aquatic larvae, small crustaceans, mollusca and even frog's spawn when in the water. Food is detected by sight and smell, and swimming is achieved by the use of the tail with the limbs being usually held alongside the body.

Newts like most tailed amphibians can regenerate amputated parts such as the tail, limbs and even some parts of the head. The power of regeneration decreases with age. FAMILY: Salamandridae, ORDER: Caudata, CLASS: Amphibia. (Ill. p. 102-104.)

NIGHT ADDERS, a dozen species of *vipers of the genus *Causus* ranging from the Sahara to South Africa, with one species in Israel and Sinai. They are usually regarded as the most primitive of the vipers, their fangs being shorter and cruder than in typical vipers. FAMILY: Viperidae, ORDER: Squamata, CLASS: Reptilia.

NIGHT LIZARDS, a small family of lizards exclusively American. They become active at twilight and during the day hide in rock crevices and under stones. There are 12 species and four genera distributed over the southwestern states of the USA, a few

Californian islands, Mexico and Central America as far as Panama. One species is confined to the Oriente province in Cuba. They are similar to *geckos and like them have immovable eyelids with a transparent window in the lower eyelid. The skull characters and those of the rest of the skeleton show that they are not related to geckos but to skinks.

They are inhabitants of arid areas and some species have a very restricted distribution. For example, *Cricosaura typica* of eastern Cuba is found only among limestone boulders. *Klauberina riversiana* is found on only a few islands along the coast of California. *Xantusia vigilis*, the best known of the Night lizards, lives in the semi-deserts of the southwest of North America where the yucca grows, the Night lizard living among the rotting logs and branches of this shrub.

Night lizards feed on small insects and their larvae which they catch by short jumps when foraging at night. The female gives birth to living young, so far as we know, and each bears only a few, sometimes only one, young at a time. FAMILY: Xantusiidae, ORDER: Squamata, CLASS: Reptilia. (Ill. p. 98.)

OLIGOKYPHUS, a European genus of advanced *mammal-like reptile of Upper Triassic to Lower Jurassic age. Close relatives have been found in southern Africa, China, and North America. Together these forms constitute a group of 'near mammals' called tritylodonts. Although not directly on the mammalian line of descent they sit astride the reptile-mammal frontier as a collateral branch. Many of the features typical of mammals are present in tritylodonts such as a large braincase relative to skull size, specialized teeth for mastication, a bony secondary palate separating the nasal passage from the mouth cavity, and a lower jaw composed essentially of a single bone on each side. The tritylodont post-cranial skeleton also demonstrates many mammalian features. The particular tritylodont features concern the dentition. Behind the incisors was a gap in the tooth row, and there was probably a cheek pouch here as in modern rodents. The cheek teeth are very diagnostic for each carries from two to four, depending on species, longitudinal rows of cusps. The tritylodonts were certainly herbivores and were descended from specialized *cynodonts. ORDER: Ictidosauria, SUBCLASS: Synapsida, CLASS: Reptilia.

OLM *Proteus anguinus,* aquatic salamander living in a permanent larval or neotenous form and retaining three pairs of external gills throughout life. The single species from deep caves in Carniola, Carinthia and Dalmatia in Europe, grows to 12 in (30 cm) and is a uniform white except for the gills which are bright red. It lives in perpetual darkness and the eyes are concealed under the opaque skin. It seems the olm retains some sensitivity to light since when it is kept in the light in captivity it turns black. The olm is said to keep very well in captivity provided the temperature of the water is kept at about 50°F (10°C). The limbs are of moderate size and there are three fingers and two toes. Fertilization is internal and the eggs, laid singly, are fastened to the undersurfaces of stones and take about 90 days to hatch into larvae about 1 in (2·5 cm) long. It has been reported that sometimes the female retains the fertilized eggs in her body and the young are born alive. FAMILY: Proteidae, ORDER: Caudata, CLASS: Amphibia.

OPISTHOCOELA, amphibians with opisthocoelous vertebrae, that is, the centrum of each vertebra is flat or concave in front and convex behind. The South American and African members of the group are tongueless and belong to the well-known family *Pipidae. One of these, the African clawed toad *Xenopus laevis,* has been widely used for pregnancy tests since it was discovered that urine from a pregnant woman injected into an unmated female toad would cause it to lay eggs, whereas urine from a non-pregnant woman would not.

The European and Asian opisthocoelans form the family Discoglossidae. These have disc shaped tongues and include the Fire-bellied toad *Bombina bombina* which turns a fiery orange colour on its undersurface when disturbed. Closely related to it is the Midwife toad *Alytes obstetricans,* the male of which cares for fertilized eggs by attaching them to his legs. ORDER: Anura, CLASS: Amphibia.

PANCAKE TORTOISE *Malacochersus tornieri,* of Tanzania, also known as Loveridge's tortoise, has a flattened, flexible shell, and can squeeze into narrow crevices and between rocks. By slightly inflating its body it can resist being pulled out.

PARADOXICAL FROG *Pseudis paradoxa,* a remarkable frog, of Trinidad and the Amazon basin, in which the tadpole is more than three times the length of the adult.

PELOBATIDAE, a family of frogs belonging to the suborder Anomocoela, intermediate in structure between the more primitive Amphicoela, Opisthocoela and Procoela and the more advanced Diplasiocoela. Like the more primitive Discoglossidae and Pipidae the vertebrae are stegochordal. This means that during development the ring of tissue around the notochord ossifies only in a small arc over the notochord which then degenerates. In the other families the ring of tissue ossifies completely and replaces the notochord' to form a solid bony centrum. Like the more advanced families, however, some of the muscles of the hindlimb of the Pelobatidae are separate while in the more primitive forms they are still fused together.

The genus *Pelodytes* contains two species which are found in Europe. They are sometimes placed in a separate family, the Pelodytidae. *P. punctatus* is called the *Mud diver.

Some members of the Pelobatidae are known as Spadefoot toads. The name refers to the hard tubercle on the edge of each foot which is used for digging. The animal shuffles backwards into the ground, pushing the soil to either side with the scraper-like tubercles.

The European Spadefoot toads belong to the genus *Pelobates. P. fuscus* is found throughout Europe, usually in areas with light, sandy soil in which it can dig easily. As it burrows the soil falls over it and it takes less than a minute to disappear from sight. They are stout frogs, about $2\frac{1}{2}$ in (63 mm) long and are sometimes mistaken for toads. They can, however, be distinguished from the true toads (*Bufo*) by their smoother skin and the fact that the pupil of the eye is vertical instead of horizontal.

When disturbed the skin exudes an irritant fluid which smells strongly of garlic and in Germany these frogs are known as 'Garlic toads'. Besides this poisonous secretion they have another defence mechanism. They can sometimes be roused to what looks like a fit of rage; the frog inflates its body to a round ball and jumps repeatedly at its aggressor with gaping mouth as though to bite, while screaming loudly.

Spadefoot toads spend the day underground, emerging to hunt for food a few hours after sunset. In the breeding season the male calls underwater and during mating the large string of eggs is twisted round the stems of water plants. The tadpoles are large, sometimes reaching a length of 5 in (12·5 cm). The time which they take to develop into adults varies; occasionally the tadpoles hibernate and metamorphose the next year.

The Spadefoot toads of America belong to the genus *Scaphiopus.* Most species are found in the southwestern States in arid or semi-arid conditions. The Eastern spadefoot, *S. holbrooki* is found in the wetter east and southeast, but even here it seems to prefer the drier, sandier parts.

Spadefoot toads show several adaptations to the dry conditions in which they live. Primarily, they burrow, so avoiding the hot dry air, and remain in the soil where there is some moisture. They may bury themselves as much as 6 ft (1·8 m) below the surface. During the period of the year in which they are active they keep the entrances to their burrows clear but during the winter or in times of drought they allow the earth to collapse around them and may remain buried for several months until the conditions are right for emergence. When Couch's spadefoot *S. couchi* emerges from *aestivation it is covered with a hard layer like dried skin which forms a 'cocoon' around the frog and probably helps prevent loss of moisture in the burrow.

Spadefoots are also adapted to their dry habitat by being 'explosive' breeders. They appear in large numbers after heavy rain and breed in temporary pools. The Eastern spadefoot has the unusual habit of sometimes beginning to call while still buried. Early in

the evening a muffled chorus is heard around pools although no frogs are visible. After a while the males emerge from their burrows and continue to call while floating in the water. Most species of spadefoots have a loud voice

The eggs of spadefoots develop rapidly. In the Western spadefoot *S. hammondi* the eggs, which are attached to water plants, hatch after only $1\frac{1}{2}$–2 days. The tadpoles also develop rapidly and may change into frogs after about 2 weeks. This time varies, however, and the conditions which affect it are not fully understood. It may be connected with the drying up of the pools. Tadpoles removed from a drying pool and placed in water remain as tadpoles for several weeks while those left in the pool change into frogs just before the pool dries up. The availability of food is also probably an important factor in governing the rate of metamorphosis. In some species of spadefoot, when food is scarce, the tadpoles become cannabalistic. This ensures that at least some of them are able to survive.

Megophrys nasuta belongs to a genus of Pelobatidae found in South Asia. It has a curious appearance which forms an effective camouflage. It has a triangular projection of skin on the snout and a similar projection over each eye. It lives on the floor of rain forests and its mottled brown colour blends with the dead leaves. From above, the skin projections hide the eyes and disguise the outline of the frog.

The tadpoles of *M. montana* and several other species of the genus have greatly enlarged lips which form a large funnel around the mouth. This floats on the surface of the water with the tadpole hanging vertically beneath it. The inside of the funnel has rows of horny teeth which are used to scrape food particles off the undersides of floating leaves. ORDER: Anura, CLASS: Amphibia.

PELODYTIDAE, frogs of the genus *Pelodytes,* sometimes placed in a separate family, the Pelodytidae. They are more usually included in the *Pelobatidae. ORDER: Anura, CLASS: Amphibia.

PELYCOSAURS, extinct reptiles that flourished during the Upper Carboniferous and Permian periods, 300–225 million years ago. They were up to 12 ft (4 m) long and they had massive jaws. *Elaphasaurus* had crushing plates on its palate, possibly indicating that it fed on coarse, fibrous vegetation. The most remarkable feature of the pelycosaurs is the long neural spine on each vertebra, up to 3 ft (1 m) high, often with cross bones on them. It is supposed that these spines supported a web of skin, like a sail over the animal's back, possibly serving to take in heat from the sun, or for radiating body heat to the atmosphere. ORDER: Pelycosauria, SUBCLASS: Synapsida, CLASS: Reptilia.

PHRYNOMERIDAE, a small family of frogs, members of which are distinguished from the Microhylidae only in the possession of an extra cartilaginous element in each digit and they are sometimes included in that family. There is only one genus, *Phrynomerus,* which is found in Africa.

Phrynomerus bifasciatus is known as the Red-banded frog. It is about 2 in (5 cm) long, black with a band of scarlet along each side and a similar coloured patch on the back. It burrows into the ground and usually emerges only at night. When placed in the light for a few hours the red stripes fade, first to orange and then to pink. In stronger light all the colour fades and the frog becomes a uniform grey. It is the skin itself and not the eyes which is sensitive to the light; if part of the back is shaded this part remains coloured.

Red-banded frogs walk or run rather than jump. Although the tips of their fingers and toes are expanded into discs they are not strictly arboreal in habits. They clamber over logs and small bushes while searching for food which consists mainly of ants and termites. They are sometimes found in the chambers of termite nests.

Breeding occurs only after rains and large numbers of frogs congregate in shallow pools. The calls of the males can be heard more than $\frac{1}{2}$ ml (0·8 km) away. About 600 eggs are laid and hatch after four days. The tadpoles resemble those of Microhylidae in that, unlike most other frogs, the mouth does not have a cornified beak or rows of teeth. It is, instead, a simple aperture at the tip of the head through which the food particles suspended in the water are sucked. Metamorphosis into frogs occurs after about a month.

The habits of other species of *Phrynomerus* are not so well known as for the Red-banded frog. *P. annectens* is smaller and is found in open scrub country in Southwest Africa and Angola. It has patches of redbrown and yellow spots rather than red bands and is better adapted to running than the Red-banded frog. The front legs are longer and the toes point forward rather than outwards. It runs very quickly, more like a

mouse than a frog. It is very flattened and probably lives under stones and leaves. ORDER: Anura, CLASS: Amphibia. (Ill. p.100.)

PIPE SNAKES, once widespread, now comprise only three genera of non-poisonous snakes. They show many primitive features several of which are shared with the late Cretaceous and oldest known fossil snake *Dinilysia* and in some respects Pipe snakes are intermediate between the boas and shield-tails. Hindlimb vestiges are present as two spurs, close to the cloaca. There are two lungs but the left lung is less than a tenth the length of the right. On the underside there are enlarged belly scales, one to each vertebra, but these are not as wide as in most snakes. The skull bones are solidly joined and the jaws are not very flexible. Most Pipe snakes have a spectacle covering the eye but in the genus *Anilius* the eye is beneath the head scales.

Most Pipe snakes belong to the genus *Cylindrophis* found in Ceylon and from Burma to the Malay Archipelago. Another genus, *Anomochilus,* is found in Malaya and Sumatra. The third genus, *Anilius,* occurs in South America. All the family are ovoviviparous, giving birth to small litters of young, each of which may be half the length of the parent. All burrow underground or in surface litter. The skull is unsuitable for very large prey but they are recorded as eating eels and snakes as long as themselves. Some of the Pipe snakes have interesting protective devices. The Guyanan pipe snake or False coral snake *Anilius scytale* is banded black and red, mimicking a poisonous snake of the same country. The Malayan pipe snake *Cylindrophis rufus* lifts its tail when molested, showing the crimson below as it waves it above its body, giving the appearance of a threatening head. FAMILY: Aniliidae, ORDER: Squamata, CLASS: Reptilia.

PIPIDAE, a family of frogs, the only one in the so-called Aglossa, which means 'without a tongue', one of the adaptations to an aquatic life. Others are the absence of eyelids, a flattened body, powerful hindlegs and large webbed feet. There are four genera, and these fall into two distinct groups. There are the American forms of the genus *Pipa* and the African forms of the genera *Xenopus, Hymenochirus* and *Pseudohymenochirus.*

The strange-looking frogs of the genus *Xenopus* are known as 'platannas', a South African word meaning 'flat-handed'. All the members of the Pipidae, in fact, have this character. When swimming in the water the front legs, which are small and feeble, are held out in front of the head with the fingers spread out in a fan. They act as feelers and as soon as they touch anything in the murky water which might be food they push it to the mouth. In *Pipa* this sensory function is aided

by a star-like cluster of papillae at the end of each finger.

Pipa pipa, the Surinam toad, is found in the Amazon and the Orinoco. Its blackish-brown body is flattened making it difficult to see in muddy waters. The Surinam toad has an unusual method of breeding; the eggs develop in small pits in the female's back. During amplexus the male grasps the female just in front of her hindlegs and the two swim upwards in a loop in the water. At the top of the loop they are upside-down and at this point the eggs are released by the female and fall onto the belly of the male. They are then fertilized and move onto the female's back. They are pressed further up her back by movements of the male and then stick to her skin. The female then remains still while the skin of her back swells up around the eggs until each one is enclosed in a pit closed with a lid which is probably a hardened secretion of the female's skin. In them the eggs develop. In some species it is tadpoles which emerge while in others further development occurs and small frogs push off the lids of their pockets and swim out.

Hymenochirus is similar in some respects to *Xenopus.* Three of the toes have claws although the fingers are also partly webbed. ORDER: Anura, CLASS: Amphibia. (Ill. p.104.)

PIT VIPERS, a very important group of highly venomous snakes, of which the best known are the *rattlesnakes of North America. The Pit vipers are either placed in a separate family of snakes, the Crotalidae, or in a subfamily, the Crotalinae of the family of true vipers, Viperidae. In the latter classification the true vipers constitute the subfamily Viperinae. In this account the Pit vipers are regarded as a family in their own right because the differences between them and the true vipers, although few, are mostly clear-cut and probably indicate that the two groups are not very closely related.

Pit vipers are so called because they possess a double pit in front of, and slightly below, the eye. The two halves of this cavity are separated by a translucent membrane which is richly innervated and bears a large number of sensory nerve endings. The forward chamber of the cavity has a fairly obvious external opening, which may be more noticeable than the nostrils; hence the crotalids are sometimes known locally as 'four nostrils'. The posterior section of the pit also has an external opening, but this is usually hidden and is placed just in front of the eye. The double pit on each side of the head is accompanied in a deep hollow in the bone known as the maxilla. Experiments with rattlesnakes *Crotalus* and also with copperheads *Agkistrodon contortrix* appear to have demonstrated that the membrane in the pit is exceedingly sensitive to changes in temperature and that it is used by the snake to detect

King snakes owe their name to their habit of eating other snakes, killing them by constriction.

King snake coils around mouse to suffocate it.

Many times during the evolution of the lizards, limbs have been reduced to produce snake-like forms, the example here is *Diploglossus tenuifasciatus*.

Boyd's rain forest dragon, an agamid lizard, *Goniocephalus boydii*, from Australia.

The Eyed or Ocellated lizard of Spain
Night lizard.

Leptodactylus rugosus of tropical America, a frog of the family Leptodactylidae.

Mexican beaded lizard.

Frilled lizard.

An anolis lizard *Anolis equestris* showing its throat sac extended during aggressive display.
Another lacertid of the islands off Eastern Spain, *Lacerta pityuensis*.

The Green lizard, 38 cm long, is one of Europe's largest lizards.

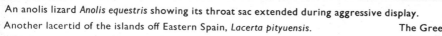

99

Red-banded frogs of Africa, of the family Phrynomeridae, *Myron richardsoni*, which is also known as a Mangrove snake.

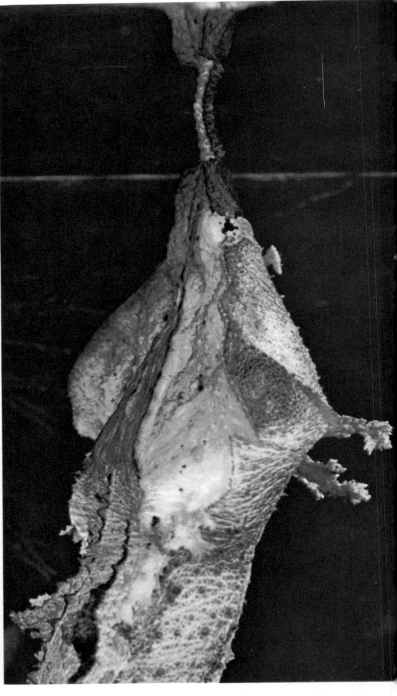

The matamata rises to the surface to take in air by its schnorkel.

Western matamata uses its schnorkel-snout to breathe while underwater.

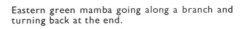

Eastern green mamba going along a branch and turning back at the end.

Male Crested newt, *Triturus cristatus*, of Europe.

Mudpuppies retain their gills throughout life, an example of neoteny.

Two male Warty newts.

The Mountain devil or moloch   *Moloch horridus*, Australian agamid lizard.

European Midwife toad *Alytes obstetricans* with eggs. Male carries eggs on his back.

Alpine newts often develop neotonously in the of Southeast Asia.

Asiatic painted frog *Kaloula pulchra*, a microhylid cold waters of high level lakes.

Yellow monitor *Varanus flavescens* of S. Asia.

Smooth newt .

The African clawed frog *Xenopus laevis* is one of the tongueless frogs which are sometimes placed in a suborder Aglossa on their own.

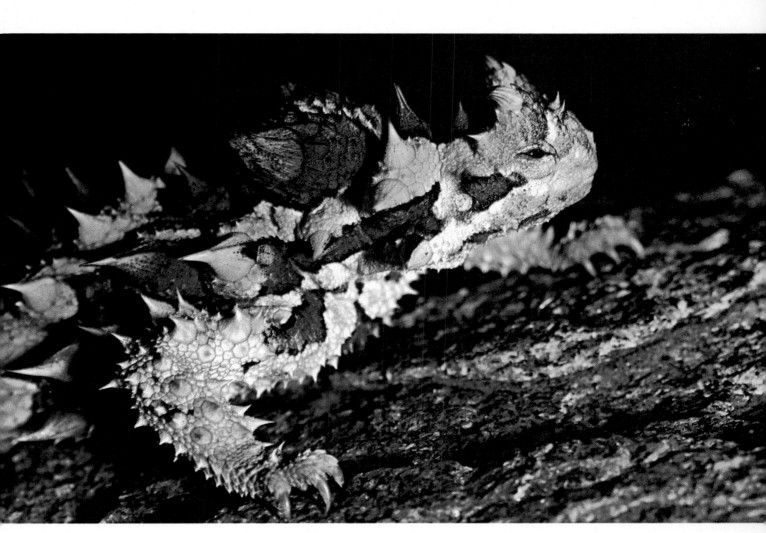

Thorny devil of the desert regions of Australia, with fearsome aspect but quite harmless.
Crossed Pit viper *Bothrops alternatus*. Pit vipers have a pit on each side, used as heat-detectors to strike at warmblooded prey.

Wall lizard of Europe.
The Nile monitor *Varanus niloticus*.

Head of a Pit viper.

the presence of animals which are warmer than their surroundings. Pit vipers which have been blindfolded are able to follow the movements of warm-blooded prey very accurately up to distances of about 6 ft (1·8 m), but they only strike when near enough to reach the prey. The only teeth present in the upper jaw are the long, curved fangs which are in paired sockets in the maxilla to allow for periodic replacement on each side. However, smaller teeth are present on the lower jaw and the pterygoid and palatine bones of the palate, so that the prey can be held very firmly once gripped. The maxilla of Pit vipers is noticeably very short and rectangular, especially compared to that of non-poisonous snakes. This shape is closely correlated with the swinging, forward movement it makes when the snake strikes with the jaws open, allowing the long fangs to assume a vertical position and thus penetrate the prey. The cavity in the maxilla and the associated sensory pit are the most important characters that distinguish the Pit vipers or crotalids from the true vipers. True vipers also tend to have longer poison fangs and shorter, thicker bodies than the Pit vipers.

Pit vipers are distributed through eastern Europe, much of Asia and Japan, and the Indo-Australian Archipelago, but their principal stronghold is in the New World, where live the rattlesnakes. Unlike the true vipers, the crotalids are absent from Africa.

The South and Central American genus of crotalids known as *Bothrops* includes several very poisonous, long fanged species. One of the most important of these is the fer-de-lance *B. atrox* which occurs throughout Brazil, Peru, Central America and much of Mexico, as well as many West Indian Islands, and attains a length of 10 ft (3 m). The fer-de-lance (literally, the iron of the lance) is named from the characteristic shape of its head. It frequently hampers the development of new areas for agriculture in many parts of tropical America since it occurs most commonly in forests and near running water. After the ground has been cleared, the fer-de-lance may return, especially to sugar and banana plantations. Although the immature snakes are tree climbers, adults of this species tend to remain on the ground. When excited, the fer-de-lance vibrates its tail vigorously against the ground and creates a rapid tapping sound which serves to alarm predators and enemies. The young probably feed mainly on amphibians such as frogs but adults prey primarily on mammals such as opossums and rats. Another well known species is the jararaca *Bothrops jararaca* which is the cause of many serious cases of snakebite in Brazil. The jararaca grows to a length of 5 ft (1·5 m) and is pale velvety brown or olive, with yellow marks having black margins on the sides of the body. The largest Pit viper is the tropical American

bushmaster *Lachesis muta* which may reach 12 ft (3·6 m) and is one of the most feared venomous snakes. The bushmaster is a forest dweller and, although widely known and respected, is nowhere common. Other Pit vipers, of the genus *Agkistrodon*, are well known in North America. The copperhead *A. contortrix* and the cottonmouth or moccasin *A. piscivorus* are both fairly common and highly venomous. Halys pit viper *A. halys* occurs over much of Central Asia and extends into eastern Europe.

Most Pit vipers, except the bushmaster and some Old World Pit vipers, are ovoviviparous, that is, the eggs hatch inside the body of the mother and the young are born alive. The bushmaster buries its eggs in the litter of the forest floor.

The non-poisonous kingsnake *Lampropeltis* is one of the few enemies of rattlesnakes. When a rattlesnake is threatened by a kingsnake it lowers its head and arches the middle section of the body off the ground and attempts to fend off its attacker with the arched body loop. This posture makes it difficult for the kingsnake to grasp its prey's head in order to swallow it.

In areas having cold winters rattlesnakes often aggregate in large numbers, together with tortoises and frogs, to hibernate. For example, hundreds of Great Basin rattlesnakes *Crotalus viridis* annually congregate in underground channels near Lake Bonneville, Utah. It is clear that many must travel long distances in order to assemble there and it is possible that this annual migration represents a learned behaviour pattern on the part of the adult snakes. FAMILY: Crotalidae, ORDER: Squamata, CLASS: Reptilia. (Ill. p. 105, 106.)

PLESIOSAURS, extinct marine reptiles whose remains are found in Jurassic rocks almost throughout the world. They had broad flattened bodies, long necks and, usually, small, flattened triangular heads, a short tail and four flippers. The best description ever given, by Dean Buckland of Oxford, was that a plesiosaur resembled 'a snake threaded through the shell of a turtle'. The skull had a pineal opening on top and the nostrils were set high up on the head, near the eyes, so presumably a plesiosaur, like a crocodile, could surface to breathe exposing little more than the rims of the nostrils. The jaws were armed with strong pointed teeth marked with striations. The turtle-like flippers were covered with a tough skin and the fingers and toes within were lengthened by having many bones, each digit looking in skeleton like a string of bony bobbins. The flippers were probably moved with a rowing action, and plesiosaurs, probably not fast swimmers, would have been able to seize prey by a darting movement of the long neck. The remains of fish and hooks of squid have been

found fossil where the plesiosaur's stomach would have been.

Plesiosaurs varied in size up to 40 ft (12·2 m). Some had very long necks. *Elasmosaurus*, for example, had a neck 20 ft (6·1 m) long, with 76 neck vertebrae. The females laid eggs on the shore. SUBORDER: Plesiosauria, ORDER: Sauropterygia, CLASS: Reptilia.

PLETHODONTIDAE, a family of tailed amphibians known as the *Lungless salamanders. See also salamanders.

PLEURODIRA, or side-necked turtles, a suborder of the Testudines (= Chelonia). They are found only in the southern hemisphere and differ from the *Cryptodira in withdrawing the head by a sideways movement of the neck. See turtles.

PROCOELA, a suborder of tailless amphibians (Anura) characterized by the possession of procoelous vertebrae, that is, vertebrae which are concave on the anterior face. The suborder contains ten families and hundreds of species, including the South American Horned toads, *Ceratophys* (family Leptodactylidae), Darwin's toad *Rhinoderma darwinii* (family Rhinodermatidae), the Tree frogs (family Hylidae) and the true toads (family Bufonidae). ORDER: Anura, CLASS: Amphibia.

PROTEIDAE, aquatic salamanders that remain larvae throughout life, retaining the external gills. The family is composed of two genera: *Proteus* with a single species, the olm *Proteus anguinus*, from Europe, and the four species of mudpuppies *Necturus* from North America and southern Canada.

Proteus and *Necturus* are sometimes placed in separate families. Recent evidence shows that the olm and the mudpuppy have the same chromosome number (19) and this may indicate that they are closely related.

The first fossil salamanders from the Upper Jurassic of Wyoming and the Lower Cretaceous of Belgium are probably relatives of the Proteidae. See mudpuppy and olm. ORDER: Caudata, CLASS: Amphibia.

PSEUDIDAE, a family of frogs with only two genera and these sometimes considered to constitute a subfamily of the *treefrogs (Hylidae). Like the treefrogs they have an extra element in each finger and toe but while in the treefrogs this is small and enables the adhesive disc to remain pressed against a flat surface while the digit is at an angle to it, in the Pseudidae its function is to lengthen each digit. This is an adaptation to a strictly aquatic habit. The long toes are completely webbed and the fingers are used for sweeping through the mud at the bottom of ponds searching for particles of food.

Pseudis bolbodactyla, a stout frog about 2 in (5 cm) long with long, powerful legs, has bulbous eyes and a granular skin. The toes and fingers are slightly expanded at the tips. The end bone in each digit has a disc of cartilage attached to the tip. This frog is found in shallow lakes in Brazil where it floats among the water plants with only its eyes and snout above the surface. It breeds at the beginning of the rains in September. The males have a large internal vocal sac and call during the daytime, the call sounding like the grunting of a pig. The eggs are laid in the water in a frothy mass. The tadpoles are large and are caught by the local peoples for food. Other members of this genus also have unusually large tadpoles. In the best known, *P. paradoxa,* the adult is about 3 in (7·5 cm) long while the tadpole is about 10 in (25 cm) long. When the tadpoles were first discovered they were given a separate name since it was not realized that they changed into the frogs. ORDER: Anura, CLASS: Amphibia.

PTERANODON, an extinct reptile, was the largest flying animal that has ever lived. Its wings spanned over 27 ft (9 m); the largest bird, the albatross, only has a wing-span of 11 ft (3·3 m). Although so large, it weighed no more than 40–50 lb (19–23 kg). Even the teeth had been lost, so shedding weight, and the jaws were covered by a light horny beak, as in birds. The low body weight combined with the large size made *Pteranodon* a remarkably efficient glider; it showed many of the modifications later discovered by man and used in aeroplanes. For example, the bones of the wing were hollow and strengthened internally by fine crosswise struts of bone—a design used in plane wings. *Pteranodon* was also equipped with air-brakes in the form of small membranes at the front of its wings which could be raised to reduce its speed.

At the end of the Cretaceous, 70 million years ago, *Pteranodon* became extinct, possibly losing out in competition with the fast-evolving birds. ORDER: Pterosauria, CLASS: Reptilia.

PTERODACTYL, the name which has come to be generally used for all flying reptiles or *pterosaurs, although originally applied to the first specimens discovered and named by Cuvier *Pterodactylus.*

PTEROSAURS, winged reptiles that lived 100–70 million years ago. The smallest, such as *Ptenodracon,* were no bigger than a sparrow, the largest, *Pteranodon,* had a wing-span of over 27 ft (9 m). The largest living bird, the Wandering albatross, has a wing-span of only 11 ft (3·3 m). The various species became highly specialized for different kinds of flight.

The precise origin of the pterosaurs is not known but they are presumed to have been derived from thecodonts. These are the most primitive members of the subclass *Archosauria and are said to have given rise to all later archosaurs, including two kinds of dinosaurs, the crocodiles and birds, as well as pterosaurs. The theory is that a type of small, agile thecodont took to forest living. Thecodonts were bipedal with strong hindlegs and long tails which balanced them when they stood upright. As the arms were not needed for walking, they were free to evolve into wings. These ancestors of the pterosaurs may have taken to the air to escape from enemies, or in pursuit of insects, which formed an abundant food supply.

Presumably, after an initial parachuting stage, the pterosaurs evolved true wings. These were supported by the fourth finger only, unlike bats, in which four of the fingers are included in the wing membrane. Short broad wings are the most useful for flapping flight and these were present in the earlier Jurassic pterosaurs. To produce the necessary power for flight, strong pectoral muscles were needed; these arise from the sternum or breastbone, part of the pectoral girdle. In pterosaurs, the sternum became large and keeled and the whole pectoral girdle strong to withstand the force of the flapping wings. In fact the whole body changed to form a short, rigid box to furnish support for the all-important wings.

Primitive pterosaurs were fairly small animals—they could not have been too large as their wings would have caught in the trees. A typical example is *Rhamphorhynchus,* which had a 4 ft (1·3 m) wing span. It had a long tail which helped to stabilize it while flying. *Rhamphorhynchus* was a carnivore, with forwardly-directed, sharply-pointed teeth. From such early forms, pterosaurs evolved to fill various ecological niches. For example, for flying over water, gliding, rather than flapping the wings, became advantageous, and rising air-currents over cliffs can be used for gliding, to conserve muscular energies in most seabirds. *Pteranodon* represents the peak of this evolution. It was the most highly evolved living glider there has ever been and incorporated many features later 'rediscovered' by man. An efficient glider must have a light body supported by a large wing area. This ensures that it sinks only slowly through the air and so makes longer glides possible. The ratio between body-weight and wing-surface in *Pteranodon* was remarkably low and has only been excelled by some insects. Each square foot of wing only carried 1lb of weight. In man-made gliders a load of at least 4 lb/sq ft is usual. *Pteranodon* had attained an enormous wing area by extreme elongation of the wing-finger with the flying membrane sweeping from wing-tip right down to the ankle. The body weight of *Pteranodon* had been reduced by many

means. The hindlegs were much reduced. The heavy tail and teeth seen in early pterosaurs had been shed and the bone of the skeleton had become surprisingly thin. In the long wing-bones it was no thicker than blotting paper: the hollow bones of birds are massive compared with the delicate tubes which supported pterosaur wings.

The achievement of such a low body-weight/wing-span ratio allowed *Pteranodon* to glide at exceptionally low speeds. It could remain airborne without stalling at only 15 mph (24 kph). This flying speed was so low that take-off and landing (into wind, as in modern birds and aeroplanes) would have been easy. In fact, in winds above 15 mph *Pteranodon* would only need to spread its wings to become airborne, with negligible effort. But probably it more frequently took off from cliffs than level ground as it was an oceanic animal and was likely to have nested on cliff sites: but if it landed on the water it could easily have taken off from the crest of a wave. The low gliding speed also facilitated easy and gentle landing. It was most important that *Pteranodon* should have suffered no great shock on impact as its large, fragile body would have been smashed to pieces. It avoided this by landing in slow motion when it came soaring home to its cliff-top home.

Pterosaurs are usually spoken of as flying reptiles, but reptiles are always cold-blooded and usually covered in scales. Birds and mammals, on the other hand, are warm-blooded and have their bodies covered in feathers or fur respectively. They have evolved mechanisms which enable them to keep their body temperature at a constant level, making them less dependent on climatic conditions. Reptiles must live in fairly warm places as they need to bask in the sun to heat themselves up before they can pursue their day's activities. Pterosaurs, like birds and mammals, had crossed the 'thermal barrier' and were warm-blooded. Flying is an active way of life and consumes much energy. Heat is generated by this increased metabolism, but this heat then needs to be conserved in the body to keep it warm. Birds use an insulating covering of feathers to do this, and mammals fur, and pterosaurs also had a thick furry covering but as in bats this did not extend to the wings.

Why did the fur originate? As mentioned before, pterosaurs may have evolved from small thecodonts that had taken to forest living. The temperature among trees is some degrees lower than that of open plains, because there is far more shade. This lowered temperature may have been responsible for stimulating the development of fur for warmth. The feathers of birds may have evolved for the same reason, only later being utilized for flight. The naked wing-membrane of the pterosaurs could have been used to dissipate excess heat which would have been produced during long flights.

As pterosaurs were warm-blooded, they could not have laid eggs in the reptilian manner and then abandoned them. If egg-laying had occurred, the eggs must have been kept warm and brooded in the manner of birds or the platypus. The brain of pterosaurs was highly developed and they were quite capable of the behaviour involved in caring for the young. It is inconceivable that the later giant pterosaurs laid eggs commensurate with their size—the weight involved in carrying such eggs would have been too much extra loading. The young were more likely to have been hatched from diminutive eggs and then reared by the parent. Some pterosaurs had a throat-sac that may have served to carry food which was later regurgitated for the baby pterosaurs. So perhaps, as one paleontologist has suggested 'they reared their young with affectionate care!'

Why did the pterosaurs, who were so successful on Earth for so long, become extinct? This is a problem that has never been fully answered. One suggestion is that the giant Cretaceous forms were too highly specialized—that they could only survive under certain special ecological conditions, and if any change had occurred in their environment they would have been unable to adapt to it. This seems to be the fate of most specialized and highly developed species of animals. It is normally only the primitive and less advanced forms that retain their evolutionary vitality and can adapt or give rise to fresh groups of animals. Another suggestion is that the pterosaurs 'lost out' in competition with the birds. By the close of the Cretaceous birds had evolved and radiated into many environments. They were similar to present day forms. Perhaps some sea-going species came into competition with *Pteranodon* and the other giant gliders. The birds may have fed on the same fish, or crowded the pterosaurs from their cliff-top homes. ORDER: Pterosauria, SUBCLASS: Archosauria, CLASS: Reptilia.

PUFF ADDERS, African snakes of the genus *Bitis,* highly venomous, so called because of their loud hissing or blowing air from the lungs, that is, they puff. The name is also one of several common names for the North American *Hog-nosed snake which, although non-venomous, also tends to blow air loudly, as if in warning, when disturbed. See vipers.

PYTHONS, the Old World equivalent of the New World *boas, and like them bearing small spurs that represent the vestiges of hindlimbs. These two snakes are clearly the closest living relatives of the ancestral snake type. There are seven genera in the subfamily Pythoninae inhabiting the warmer regions

Above: young python leaving the egg. Below: Ball python, of Africa, constricting its prey.

from Africa to Australia. The largest and best-known, the true pythons, belong to the genus *Python.* They all have bold colour patterns mainly in browns and yellow. Three live in Africa, the African python *P. sebae,* which reaches a length of 32 ft (9.9 m), the Ball python *P. regius,* which, when molested, rolls itself into a tight ball with its head inside, and the Angolan python *P. anchietae.* Several other species are found from India to China and the East Indies. The largest species, the Reticulate python *P. reticulatus,* reaching a

length of 33 ft (10 m), ranges from Burma to the Philippine Islands and Timor. Although so large it has been found to be remarkably inoffensive in the wild and most accounts of its attacks on humans are exaggerated or invented. The Indian python *P. molurus* with a length up to 20 ft (6 m) is found from India to China and on some of the islands of the East Indies.

As distinct from the true pythons there are several other genera of pythons found in the East Indies and Australia. The Rock pythons

109

Egg of Royal python *Python regius* in process of hatching. The shell is parchment-like.

Liasis are all found in the Australasian region. The largest of these is the Amethystine rock python *L. amethystinus* which reaches a length of 20 ft (6 m). The Rock pythons have larger and more regular head shields than the true pythons and they are usually an olive colour above and yellow below without the bold patterns of the true pythons. Another smaller group is the Australian womas *Aspidites* which, unlike most pythons, eat other snakes. Two other pythons that are interesting because of their complete adjustment to different ways of life are the Green tree python *Chondropython viridis* of New Guinea which hunts for its prey in the treetops and the Burrowing python *Calabaria reinhardti* of West Africa which spends its time underground feeding on small rodents.

The pythons live in a wide variety of habitats. Some live near water like the Indian python which is almost semi-aquatic, others prefer jungles and climb trees while the African python lives in open country. The Reticulate python has a preference for living near human settlements. They kill their prey by constriction, small mammals being preferred but birds, reptiles, frogs and even fish are also taken. The larger African pythons also take small antelopes. A large python can swallow prey weighing up to 120 lb (54 kg) and one 18 ft (5·5 m) African python is known to have eaten a leopard.

All the pythons lay eggs usually 3–4 months after mating. The number varies considerably from eight to over a hundred. The female pushes them together in a heap and coils herself around them, brooding them for 2–3 months. Most pythons merely guard their eggs but some, including the Indian python, actually incubate them by keeping their body temperature several degrees above that of the surrounding air. When hatched the young grow rapidly but they have many enemies. As they grow larger, however, fewer animals can overpower them. Crocodiles, hyaenas and tigers have been found with the remains of pythons in their stomachs and there is one account of a 17 ft (5 m) Indian python being killed by a pair of otters which apparently attacked it from either side, avoiding harm by their agility. FAMILY: Boidae, ORDER: Squamata, CLASS: Reptilia.

R

RACERS, five species of snakes of the genus *Coluber.* The eastern Black racer *C. constrictor constrictor* and the midwest Blue racer *C. c. flavoventris* and three others are fast, active snakes of the United States. They often travel with elevated heads, over shrubs as well as on the ground. They are all egg-layers, producing clutches of about 12 eggs which hatch into young whose spotted bodies do not resemble the even-coloured adults. These harmless snakes are sometimes erroneously called the 'hoop snakes'. Racers average about 4 ft (120 cm) and eat whatever they can catch, from insects to mice. FAMILY: Colubridae, ORDER: Squamata, CLASS: Reptilia.

RACERUNNER *Cnemidophorus,* active diurnal *Teiid lizards ranging from the United States southwards through Central America to northern Argentina.

RANIDAE, family of frogs containing the large genus *Rana* to which the term 'frog' was first applied, the species of which are 'typical' frogs. The whole family is therefore dealt with under frogs. ORDER: Anura, CLASS: Amphibia.

RATTLESNAKES, named for the rattle on their tail, belong to two genera *Crotalus* and *Sistrurus.* They are unique to the Americas. There are about 30 species and 60 subspecies ranging from Canada southwards through South America. In the United States, they are the most respected and feared snakes. All species north of Mexico have a haemotoxic or blood poison while many south of this have a mixture of blood and nerve poison. Fortunately, a single polyvalent antivenine is now available for all rattlesnake bites.

Most species of rattlesnake belong to the genus *Crotalus* characterized by many small scales on the top of the head. Species belonging to the other genus, *Sistrurus,* are either small swamp rattlers called *massasaugas *S. catenatus* or dry land Pigmy rattlers. All are distinguished by having but nine scales covering the head.

The rattle, the most outstanding feature of these snakes, is composed of a material similar to our finger nails. The baby rattlesnake is born with a button at the end of the tail and the first time it sheds its skin the piece next to the button remains, and each time the skin is shed, normally three or four times a year, a new segment is added to this, so

Eastern diamondback rattlesnake coiled defensively, ready to strike if further disturbed.

building up the rattle. Each new segment is convoluted to fit loosely into the previous segment, and it is the clicking together of these segments that produces the characteristic rattle. The rattle is vibrated so fast it may appear as no more than a blur and the noise it makes is like the hiss of escaping steam or the rapid crackling of frying fat. When wet, the rattle makes no noise. Occasionally a snake is caught with fifteen or more segments to the rattle but only rarely, for the segments of the rattle are brittle and break easily. One view is that the sound of the rattle is for defence, warning other animals to keep away. Another view is that it acts as a lure to attract small animals, mainly rodents, which draw near out of curiosity and serve as prey. There is, however, the contradiction that some snakes rattle almost continually while others refuse to buzz at all. Nevertheless, experiments with weasels in captivity have shown they will not attack rattlesnakes with their rattles intact but will readily attack, kill and eat one that has had its rattle removed.

Rattlesnakes are *Pit vipers. The pits, one on each cheek, between the eye and the nostril, are extremely sensitive heat detectors. Rattlers have movable fangs which fold parallel to the roof of the mouth when not in use and are shed about every three weeks. New fangs move in behind the old ones just before they are shed. Rattlers have eyes equipped for both day and night vision. A vertical elliptical pupil dilates after dark to become round, admitting more light. All rattlers give birth to living, poisonous young.

Rattlesnakes are not particularly aggressive. They will not go out of their way to bite but are decidedly active when on the defence. A rattlesnake coils up except for the forepart of the body which is raised ready for action and normally the rattle is buzzing. The striking range is proportional, usually from one-third to one-half of the snake's length, although it is possible for a rattlesnake to strike its full length. Some rattlers will strike repeatedly.

The first rattler encountered by the white settlers in North America was the Timber or Banded rattlesnake. Based on early accounts it was eventually named *Crotalus horridus,* for obvious reasons. It averages 4 ft (120 cm) in length and may attain 6 ft (182 cm). The black or brown bands on a brown or yellowish body camouflages it too well on the forest floor. It is found throughout much of the eastern half of the United States. Actually, *C. horridus* is one of the more gentle species.

The next important snake the settlers had to contend with was *C. adamanteus,* the Eastern diamondback rattlesnake. *C. adamanteus* is one of the truly dangerous snakes of the world and inhabits the southeastern area of the United States.

Although accounts vary, it is quite certain that 8 ft (2·4 m) specimens have been captured. Such a snake would weigh well over 15 lb (6·8 kg) and be 15 in (38 cm) in circumference. An adult Diamondback could have fangs ¾ in (19 mm) long, capable of being driven through almost any boot and of injecting well over a lethal dose of venom into a victim.

The country over which it ranges is subtropical and the snakes do not have to find dens for winter, so are widely scattered. Persistent hunting has reduced their numbers and large specimens are rare. The Eastern diamondback is easily recognized, even when young. It has a grey body with numerous large black, white bordered, diamond-shaped marks along its back. The last several inches of its tail has alternate black and white bands.

Travelling west, another large Diamondback, *C. atrox,* can be found. It is lighter in colour than *C. adamanteus* but has the same pattern and although slightly smaller, it has a far nastier disposition. It ranges through much of the southwest and into Mexico. *C. atrox* is the snake responsible for most deaths due to snake bite in the United States.

In their more northern range, some areas become so heavily populated with this rattler that great hunts are organized. Several cities in the southwest have hunts each year and they attract people from all over the world. Hundreds of pounds of snakes are so destroyed.

Much of the western great plains are infested with the little Prairie rattler *C. viridis.* It is too small normally to cause death to a treated human, but untreated horses and cattle bitten on the nose while grazing occasionally die as the resulting swelling blocks the air passage. *C. viridis* seldom exceeds 4 ft (120 cm) in length and averages about 2 ft (60 cm). It is grey green with a series of dark blotches on the back. Its range extends from Canada to Mexico.

Because of the nasty disposition of this snake and its great numbers, a different method is used to thin it out. The plains offer few good denning sites and due to the severity of the long, cold winters, the snake must get well under the frost line to survive. Mesas and buttes, as the rocky, fractured small hills are called, offer some good dens. The cattlemen place boxes or barrels at the exit. The snakes fall in and are trapped when they come out in the spring and are then destroyed.

Among several species of rattlesnakes to be found in the southwest United States, none is more unusual than the sidewinder *C. cerastis,* up to 2 ft (60 cm) in length, also called the Horned rattlesnake because two head scales over its eyes have been elongated into horn-like growths. Because it lives in loose sand this snake uses an odd method of locomotion. It lifts half its body to a new position, then brings up the other half. So it travels sideways leaving a trail resembling a line of J's in the sand. When the sun grows too hot the snake wriggles into the sand leaving just its eyes exposed, the 'horns' preventing the sand from falling over its eyes.

There are a number of medium-sized rattlers with a more restricted distribution. *C. oraganus* is closely related to the *C. viridis* but inhabits the northwest. The southwestern United States has many little known species, such as the Speckled rattler *C. mitchelli pyrrhus* and the Banded rock *C. lepidus klauberi.*

Mexico, Central America and South America have many average to small species and the islands of both coasts occasionally have a rattler found nowhere else, like the Aruba Island rattler *C. unicolor.* They are much like the North American snakes except that some of them have a mixed venom which is much quicker acting and much harder to treat. *C. basaliscus, C. durissus,* and *C. terrificus* are all much the size of *C. atrox* but, with the addition of the nerve poison, are far more dangerous.

The genus *Sistrurus* embraces the little rattlers of the eastern United States. These are dangerous because their tiny rattles sound like insects and because their dark colours hide them in the swampy or wooded areas where they live. They too like mice but, unlike the *Crotalus,* will also eat frogs. FAMILY: Crotalidae, ORDER: Squamata, CLASS: Reptilia.

REAR-FANGED SNAKES, also called Back-fanged snakes, make up about a third of the family Colubridae. They used to be classified in a subfamily the Boiginae, but it is now accepted that they do not necessarily represent a group of related species. They include well-known species like the *boom-slang and the Indian water snake *Homalopsis buccata.* Rear-fanged snakes are so-called because their fangs are at the back of the jaws instead of the front, and they are merely grooved on the front surface, instead of being hollow as in the front-fanged snakes, for conducting the venom into the victim's body. Such snakes prey on fairly small animals, usually lizards and frogs, because they need to use a chewing action in order to bring their prey to the rear fangs to inject the poison. It is usual to refer to the rear-fanged condition as opisthoglyphous. FAMILY: Colubridae, ORDER: Squamata, CLASS: Reptilia.

RHACOPHORIDAE, a family of frogs most of which are arboreal and differ from the true frogs only in possessing an extra element of cartilage in each finger and toe. Some authorities consider this character not of sufficient importance to make a distinct family and include them in the Ranidae. As in the other large family of treefrogs (Hylidae) the extra element provides an extra joint in the fingers and toes which enables the adhesive disc at the tip of the digit to be pressed flat against a smooth surface no matter at what angle the hand or foot is held. There are a dozen genera and they are found in Africa, South Asia, Japan and the East Indies.

The genus *Rhacophorus* contains about 80 species of treefrogs in Asia and the East Indies. In all the toes are completely webbed but in some the fingers are also completely webbed and are used as gliding membranes. Such frogs are known as 'Flying frogs' and, although their flying abilities have been greatly exaggerated, they can nevertheless glide quite efficiently. They leap from trees and hold their hands and feet outstretched. The webs increase the air resistance and they float down to the ground at an angle, covering a distance of perhaps 30–40 ft (9–12 m). In *R. malabaricus* from South India the body is bright green and the frog is difficult to see as it sits on the leaves but the webs are bright red and the underside of the body bright yellow and this makes the frog very conspicuous when it jumps.

Species of *Rhacophorus* are 'foam-nesters'. The eggs are laid in a foam mass produced by the female. In *R. pardalis* which is found in the Philippines and Borneo the pairing of the adults occurs out of water in low bushes

The Indian water snake, one of the rear-fanged snakes.

The Running frog of West Africa, a member of the family Rhacopharidae. Most of its near relatives live in trees.

overhanging pools. Before the female ejects the eggs she releases a small quantity of sticky fluid. She beats it into a froth with her hindlegs and then more fluid, together with the eggs, is released. The male fertilizes the eggs and the female then beats these into a foamy mass which is about 3 in (7·5 cm) across and contains about 50 eggs. The male and female then drag themselves out of the foam, leaving it hanging from the leaf or branch. After a short time the outside of the mass dries to form a hard crust. The eggs in the centre develop into tadpoles which live in the liquified froth inside the crust and breath the air which was beaten into it. Rain is probably necessary to soften the crust to enable the hatched tadpoles to escape. Completely dried nests with dead tadpoles in them are sometimes found. When they break out of the nest after about eight days the tadpoles drop into the pool below where they continue their development, changing into frogs after 2–3 months. Most species in the genus have similar breeding habits but in some, *R. schlegeli* from Japan, for instance, the foam nest is deposited in a hollow dug in the banks of ponds.

Chiromantis is another genus whose members are also treefrogs and also produce foam nests. They are, however, found in Africa and have several distinctive features. As in the previous genus the toes and fingers have well-developed discs but the fingers are arranged in opposable pairs. The first two fingers are set at right angles to the other two and the hand is thus able to grasp twigs like a pair of pincers.

The Grey treefrog *C. xerampelina* is large and placid about 3 in (7·5 cm) long with a rough, grey skin. It usually sits on horizontal branches; its suckers do not seem strong enough to hold it onto a vertical surface for very long. It is remarkable for the long periods it spends in one place—one was seen in the same spot for seven months. It avoids water and, unlike most frogs, moves into a sheltered spot when it rains. How it conserves moisture even though it may sit in the sun for long periods is not known. Its breeding habits are similar to those of the previous genus. Frothy egg masses about 8 in (20 cm) across and containing about 150 eggs are deposited on leaves and branches. They are only found on those branches directly overhanging water usually at a height of about 4 ft (1·2 m) but occasionally as high as 50 ft (15 m). The egg masses are deposited at night and how the frog knows which branches are above water is not known. The eggs develop into tadpoles after about five days and these wriggle in the liquified jelly until they drop into the water.

The Forest treefrog *Leptopelis natalensis* also lays its eggs out of water but they are not beaten into a frothy mass. About 200 eggs are laid in mud or decaying leaves from 1–3 ft (30–90 cm) away from water. After about two weeks the tadpoles break out of the eggs and wriggle in a mass over the ground towards the water. They are probably attracted to it by smell and if the mass of tadpoles is placed on the opposite side of the pool they all turn round and continue wriggling towards it. They change into adults after about six weeks.

The adults are about 2½ in (6·3 cm) long and a bright green or buff, with large bulging eyes. The fingers and toes have adhesive discs on their tips and the frogs rest on leaves during the day, becoming active at night.

Another species, *L. bocagei,* does not have adhesive discs and shows no inclination to climb. It spends most of the time buried underground, occasionally coming out to feed.

Kassina senegalensis is another member of the Rhacophoridae which is not arboreal. It is known as the Running frog. It has a long slim body about 1½ in (3·7 cm) long and is grey or tan with black or brown stripes running along the body. It does not hop but crawls rather slowly with the body raised well clear of the ground.

Frogs of the genera *Afrixalus* and *Hyperolius* are small long-bodied frogs with adhesive discs on their fingers and toes. They are not really treefrogs, however, since they live in open situations in the reeds and sedges around pools and swamps.

The Spiny reed frog *Afrixalus fornasinii* is about 1½ in (3·7 cm) long and is white or light brown with a dark brown stripe down the middle of the back. It sits at the bases of reeds during the day facing up the stem. When disturbed it backs rapidly into the water. The spines referred to in the name are present in many species of this genus. All the parts of the skin which are exposed when the frog is sitting on a leaf are covered with small white warts. Each wart has a small black spine in its centre.

The Spiny reed frog has a very unusual method of protecting its eggs. They are laid on the leaves of reeds about 3 ft (90 cm) above the water in batches of about 40. The two edges of the leaf are then folded over and glued together so that the eggs are protected in a tube. When the tadpoles hatch, after about five days, they drop into the water.

Other species in the genus have similar habits although in the Golden spiny reed frog *A. spinifrons* the eggs are deposited on a leaf under water rather than above it.

Species of *Hyperolius* are similar in appearance to *Afrixalus,* but the pupil is horizontal instead of vertical. It is a large genus, containing some 200 species, and there is great variation in the colours and patterns even within a single species so that identification is often difficult. Most of them are known as Sedge frogs and live in the vegetation around pools.

The Arum frog *H. horstocki* is found particularly in the white flower of the Arum lily, where it feeds on the insects which are attracted by the scent of the flower. At such times it becomes white and in a vivarium several frogs are often found piled on top of each other. They have been attracted to the nearest white object which in this case is another Arum frog. When the Arum lily is not in flower the Arum frog is found on other plants and is then brown. The eggs are laid in water in groups of 10–30 and are attached to the roots of water plants.

Most species in the genus lay their eggs in water but some have more unusual breeding habits. The Yellow-green reed frog *H. tuberilinguis* lays its eggs in a sticky mass containing 300–400 eggs on leaves or grass a few inches above the water.

The Waterlily frog *H. pusillus* lays its eggs in a single layer between the large overlapping leaves of waterlilies which are thus stuck together and protect the eggs. After about five days the tadpoles hatch and wriggle from between the leaves into the water below. ORDER: Anura, CLASS: Amphibia.

RHAMPHORHYNCHUS, a small Jurassic *pterosaur (flying reptile) with a wingspan of 4 ft (1·2 m). As in all pterosaurs, its wings were supported by the greatly elongated fourth finger. The tail was longer than its body and had a small flap of skin at the end, so it could have been used for steering and balance. Its jaws were armed with sharp forwardly-directed teeth, used to catch the fish. *Rhamphorhynchus* was primitive. The heavy tail and the teeth were lost as the pterosaurs grew larger and lighter. ORDER: Pterosauria, CLASS: Reptilia.

RHINOCEROS VIPER *Bitis nasicornis,* a species of Puff adder, up to 4 ft (1·3 m) long, gaudily coloured and with large pointed and erectile scales on the tip of the snout. It is sometimes called the Nose-horned viper but, in fact, its near relative, the *Gaboon viper, has similar hornlike scales on the snout.

Horned vipers are two distinct species, *Cerastes cerastes* and *C. cornutus,* living in the sandy deserts of northeast Africa and southwest Asia. They have a hornlike scale over each eye. They bury themselves in the sand and it is supposed that the 'horn' keeps sand grains out of the eyes when the head is almost completely buried. FAMILY: Viperidae, ORDER: Squamata, CLASS: Reptilia.

RHINODERMATIDAE, a family of frogs sometimes used to accommodate the unusual Mouth-breeding or Darwin's frogs of the genus *Rhinoderma*. These are now usually placed in the Leptodactylidae. ORDER: Anura, CLASS: Amphibia.

RHINOPHRYNIDAE, a family of frogs

containing a single species, the Mexican burrowing toad *Rhinophrynus dorsalis*. This is highly specialized for its burrowing habits and is difficult to classify. It appears to be most closely related to the *Pipidae. It is characterized by having a shoulder girdle which is arciferal (that is, the two ventral halves overlap in the midline) while the sternum is absent. It is found in wooded areas of Mexico and Guatemala where it lives in holes in the ground. It reaches a length of about $2\frac{1}{2}$ in (63 mm) and has a fat, egg-shaped body with a small triangular head. Its skin is smooth and brown with yellow or pink markings. The first toe on each foot has a large scraper-like tubercle with which the frog is able to dig into the ground. Other adaptations to its burrowing habits include the robust structure of its forelimb bones and the position of the nostrils, which are set well back on the snout near the eyes. It feeds largely on termites and has no teeth and a tongue which is attached at its posterior end and is protruded like a mammal's tongue, rather than flipped out like that of most frogs.

The eggs are laid in water and the tadpoles which hatch out resemble those of the Pipidae in having a long tentacle on either side of the mouth. ORDER: Anura, CLASS: Amphibia.

RHIPIDISTIA, a group of fossil fishes. The earliest are from the Lower Devonian, some 390 million years ago, and they finally became extinct in the Lower Permian 260 million years ago. Together with the Actinistia or coelacanths they comprise the *Crossopterygii one of the major groups of bony fish. The vast majority of rhipidistians were freshwater. They are of great interest because it is generally agreed that the ancestor (or ancestors) of all tetrapods was a rhipidistian fish. Anatomically they have much in common with their immediate descendants the early Amphibia.

In the most primitive Rhipidistia the dermal (external) bones of the skull and shoulder girdle and the complete covering of scales behind them are covered with a layer of cosmine, closely comparable with the dentine of our teeth, and like our teeth the most superficial layer is of hard shiny enamel. The head was that of an active predatory fish, with a long gape and the margins of both jaws armed with sharp slightly recurved teeth. In addition there was a series of tusks in a row inside the upper jaw margin paralleling the external maxillary teeth. The arrangement of teeth and tusks, as well as their microscopic structure, closely parallels that of the *labyrinthodont Amphibia.

Unlike their labyrinthodont descendants the Rhipidistia retained gills of the type found in living bony fishes as evidenced by the preserved bony gill covers. They also had lungs, which were inherited by their land-living descendants. Lungs for breathing in

poorly oxygenated water appear to have been a characteristic of all true primitive bony fish and have been converted to a single or paired swimbladder in most primitive species. Thus it is the loss of fish gills not the origin of lungs that characterizes tetrapods.

The fins of Rhipidistia also emphasize their claim to be ancestors of tetrapods. Apart from two median dorsal fins, a tail fin and a ventral fin, they had, in common with all bony fishes, paired pectoral and pelvic fins corresponding to the arms and legs of tetrapods. Particularly in the pectoral fin skeleton it is possible to trace many elements of the tetrapod foreleg. The bone which articulates with the shoulder girdle is a true humerus and is succeeded by a series of three bones, the next of which corresponds to the ulna. The four bones (basals) together form the axis of the fin and projecting from them was a series of radials, the first of which corresponds to the radius of the forearm.

The Rhipidistia are usually divided into three families. The first represented by *Osteolepis,* a common fossil in the Middle Devonian of Scotland and elsewhere, were primitive forms with heavy scales and an asymmetrical (heterocercal) tail fin which gave lift to the heavy body. In spite of their primitive nature the Osteolepidae were the last family to become extinct and are common in Coal Measure faunas.

The second family, the Rhizodontidae, is represented by *Eusthenopteron*. These were advanced forms with scales and bones lightened by the loss of cosmine and enamel and with a symmetrical tail. *Eusthenopteron* can claim to be one of the most thoroughly studied of fossil fishes, largely due to the work of Professor Jarvik in Stockholm who has reconstructed the anatomy of the skull in minute detail from sections.

The third family, the Holoptychidae, are aberrant deep-bodied forms with narrow fins

and an extra pair of external nostrils in addition to the paired external and internal nostrils which rhipidistians share exclusively with tetrapods. The earliest known rhipidistian is assigned to this family.

His detailed study of skull anatomy, particularly that of the snout, has led Jarvik to suggest that the ancestry of caudates (newts and salamanders) can be traced back to the holoptychids, while osteolepids or rhizodontids gave rise to the frogs and all other tetrapods. This theory, however, is not generally accepted outside Sweden and no linking intermediate·fossil forms are suggested in either case. SUBCLASS: Crossopterygii, CLASS: Pisces.

RHYNCHOCEPHALIA, order of reptiles now extinct except for a single species, the *tuatara *Sphenodon punctatus,* of New Zealand.

The rhynchocephalians first appeared in the Lower Triassic period 200 million years ago and were relatively abundant in the Middle Triassic. Their remains are fairly common in the continental formations of East Africa, Brazil, and Argentina. Occasionally small rhynchocephalians are found in the Lower Cretaceous of Europe and South America, but beyond this point there is no more recent fossil record. It seems that the group became restricted to its present limited distribution some 63 million years ago in the Tertiary Period. The rhynchocephalians have probably been derived from a group of fossil reptiles known as the eosuchians which were in turn evolved from the *stem-reptiles or cotylosaurs. An important diagnostic feature of the cotylosaurs which were the most primitive of reptiles and gave rise to all known groups of reptiles, is the presence of an almost complete armour of bones (dermal bones) which sheathed the head above, below and at the sides. Such a

The tuatara of New Zealand sometimes shares a burrow with a shearwater or mutton-bird.

skull condition is termed anapsid. In the eosuchians and the rhynchocephalians there has been considerable modification in the pattern of the dermal bones particularly in the temporal region. In these two groups the temporal region has two areas which lack the dermal covering bones. These areas are termed the temporal fossae and were probably evolved to facilitate the action of the jaw muscles. In the eosuchians and the rhynchocephalians the upper temporal fossa is separated from the lower by a bar of bone (composed of the two dermal elements termed the squamosal and the post-orbital) and the lower fossa is bounded ventrally by bone (largely the dermal bone named the jugal). The presence of these two complete fossae is a diagnostic feature of the eosuchians and the rhynchocephalians including the tuatara. In modern lizards the bar of bone below the lower temporal fossa is absent. Despite the similarities between the rhynchocephalians and the eosuchians the two groups differ in a number of ways. The skull in the rhynchocephalians is characterized by the presence of an overhanging beak on the upper jaw which is not found in the eosuchians. In fact Rhynchocephalia means 'beak-headed'. The ribs in the Rhynchocephalia are single-headed rather than double and in this feature resemble those of modern lizards rather than those of the eosuchians. However, the ribs of rhynchocephalians also resemble those of birds in that they have uncinate processes. The teeth of rhynchocephalians are fused to the surface of the jaw, and are termed acrodont, whereas those of the eosuchians are set in sockets.

An early offshoot of the rhynchocephalian stock are the Triassic family the Rhynchosauridae, the members of which are known from all the continents except North America. Two members of this family are *Rhynchosaurus* and *Hyperodapedon* which had elongate beak-like, toothless upper jaws. They were probably egg-eating, shore-living forms. A third member of this group is *Scaphonyx* which reached a length of 6 ft (1·8 m) and was herbivorous. The skull is short and broad with a characteristic 'parrot-like' beak. The palate has a large tooth plate on either side and the upper edge of the lower jaw is modified to form a chopping blade which fits into a longitudinal groove in the upper tooth plate.

Homoeosaurus which is found in rocks 140 million years old from the Upper Jurassic is almost identical in structure to the modern tuatara. It seems therefore that the rhynchocephalian pattern of structural organization has remained relatively unchanged for many millions of years and the ancestry of the modern form can be traced back via a form resembling *Homoeosaurus* to the eosuchians and thence to the stem-reptiles. CLASS: Reptilia.

RINGHALS *Hemachatus haemachatus,* a 'spitting' cobra with strongly keeled scales. It rarely exceeds 4 ft (1·2 m) in length. It is restricted to South Africa.
Unlike other *cobras it bears live young. FAMILY: Elapidae, ORDER: Squamata, CLASS: Reptilia.

RUSSELL'S VIPER *Vipera russelli,* the common *viper of the Indian Peninsula and one of the most feared snakes in India.

S

SALAMANDERS, a general term for the tailed amphibians which belong to the following families: Hynobiidae, Cryptobranchidae, Sirenidae, Proteidae, Amphiumidae, Ambystomatidae and Plethodontidae. The family Salamandridae comprises mainly the newts but it also includes the European salamander.

The salamanders are long-bodied amphibians which retain a tail throughout life and hence differ from the frogs and toads (order Anura) which lose their tail after the larval or tadpole stage. The limbs of salamanders

The male European or Spotted salamander *Salamandra salamandra* makes a clumsy attempt to embrace the female by clambering onto her back but, as in other salamanders, there is no coition, he lays a spermatophore which the female picks up with her cloaca.

are usually relatively small and in no case are they modified for jumping. The forelimb usually has four toes and the hindlimb five. There is a tendency towards a reduction in the number of toes and in some cases limbs may also be reduced in size and even lost. For example, the Great siren *Siren lacertinia* (family Sirenidae) lacks hindlimbs, and the Mud siren *Pseudobranchus striatus* is also without hindlimbs and has only three toes on the forelimb. For rapid movement salamanders do not use their limbs to any great extent but wriggle with the belly touching or close to the ground. The movement resembles that of a fish swimming and is produced by the serial contraction of the muscle blocks or myotomes arranged along the body. The movement is probably similar to that used by the first land vertebrates and is essentially 'swimming on land'. In slower, more methodical movement the body is supported by the limbs.

Externally, salamanders resemble the ancient forms from which they have evolved, but internally a good deal of modification has occurred. One major change has been a reduction in the amount of bone. The brain in the ancestors of salamanders was surrounded by a bony braincase which was in turn sheathed by a series of superficial bones, known as dermal bones, which almost completely enclosed the brain case. Openings for the eyes and the external nostrils were found in the dermal shield and there was also a dorsal opening in the parietal bone for a third or pineal eye. In modern salamanders there has been considerable reduction in the number and extent of the dermal bones and the skeleton of the head may have large areas of cartilage. Similar reductions have occurred in the dermal elements of the lower jaw and the limb girdles. The reduction of bone in the pectoral and pelvic girdles is especially marked in the aquatic salamanders. In the Mud siren which lacks the hindlimbs the pelvic girdle is also absent.

Breathing in modern salamanders is accomplished by movements of the hyoid apparatus in the floor of the mouth and by gulping movements which result in air being 'swallowed' into the lungs. In all salamanders the skin is an important area of respiration and in many species the lungs are reduced in size. This is especially so in those salamanders such as *Ranodon* and *Onychodactylus* (family Hynobiidae) which inhabit fast-moving waterways. The presence of large lungs in such forms would increase the animal's buoyancy and the possibility of its being carried away by the current. The ultimate in lung reduction is found in the family Plethodontidae in which lungs are entirely absent.

The skin in salamanders is well supplied with small blood vessels (capillaries) which often run close to the surface of the skin and hence facilitate the uptake of oxygen. The lining of the mouth cavity may also be richly supplied with blood vessels and may be used as an area of oxygen uptake. This is especially important in some plethodontids which take up to 20% of their oxygen in this way. The heart in all amphibians has a single chamber (ventricle) for pumping the blood. This allows extensive mixing of blood returning from the right and left sides of the heart. Some of the blood from the ventricle is carried to the lungs in the pulmonary artery and some to the skin in a series of segmental arteries. In frogs and toads which have very short bodies the blood to the skin is carried in a pair of cutaneous arteries. In the Lungless salmanders the

pulmonary artery is reduced to a tiny vessel which runs to the body wall.

The skin in salamanders is kept moist by the secretion of mucus from small flask-shaped glands below the epidermis. In some species, such as the Slimy salamander *Plethodon glutinosus,* this secretion is very sticky. The granular or poison glands have a similar structure to the mucous glands but secrete noxious substances of variable toxicity.

In some species the male salamander has special tubular glands, the hedonic glands, which produce a secretion attracting the female during courtship.

The entire outer body surface of salamanders is shed at regular intervals. The time between successive moults is very variable and in many species the animal eats the old skin. Modern salamanders exhibit a great diversity in colour and many species have bright patches of yellow, orange or gold, but some species are dull and drab. In some, such as the olm *Proteus anguinus* (family Proteidae), the animal may be uniformly white.

Eyes are usually well developed in salamanders and their surface is cleansed by the secretion of a gland which runs along the lower eyelid and has several openings onto the eye. The secretion is carried away from the eye to the nasal chamber by a lachrymal

The Striped salamander *Salamandra salamandra.*

duct from the inner corner of the lower lid. This is very similar to the tear duct in higher vertebrates. The Grotto salamander *Typhlotriton spelaeus* has functional eyes during the larval period which it spends at the mouth of caves. Later it retreats into total darkness the eyelids grow together, partly fuse and the eye degenerates. If the larva is allowed to develop in the light the eyes remain functional.

Male and female Spotted salamander are alike externally except that the female is slightly larger.

The sense of smell is important in salamanders and is often used to locate food and also during courtship. Air is taken in via the external nostrils and passed through a sensory nasal cavity. This nasal sac communicates with the cavity of the mouth by an internal nostril or choana, and hence the air from the nasal chamber usually enters the oral cavity. Many salamanders possess an accessory chamber or area of nasal epithelium which forms the Jacobson's or vomeronasal organ. This structure is used to test the contents of the mouth

Salamanders occupy a variety of habitats and may be aquatic, semi-terrestrial, fully terrestrial and even arboreal. They are generally secretive and are found in out of the way places such as caves, under logs, in crevices and in the humus of the forest floor. Many salamanders occur in lowland areas but some are found in high cloud forests and high mountain streams up to a height of 13,000 ft (4,000 m). They vary greatly in size, from the Pigmy salamander *Desmognathus wrighti* (family Plethodontidae) 2 in (5 cm) long, to the Japanese giant salamander *Megalobactrachus japonicus* (family Cryptobranchidae) which may reach 5 ft (1·5 m). Salamanders are usually solitary but the Arboreal salamander *Aneides lugubris* (family Plethodontidae) is often found in small groups. Unlike frogs and toads, salamanders are usually voiceless, although the Pacific giant salamander *Dicamptodon ensatus* (family Ambystomatidae) is said to produce a low pitched sound resembling a bark, and a high pitched 'scream' when alarmed. The Arboreal salamander and the Monterey salamander *Ensatina eschscholtzi* (family Plethodontidae) produce a mouse-like squeak.

Male salamanders often stage an elaborate courtship display in front of the female prior to breeding. Fertilization is usually internal and the female picks up with her cloaca a packet of sperm, known as a spermatophore, dropped by the male. In the hynobiids, such as *Hynobius shihi,* and in the sirens and Giant salamanders fertilization is external. The eggs of salamanders contain yolk and usually develop in water into a larva which has external gills and also gill slits. These are usually lost at metamorphosis. Some of the terrestrial salamanders lay their eggs in damp places on land and there is no aquatic larval phase. Within the group there are many instances in which larval characters are retained for prolonged periods, and there are many cases of permanent larval forms capable of breeding (neotenous forms). Those species which retain external gills throughout life are often termed perennibranchiate (persistent gills) and those which lose their gills as caducibranchiate (deciduous gills). Neotenous salamanders of some species may be induced to metamorphose by changing their environment.

Many aquatic salamanders and aquatic larvae of semi-terrestrial forms retain traces of a sensory system similar to the lateral line system of fishes. This is sensitive to low frequency water-borne vibrations. The lateral line system in salamanders functions in the same way and consists of specialized cells often in definite rows which may be marked by small pits in the surface of the skin. When aquatic larvae become terrestrial the lateral line system usually disappears.

Salamanders are not considered to be of economic importance although the axolotl is said to be eaten by the locals in Mexico City. Salamanders feed largely on insects and small invertebrates and they undoubtedly destroy useful as well as harmful animals. Food is not generally chewed but is swallowed rapidly and in many salamanders the tongue is used in the capture of the food. Salamanders have the ability to shed their tail to avoid capture and many of the plethodontids have a constriction at the base of the tail which is the point at which the tail breaks off. The ability to regenerate the tail is extensive in salamanders and they are capable of regenerating limbs and even parts of the head. In addition they are relatively easy to keep in captivity and have therefore been widely used in fundamental biological research on regeneration and developmental biology. (See Ambystomatids, Amphiuma, Cryptobranchidae, Giant salamander, Hynobiids, Lungless salamander, mudpuppy, newts, olm, Proteidae, sirens. ORDER: Caudata, CLASS: Amphibia.

SALIENTIA, alternative name for the *Anura or tailless amphibians.

SANDFISH, common name for eight species of *skinks *Scincus,* a kind of lizard, ranging from Algeria to West Pakistan, which wriggle into and through loose sand as if they are swimming. They have rather broad snouts that sharpen to an edge and their toes are flattened and have fringes of projecting scales which enable them to move over the surface of loose sand. Although they can comfortably negotiate the areas above ground, the 'sandfish' spend most of their time under the surface searching for insects. FAMILY: Scincidae, ORDER: Squamata, CLASS: Reptilia.

SAUROPTERYGIA, order of extinct aquatic reptiles characterized, among other things, by having a series of abdominal ribs closely intermeshed. The earliest sauropterygians, of the Triassic 200 million years ago, had fairly normal limbs, suitable for use on land as well as in water. These included the nothosaurs and placodonts. The *plesiosaurs, which came later, in the Jurassic and Cretaceous periods, 200–70 million years ago, had flippers and were fully aquatic. CLASS: Reptilia.

Permanent larval form of the axolotl.

SAW-SCALED VIPER *Echis carinatus,* although no more than about 2 ft (60 cm) long has the most powerful venom of any of the *vipers. It is found throughout the desert region of North Africa, eastwards through India to Ceylon.

SEA SNAKES, poisonous snakes that live permanently in the sea and are fully adapted to that way of life, having the body flattened from side to side and the tail flattened and paddle-shaped. They swim with a sculling action of the tail, keeping mainly near the surface but able to submerge, closing the valvular nostrils on the top of the snout. They

The Banded slender-necked sea snake *Hydrophis fasciatus* does not normally come ashore.

are, however, fully air-breathing and must surface periodically or drown. The head is characteristically small and the front half of the body slender with the hindquarters more fully rounded. Some Sea snakes reach a length of 10 ft (3 m) but the majority are 4–5 ft (1·2–1·6 m) long. All have venom glands with cobra-like fangs, hollow and permanently erect in the front of the mouth. The 50 species are confined to the tropics, especially in the eastern Indian Ocean and western Pacific, mainly living in inshore waters. Some Sea snakes swarm in the cracks and crannies of rocks in the intertidal zone. A few are known to enter tidal rivers up to 100 miles (160 km) inland. One species only, *Hydrophis semperi,* is confined to freshwater, in the Philippines. One of the commonest and most widely distributed is the Yellow-bellied sea snake *Pelamis platurus* which is black on the back and yellow or pale brown on the belly, the two colours being sharply separated. The tail is dappled black and yellow. Some species, living among seaweeds, are cross-barred with brown on a dun or grey background.

The slender front part of the body serves as a long neck allowing the snakes to strike downwards or sideways at prey, killing them with their venom which is powerful enough to immobilize small fishes in a matter of moments. Some Sea snakes feed exclusively on eels but those that habitually lie among seaweeds or under floating objects eat the small fishes that go there to shelter. Crustaceans are also eaten.

Sea snakes are not the same thing as 'sea serpents' and yet it is possible that they may have contributed something to this sea legend from their habit of congregating in large numbers in long narrow bands writhing at the surface. The largest ever recorded was seen from a steamer in the Malacca Strait and the total mass formed a band 10 ft (3 m) wide and over 60 miles (96 km) long. The reason for these congregations is not known but it may be connected with breeding.

Members of the subfamily Laticaudinae go on land to lay eggs, usually in caves on the shore, and in the Philippines Japanese fishermen killed large numbers at such times. Sea snakes of the subfamily Hydrophinae give birth to living young in the sea. The killing of the Sea snake *Laticauda semifasciata* by the Japanese was for the sake of its skin from which leather was made. Its flesh was also eaten. Other species in other parts of the Sea snakes' range are also used to a limited extent for the leather they yield, while the flesh is sold as an aphrodisiac. Sea snakes are preyed upon by seabirds and by predatory fishes.

Although the venom of a Sea snake is potent to small fishes there are relatively few reports of fatal accidents to fishermen. FAMILY: Hydrophidae, ORDER: Squamata, CLASS: Reptilia.

SEYMOURIA, a primitive tetrapod which lived in the early part of the Permian period, about 260 million years ago, in Texas and adjoining states of the USA where it is found

fossil today. The name refers to the town of Seymour in Baylor County, Texas.

Most of the anatomical characters of *Seymouria* are those of a strongly built terrestrial, if very primitive reptile. However, the skull structure relates it to the *Labyrinthodontia, a group of early Amphibia. For many years paleontologists debated whether it was reptile or amphibian, but its amphibian status was suggested when young specimens showed grooves for lateral line canals indicating a freshwater life for the young and this was clinched when related species were found fossilized in the tadpole stage. ORDER: Seymouriamorpha, CLASS: Amphibia.

SHIELD-TAILED SNAKES, forty species of primitive snakes related to the *Pipe snakes and showing many adaptations to burrowing. There are usually two lungs but the left is only of a moderate size and the skull is a rigid compact structure with peculiar features in the supporting axis and atlas vertebrae. There are no specialized enlarged belly scales. The eyes are minute and are hidden under the head scales. The tail shows varying degrees of modification in different species. Some simply have a large scale at the end of a short tail, but in others this is embellished with two or three spines. Most, however, have the scales replaced by a single circular spiny shield at the tail end. It is believed the shield is thrust into the soil to provide a firm anchorage while the small pointed head is pushed forward, but it has also been suggested that it is used to plug the entrance to the snake's burrow. Shield-tailed snakes are mostly 1 ft (30 cm) or less in length. The largest on record was 29 in (73·8 cm). These quiet, inoffensive snakes have a limited distribution in peninsular India and Ceylon, being found burrowing in the soil and under stones and logs from sea-level to 7,000 ft (2,500 m) in the forested areas. They give birth to between three and eight young at a time. With their rigid skulls Shield-tailed snakes seem unable to eat large items and their food consists of soft-bodied grubs and worms. FAMILY: Uropeltidae, ORDER: Squamata, CLASS: Reptilia.

SIDEWINDER, name given to several species of snakes which exhibit a peculiar sideways looping when moving rapidly. Sidewinding snakes occur among the *rattlesnakes or Pit vipers, family Crotalidae, and also the True vipers, family Viperidae.

A snake sidewinding is orientated with its body pointing obliquely at an angle of about 130–140° from its direction of travel. Although the body tends to point away from its general direction of movement, the head itself points forwards. At the start of the winding sequence the snake lifts its head and front part of the body off the ground and swings them forwards in a horizontal arc to a new position in the general direction of progress. The head is rapidly and forcefully driven on to the ground and the body loop between the head and tail immediately swings forward off the ground and completes the movement of the snake's body to a new position which is in front of and parallel to the former one. It should be noted that only that part of the body which is between the old and new tracks or positions moves at any one time. As soon as the tail has been shifted clear of the old position and placed into the new track (or even before this has occurred) another cycle is commenced by lifting the head to a new position once more. Thus it can

be seen that the tracks produced by a snake sidewinding are oblique to the general direction of locomotion and are not continuous. Each separate track is roughly equal in length to the snake itself, and often bears the clear impression of the ventral scales. When travelling across loose sand the snake produces fringing ridges of sand on each side of the tracks, which seem to prevent excessive lateral slip movement. Sidewinding should be seen as a special method of movement which has been developed by some snakes in order to progress rapidly across smooth and even surfaces, especially soft sand. Sidewinding snakes may travel up to three times as fast as snakes employing other methods of locomotion. Most species which sidewind live in deserts where very hot sand and rock surfaces may separate the few places suitable as shelter from predators and extreme heat. Snakes which are capable of sidewinding can also move by the usual methods of snake locomotion, by lateral undulations caused by contraction and relaxation of segmental muscles or by the rectilinear method employing waves of contraction in the belly musculature.

Although several species of rattlesnake exhibit sidewinding, the true sidewinder is the Horned rattlesnake, *Crotalus cerastes,* which occurs in the deserts of the southwestern United States. This very venomous snake has a small horn above each eye and is, therefore, reminiscent of the sidewinding Horned viper, *Cerastes cerastes,* of the deserts of North Africa, Asia Minor and the more western areas of Asia. The Horned viper lives buried in fine sand with only its eyes and horns projecting, awaiting the approach of a jerboa, Desert lark or locust. FAMILIES: Crotalidae, Viperidae, ORDER: Squamata, CLASS: Reptilia.

SKINKS, with over 600 species, comprise one of the two largest lizard families. They are

generally smooth-scaled and cylindrical, with conical heads and tapering tails, short legs or none at all, overlapping scales and a protrusible tongue. The majority are under 1 ft (30 cm) in length and most are less than 8 in (20 cm), the smallest being barely 3 in (7 cm) long. They are mostly ground-dwellers and burrowers, but many climb about in bushes or trees, although only one has a prehensile tail and thereby shows some specialization for arboreal life. This, the Solomon Islands Giant skink *Corucia zebrata,* is also the largest of the family and just exceeds 2 ft (61 cm) in length. No skink is truly aquatic and there are no real runners among them; they only crawl or scamper. They are secretive and many species spend much of their lives underground. Adaptations for burrowing are evident in the body shape, in the shovel-shaped snout and in the reduction in size or even absence of the limbs in some species. Another feature is the degenerate eye, which is covered by a scaly lower lid or by a transparent non-movable disc. The ear opening is closed and the inner ear degenerate.

Skinks are the most abundant of the lizards in Africa, the East Indies and Australia. In Australia the number of species of skinks exceeds that of any other family of reptiles. Half or more of the species occur in southeastern Asia and the East Indies, and only about 50 species are found in the Western Hemisphere. However, some skinks are found on every continent except Antarctica.

Half the species lay eggs, others give birth to living young, and one genus includes both egg-layers and live-bearers. The egg-layers may have clutches of 2–23 eggs, but live-bearers seem to have smaller broods as a general rule. Some American skinks actively tend their eggs from the time they are laid in the nest until they hatch, and one species even cares for its brood after hatching, an exception to the rule that reptiles lay their eggs or deposit their young and subsequently ignore them.

The smaller species of the skink family feed mainly on insects, the largest skinks are wholly or partly vegetarian.

For protection from their enemies, skinks rely mainly on their retiring habits and the ability to throw off and then replace all or part of the tail. When alarmed or threatened, a skink raises its tail in the air, turns it towards its enemy and waves it slowly back and forth. The tail, once broken off, will wriggle violently for some time, diverting attention from its former owner. It takes some months for the new tail to grow to the original length and the scales on it tend to be more simple in structure, while the new colour and pattern are also less complex. Multiple tails are especially common in skinks; as a result of a complete or more often a partial break in the tail, regeneration may result in the formation

The thick tail of the West African skink *Riopa fernandii* contains a store of fat.

121

of two, three or even four tail buds, which in turn develop into new tails.

The colour patterns include crossbars, stripes and spots but some species are a plain monochrome. Stripes are the most common, sometimes broad, sometimes narrow, and they may be on the back or on the sides. The colours are generally sombre, brown and olive predominating, although a bright colour may appear occasionally, especially in the males at the breeding season.

One of the best known skinks is the Australian Blue-tongue skink *Tiliqua scincoides,* 12–15 in (30–40 cm) long, frequently kept as a pet. The name refers to the light or deep blue tongue, which is slowly but constantly flicked in and out whenever the animal is alert or on the move. The young of this species are heavily banded, the bands tending to break up as the animal matures. Another attractive Australian skink is the Shingle-back lizard *Trachysaurus rugosus* up

to 18 in (45 cm) long, also known as stumpy-tail, bobtail, Double-headed lizard, boggi, and Pine-cone lizard. Unlike the other Australian skinks, the shingle-back generally has only two young at one time, only occasionally triplets. It is a sluggish animal, and feeds on flowers and fruit, as well as snails and slugs.

The most bizarre genus *Tribolonotus* has a bony casque on the head. FAMILY: Scincidae, ORDER: Squamata, CLASS: Reptilia.

SLOW WORM *Anguis fragilis,* a limbless and smooth-scaled lizard with eyelids, without lateral grooves, rather stiffly cylindrical, the head, trunk and tail being not easily distinguishable, and with the ability to cast its tail. The young are silver-grey or light bronze, with a blackish mid-dorsal stripe and underside. Adults, up to 20 in (50 cm), are darker and duller olive-grey or bronze. The females retain the 'juvenile' stripe whereas

males, which have relatively shorter trunks and longer tails, are usually less heavily marked and often show bluish markings dorsally.

Slow worms are found over temperate Eurasia west of the Caucasus mountains, but not in Ireland and some other islands. In parts of North Africa and the Middle East to Iran they are found in sheltered non-arid situations; elsewhere their habitat is usually rocky or wooded. In Britain, pairing takes place soon after emergence from hibernation and before dispersal for the summer. Three to 23 or even more young are born ovoviviparously or viviparously, late in the summer. The young are independent from birth. Slow worms eat many slugs, earthworms and insect larvae, so it is regrettable that these lizards, harmless to man and his livestock, are so often killed in mistake for venomous snakes. FAMILY: Anguidae, ORDER: Squamata, CLASS: Reptilia.

Burton's snake lizard of Australia eating a gecko.

SNAKE-LIZARDS, a group of legless lizards found only in the Australian region, their family being the only family of reptiles entirely confined to that region. About a dozen species occur on the Australian mainland, and two species in New Guinea.

Snake-lizards are all slender, snake-like lizards not easily distinguished from snakes. The principal external features by which they differ from them are their flat, fleshy tongues (slender and deeply forked in snakes) and long, fragile tails which can be regenerated when broken. In most snake-lizards the tail is at least as long as the body, whereas in snakes the tail is much shorter than the body and cannot be regenerated if any part is lost. Many snake-lizards have ear-openings, and these are absent in snakes.

All vestiges of forelimbs have been lost in snake-lizards, while the hindlimbs are so small they are no use in locomotion and movement is identical to that of snakes. The hindlimbs are best developed in the Flap- or Scaly-footed snake-lizards *Pygopus* and *Delma,* in which they are represented by small scaly flaps, one on either side of the vent. These flaps have limited movement and are normally held flat against the body. Within each flap is a much-reduced set of limb bones, with four toes. In other snake-lizards, the hindlimbs are no more than tiny spurs and the size and number of bones has been even further reduced.

Despite the great differences in their external appearances, snake-lizards are most closely related to *geckos. This relationship is based almost entirely on internal resemblances, but they have some other interesting features in common. Like most geckos, snake-lizards have no eyelids and the eyes are kept clean by the action of the fleshy tongue, which is frequently used to wipe each eye. Both geckos and snake-lizards are vocal, although most snake-lizards produce only a low squeaking sound.

Several genera of snake-lizards are known only from a handful of preserved museum specimens and virtually nothing is known of the habits of these rarities. One group *Aprasia* are light grey or brown worm-like burrowing lizards which feed on small insects. They rarely exceed 6 in (15 cm) in length and are largely restricted to southern Australia. The most common is Burton's snake-lizard *Lialis burtonis* which is found throughout mainland Australia and in parts of New Guinea. Growing to about 2 ft (61 cm) this species has a characteristic sharp, wedge-shaped snout. It varies greatly in colour; it may be cream, grey, brown, reddish or black, with or without darker stripes and spotting. It is a ground-dwelling lizard which hides in grass or litter.

The Scaly-footed snake-lizards are all diurnal, terrestrial lizards which feed largely on insects. Most average 1–2 ft (30–60 cm) in

The Flying snake *Chrysopelea ornata*, a tree-dwelling snake, gliding from a high branch to a lower one.

length and are usually brown or grey, often with dark bands on the head and nape.

All snake-lizards are egg-layers, but details of the breeding habits of most species are otherwise unknown. FAMILY: Pygopodidae, ORDER: Squamata, CLASS: Reptilia.

SNAKES, elongated legless reptiles. Because there are several kinds of lizards without external trace of limbs there is no easy test of outward appearance by which to distinguish all snakes from all lizards. In each part of the world in which limbless lizards occur with snakes it is necessary to learn the particular distinctions that apply locally.

Snakes lack moveable eyelids and a tympanic membrane to the ear. The features that distinguish all snakes from all lizards are, however, details of internal structure mainly concerned with the eyes, the skull and the viscera. The differences in the eyes lie in the wall of the eyeball (sclera) and in the rods and cones of the retina. The differences of the skull concern the braincase and, in particular, the relationships between the two rods of cartilage (trabeculae) that form the floor of the embryo braincase (before the formation of bone), the bony forward extension of the posterior braincase floor (parasphenoid) and the anterior braincase roofing bones

Boa constrictor *Constrictor constrictor*, famous South American snake which suffocates its victims.

(frontals). The differences in the viscera concern the relative positions of the thymus bodies, the gall bladder and the kidneys. A further difference is that all limbless lizards have some trace of shoulder girdle while all snakes have none.

Apart from the rather technical diagnostic features there are other features of more evident functional significance that are generally found in snakes but, either do not occur universally, or are matched in only some lizards. The tongue is deeply forked and can be protruded from the mouth. One of the immediate responses of a snake when aroused is to flick out the tongue and test the surroundings. When it is withdrawn into the mouth it is believed that the points are inserted into the openings of *Jacobson's organs in the roof of the mouth. The tongue thus mediates a chemical sense by which a snake can follow a scent trail. There is generally a hinge between the bones of the snout and the braincase which facilitates the swallowing of large prey, but more essential to this is the great looseness of attachment of the jaws. Each upper and lower jaw can move as a separate unit. Each of the upper jaws has four attachments to the skull and each lower jaw is suspended by a bone (quadrate) that is itself movably attached to the skull. The two lower jaws are joined at the chin by an elastic ligament. In swallowing, as the jaws on one side hold the prey the jaws on the other side are relaxed and pushed forwards to get a fresh grip, the prey being drawn in with a see-saw movement. All snakes have rather extensively developed labial glands the secretion of which helps to lubricate the prey during swallowing. At full distension of the jaws ordinary breathing would be impossible so the snake thrusts the windpipe forwards to the gap between the two halves of the lower jaw, opens the glottis, takes a breath and withdraws the windpipe.

The arterial arches carrying blood to the head (carotid arches) are extremely long. In the head there are transverse arteries connecting the blood supplies of right and left sides. This would seem to mean that if one main artery is squeezed during the swallowing of a large prey the other can still deliver blood to both sides of the head via the transverse arteries. However, in the majority of snakes the right artery is lost in development so that the blood to both sides of the head comes by the left vessel only.

All snakes lack all trace of shoulder girdle; most also lack all trace of the hip girdle and hindlimbs. Where hindlimb vestiges remain they have nothing to do with locomotion which is accomplished by movements of the trunk. The vertebral column needs therefore to combine strength and flexibility. Snakes have two articular facets between the vertebrae in addition to the usual three. This still permits vertical and horizontal bending but, particularly, prevents rotation between vertebrae.

Origin of snakes. The origin of snakes raises two questions: how did snakes arrive at their present condition and from what sort of four-legged ancestors did they arise? Beyond reasonable doubt snakes are closely related to lizards and arose from ancestors that we would call lizards if we knew them. However, since there are no known fossil remains of animals intermediate between lizards and snakes we have no direct evidence of their ancestors. We must rely on comparative studies of living animals.

Important evidence comes from study of the eyes. In snakes with good eyes both their structure and the mechanism of focussing are quite different from those of lizards, and all other vertebrates. The snake eye has evidently been extensively rebuilt. The structure of the retina indicates that snakes' ancestors had both rods and cones, unlike modern lizards which, even when nocturnal or burrowing, have only cones or cells derived from cones. These lines of evidence suggest that the ancestral snakes were nocturnal and that their eyes were reduced and simplified in association with burrowing, or at least strongly secretive, habits.

In all snakes, even including Tree snakes, the brain is more completely enclosed by bone than it is in lizards. Those lizards whose braincase most closely resembles the condition found in snakes are all burrowers. The snout of an animal that burrows without the use of limbs requires extra support and in all burrowing lizards some of this support is given by the upper jaws as well as by the braincase. There is one group of snakes (Blind or Worm snakes), in which the upper jaws remain mobile and the snout is supported entirely by the braincase. If the ancestral snakes were likewise burrowers that had mobile upper jaws then we would have a good reason for the snake braincase being more completely bony than in any burrowing

Snake charmer and cobra, West Pakistan.

A common snake of Africa, *Psammophis philipsi*.
Snake charmer in Morocco.

lizard. On this view those burrowing snakes, such as *Pipe snakes, in which the jaws participate in the support of the snout, have acquired this condition secondarily.

In no snakes is the tail as long as the head and trunk together; 25–30% of the total length is a usual proportion and in the long-tailed Tree snakes about 40% is a maximum. This means that in all snakes the trunk plays a major role in locomotion. In limbless lizards that live on the surface the tail plays an important part in locomotion and may comprise as much as three-quarters of the total length. In burrowing lizards on the other hand the tail is reduced in length and may be less than one-fifth of the total length. The bodily proportions of snakes thus may have been acquired during a burrowing phase of their evolutionary history in which the tail lost importance in locomotion.

Only one fossil is known that is important in the early history of snakes, *Dinilysia* from the Cretaceous of Argentina. It is quite certainly a snake and probably related to the small 'pythons' *Loxocemus* of Central America and *Calabaria* of West Africa. If we

Green tree snake *Dendrolaphis punctulatus* of Western Australia.

Ribbon snake *Thamnophis sauritus* on edge of Okefenokee swamp, United States. Its longitudinal markings make it resemble a Garter snake.

Jacobson's organ, the specialized region of the nasal sac, shown here in the mouth of a snake.

A snake *Liasis childreni*, representing one of the main groups of reptiles.

believe that snakes originated before the appearance of modern type lizards then we must look back to the Triassic to find truly ancestral snakes. In Cretaceous times there are already snakes assignable to the modern families *Boidae and Aniliidae (Pipe snakes). It is clear therefore that some of the more primitive snakes existing today had appeared long before the close of the Age of Dinosaurs. The advanced snakes (Colubridae, Viperidae and Elapidae) do not appear in the fossil record until the Miocene. This means that the

The completely sloughed skin of the head of the Four-lined snake *Elaphe quatuor-lineata*.

Tree snake swallowing a lizard.

major radiation of snakes has taken place during the last 20 million years. It has been suggested that this coincided with the rise and diversification of rodents, small mammals that comprise an important part of the diet of many snakes.

The particular relationship of snakes with lizards is in dispute. One view is that snakes are related to the Varanoidea or Platynota that includes the present day *monitors, Bornean *Earless monitor and *Gila monster. This group of lizards was already well established and diverse in Cretaceous times so, in its origins, it may well be old enough. An alternative view is that snakes are too different from any modern lizard group to be derivable from them or their immediate ancestors. As modern lizard families are already present in the Cretaceous and modern infraorders are present in the Jurassic, this would put the divergence of snakes from lizards back into the Triassic at which time the earliest known lizards, of a type more primitive than any of the modern groups are found.

Some other features of snakes. For most snakes the chemical sense mediated by

Jacobson's organ is probably the most important sense, with vision playing a supporting role. All snakes show play of the tongue when they are curious; it is usually dabbed on the ground but Tree snakes vibrate it rapidly in the air. By using the tongue a snake can recognize and trail its prey. In burrowing and secretive snakes these cues are probably entirely sufficient. In snakes that live in the open vision is certainly important in striking at the prey once recognized. Some boid snakes and *Pit vipers have radiant heat detecting sense organs by which they can recognize and strike at warm-blooded prey in total darkness. Snakes are sensitive to vibration of the ground and although there is no trace of an external ear there is now evidence that they can pick up low frequency airborne sounds from around middle C to high C.

The most general mode of locomotion of snakes involves lateral undulations of the body, known as 'serpentine' locomotion. The sides of the body press against irregularities of the surface and, as the waves pass back, the snake glides forwards on its smooth overlapping belly scales. This carries the snake forwards over all but the smoothest surfaces

and serves equally well in swimming; many snakes can glide over the surface of the ground, come to a body of water and continue forwards with no obvious change of their movements. Tree snakes, too, are able to move in this way. Another mode of locomotion, adopted mainly by heavy-bodied snakes when moving slowly, is the 'caterpillar crawl'. This relies on the free edges of the smooth overlapping belly scales; in succession, the individual scales are slightly raised and drawn forwards and then lowered and drawn back with the free edges gaining a purchase on the irregularities of the ground.

A variation of serpentine locomotion employed in narrow passages is 'concertina' locomotion in which the snake alternately draws up the rear of the body forming a series of loops that gain a purchase on the sides of the passage and then pays out the front end forming a fresh set of loops further forwards. On shifting sand against which a lateral thrust is not possible some snakes move by 'sidewinding'. The body makes two areas of parallel rolling contact with the sand and between these is a raised S-loop of the body being carried across from one area of contact to the next. As the tail is about to be raised at the end of one line of contact the neck is set down to start the next line of contact. Along each line of contact the snake measures its length from neck to tail with the body so oriented that the whole travels obliquely forwards.

Burrowing snakes have two principal locomotory modes. The 'drilling' burrowers, Worm snakes, Thread snakes, Shield-tailed snakes, make tortuous burrows in which each bend gives a purchase from which the head can be thrust forwards. The 'undulating' burrowers, Pipe snakes, Sunbeam snakes and some boid snakes, live near the surface in loose material and move by a caterpillar crawl using the snout to shovel aside the sand or litter in which they live.

Snakes eat various invertebrates such as soft bodied earthworms, slugs and snails and hard bodied arthropods such as ants and other insects, centipedes and crustaceans including crayfish and crabs. Vertebrate prey include fish, fish eggs, amphibians, with some species specializing in eating toads, lizards, snakes—a good many snakes specialize in eating other snakes, birds, birds' eggs and mammals. The larger vertebrate prey may be more than twice the diameter of the snake's head.

All snakes swallow their prey whole without any mastication. It is seized in the jaws and may be subdued by constriction or venom prior to swallowing. All the soft parts of the prey are digested and only arthropod cuticle, birds' feathers, and mammalian hair and claws remain undigested.

The mating behaviour of snakes shows the importance of the chemical sense. Female snakes in breeding condition evidently produce a secretion to which the male responds. A male will follow the scent trail of a female and, on catching up, address himself to her with much play of the tongue and sometimes chin rubbing, up and down her back. This culminates in mating during which the male may throw some loops of his body over the female before eversion of the *hemipenis. A majority of snakes lays eggs, but some produce living young. Production of living young is found particularly amongst the more highly adapted aquatic snakes.

Snakes have a large right lung that extends well down the body past the liver. In some Water snakes the lung extends further back almost to the rear end of the trunk. It is thought that it serves here as an organ of buoyancy like the air-bladder of a fish. Snakes' lungs typically have a rich blood supply in the anterior half and consist of a thin-walled air-sac in the posterior half. This apparently means that there is no pocket of stagnant air; the air passes over the blood vessels in which the exchange of gases takes place on the way both to and from the air-sac. In some snakes the roof of the windpipe has a rich blood supply; in extreme cases the entire pulmonary blood supply goes to the windpipe and the lung proper is a simple air-sac.

Modes of life of snakes. Snakes show a variety of modes of life most of which are dealt with more fully in separate articles. Drilling burrowers live underground in soft earth; they eat small invertebrate prey. These are all small snakes including the Blind snakes, Thread snakes, Shield-tailed snakes and some colubrids.

The so called undulating burrowers live in sand, forest floor litter or mud. They generally remain near the surface; some penetrate the burrows of animals on which they prey. They tend to be larger than the drilling burrowers and mainly eat small vertebrates. They include the Pipe snakes, Sunbeam snake, some boids and some colubrids.

There is a great host of secretive snakes that shun daylight and move around under litter, in crevices under logs and stones and between the roots of trees. These eat various invertebrates as well as small vertebrates, including other snakes, of similar habits. They include some boids and many colubrids, elapids and viperids. Many snakes hunt on the ground in the open; some are nocturnal, others diurnal. They commonly trail other vertebrates of similar habits and include forms that eat relatively large prey. Hunting snakes include some of the boids, from small to very large, and many colubrids, elapids and viperids, again including some large ones. A few of these are noteworthy for the speed with which they can move and could be called cursorial.

A variety of snakes live in trees. Their prey consists mainly of arboreal vertebrates, frogs, lizards, birds, birds' eggs and mammals and, in the case of the *Thirst snakes, molluscs. They are very slender and include a number of different colubrids and several of the venomous elapids and viperids.

Many snakes are amphibious living near bodies of freshwater or in marshes. They live mainly on fish and amphibians but a few take animals that come to drink. Amphibious snakes include the *anaconda, numerous colubrids and the *cottonmouth, a viper.

A smaller number of snakes are fully adapted to life in freshwater and may spend little or no time on land. Some particularly favour the muddy brackish water of estuaries. They may show some flattening of the tail and reduction of the broad belly scales; and they also eat mainly fish and amphibia. Freshwater snakes include a number of colubrids, and notably the Oriental fishing snakes and the Water cobras of Africa.

Some snakes are fully marine, a few of these come ashore to lay their eggs but most are viviparous and never come ashore; a few are truly pelagic and may be found far from land. These all eat fish except one or two that eat fish eggs.

Classification of snakes. This is a matter of considerable uncertainty. A number of classifications has been proposed, mostly during the last century; some were never generally adopted, others were and have since been more or less abandoned. The division of snakes into three main infraorders is reasonably secure; it is the classification of the higher snakes, the Caenophidia, that is in such disorder.

Order Squamata

Infraorder Scolecophidia.

Burrowers with a compact skull and rigid snout. A number of primitive features are retained.
Family Anomalepidae.
Family Typhlopidae (Blind snakes).
Family Leptotyphlopidae (Thread snakes).

Infraorder Henophidia.

Snout either mobile or supported by bones of upper jaw. Most retain hind-limb vestiges and primitive features of arterial and respiratory systems.
Family Aniliidae (Pipe snakes).
Family Uropeltidae (Shield-tailed snakes).
Family Xenopeltidae (Sunbeam snake).
Family Boidae (pythons and boas).
Family Acrochordidae (Wart snakes).

Infraorder Caenophidia

Snout and upper jawbones mobile. Primitive features of Henophidia lost.
Family Viperidae (vipers).
Family Elapidae.
Subfamily Elapinae.
Subfamily Hydrophiinae (Sea snakes).
"Family" Colubridae.
All the remaining Caenophidia, divided into a number of subfamilies of various degrees of certainty.

SNAPPING TURTLES, widespread and abundant in the fresh waters of North America, and named for their aggressive disposition. Instead of retreating into its shell when approached, the Common snapping turtle *Chelydra serpentina*, a foot or more (30 cm) long, turns to face the intruder, even advancing to the attack, snapping and biting.

The head of the Snapping turtle ends in a strong, hook-shaped down-turned beak. Three keels run along the dorsal carapace, made up of single knobs on each scute. The tail is about the same length as the carapace and has knobby horny scutes on the upper side. The plastron has degenerated to a small, cruciform scale on the centre of the belly. These turtles can barely swim and usually lie quietly on the bottom of shallow pools. Since, in addition, they leave the water only in order to lay their eggs, they need no special protection on the underside. If they are disturbed they are extremely irascible and are even said to be capable of biting through a cane with their knife-sharp jaws.

The Common snapping turtle, also known as the Loggerhead snapper, has a carapace of up to 15 in (38 cm) long and weighs up to 85 lb (38·6 kg). It eats mainly fish, invertebrates and a large proportion of vegetation, and also carrion. Loggerhead snappers are disliked because they also attack waterfowl and if disturbed by bathers may easily snap off fingers or toes.

Geographical subspecies are recognized according to the position of the knobs on the scutes of the carapace and the number of barbs on the chin: *Ch. s. serpentina* in the southeast of Canada and the whole of the eastern United States, *Ch. s. osceola* in Florida, *Ch. s. rossignonii* from Guatemala to Costa Rica and *Ch. s. acutirostris* in Panama and Ecuador. FAMILY: Chelydridae, ORDER: Testudines, CLASS: Reptilia.

SOFT-SHELLED TURTLES, so called because they have lost the horny plates of the shell entirely. They are confined to freshwater in North America, Asia and Africa. See turtles.

SQUAMATA, an order of reptiles containing the lizards and snakes of which there are about 6,000 species.

STEM-REPTILES, a name sometimes used for the extinct reptiles of the order Cotylosauria because they are the most primitive reptiles known and represent the basal stock from which all other reptiles have descended. They flourished during the Carboniferous and Permian periods, 300–225 million years ago. See reptiles.

STINKPOT, a widely used vernacular name for the common Musk turtle *Sternotherus odoratus* of North America. Extremely abundant, it is the only Musk turtle to occur over most of the eastern half of the United States. Adults seldom measure more than 4 in (10 cm) in length and are dun coloured, but the tiny hatchlings have brighter markings, especially on the plastron. The term 'stinkpot' derives from the animal's habit of voiding a vile smelling anal secretion when picked up or otherwise threatened. This habit is soon lost in captivity and the species makes a hardy, interesting pet. FAMILY: Kinosternidae, ORDER: Testudines, CLASS: Reptilia.

SUNBEAM SNAKE *Xenopeltis unicolor,* placed in a family of its own, is a harmless snake with many primitive features suggesting affinities with *Pipe snakes and *boas but in other respects it shows resemblances to the more highly evolved snakes. The broad blunt head with small eye and large symmetrical head shield merges into the trunk without a neck constriction. The belly scales are broad.

There are no vestiges of a pelvis, but two lungs are developed, the left half the size of the right. The skull is solid with the snout firmly joined to the cranium. The upper jaw bones are more firmly attached to each other than in more highly evolved snakes and the gape is limited. The popular name of this largely brown snake stems from its shiny iridescent scales. *Xenopeltis* grows to 4 ft (122 cm), is widely distributed, but not common, from Burma to southern China and the Malay Archipelago.
FAMILY: Xenopeltidae, ORDER: Squamata, CLASS: Reptilia.

SUNGAZER *Cordylus giganteus,* the largest species of the Girdle-tailed lizards, so named for its persistent habit of basking. See cordylid lizards.

SURINAM TOAD *Pipa pipa,* a tongueless frog of curiously flattened appearance and living wholly in water in the Amazon and Orinoco basins. See Pipidae.

SYNAPSIDA, a subclass of extinct reptiles which showed many features in their skeleton resembling those found in mammals, especially in the bony arch which corresponded with the zygomatic arch or cheek bone in human beings. These reptiles appear to have given rise to the mammals and are sometimes referred to as *mammal-like reptiles. SUBCLASS: Synapsida, CLASS: Reptilia.

TADPOLES, the larvae of frogs and toads. An aquatic larval stage is characteristic of all amphibians but in the salamanders and newts the larva is similar in appearance to the adult while in frogs and toads the tadpole looks completely different from the adult. It is more or less globular in shape, with no sharp distinction between the head and the rest of the body, and there is a long, muscular tail with a membranous crest on both its dorsal and ventral edges.

Even though the tadpole is free-living and obtains its own food it is still considered as part of the embryology of the frog or toad because until the adult form is reached all the organs of the body are not fully developed.

The development of each species of frog or toad is characteristic of that species and the time which it takes and the shape and size of the tadpole vary from species to species. There is, however, a basic pattern and this is best understood by following the development of a single species, the North American Leopard frog, *Rana pipiens*. The fertilized egg divides many times and the spherical mass of cells so formed begins to differentiate into different structures. Eventually the embryo assumes a tadpole-like shape and can be seen moving inside the egg membrane. The muscular and circulation systems then develop and bulges on either side of the head show where the gill arches are forming. The external gills develop and the tadpole hatches from the egg just before these begin to function. On hatching the eyes and mouth are not fully developed and there is a U-shaped adhesive organ under the head. With this the tadpole remains attached to vegetation. The external gills function for only a short period and internal gills develop and take over from them. A fold, known as the operculum, develops on the first branchial arch just in front of the external gills and grows backwards over them until they are covered. The operculum does not close up completely and a single hole, or spiracle, remains on the left side of the body. Water is taken in through the mouth, passes over the internal gills and is expelled through the spiracle. The operculum is complete after about 12 days and by this time the mouth has developed horny jaws and several rows of horny teeth, the adhesive organs have almost disappeared and the long, coiled intestine has developed and can be seen through the skin. The tadpole is then fully developed and remains in this form until metamorphosis occurs after about three months.

When the tadpole hatches the remains of the yolk can be seen as a bulge in the belly region. This is soon used up and the tadpole then obtains its own food, which consists of small particles of vegetation, by scraping it up with the horny teeth and beak.

At metamorphosis the tadpole changes rapidly into a small frog. The hindlimbs are already visible and the forelimbs, which have been developing under the operculum, emerge—the left one through the spiracle and the right one through the skin. The internal gills cease to function and are replaced by lungs. The tadpole skin is shed, together with the horny jaws and teeth, and the mouth widens. The gut shortens since the adult is carnivorous and does not require the long gut of the herbivorous tadpole. The reproductive organs are formed and the metamorphosed frog is ready to leave the water. In the last stages of metamorphosis the tail slowly becomes shorter and eventually disappears, although when the young frog finally leaves the water it may still have a short tail.

The rate of development of the tadpole depends on the temperature and for this reason any reference to the age of a tadpole should include a temperature. For example, the tail bud is formed after 84 hours at 63°F (18°C) and after only 66 hours at 77°F (25°C). An indication of the point of development a tadpole has reached is also given by its length, but this will also vary slightly, depending on the available food and other factors. Although tadpoles are usually smaller than the adult frog they are sometimes larger. Tadpoles of the genus *Pseudis* are as much as 10 in (25 cm) long while the adult is about 3 in (7·5 cm) long. See Pseudidae and Paradoxical frog.

Although the tadpole is only a stage in the development of the adult frog it is just as capable as the adult of being adapted to its environment. The round-bodied active tad-pole of *R. pipiens* is the commonest type and is typically a pond-dwelling form, but the tadpoles of many species are modified for other habitats. Some tadpoles live in fast-flowing mountain streams and do not swim in the water but attach themselves to rocks. Those of the Tailed frog *Ascaphus truei* and Ghost frogs *Heleophryne* have lips forming a large cup-shaped adhesive apparatus while in others, such as *Rana cavitympanum*, the ventral surface of the body is adapted to perform a similar function.

Many species of frogs lay their eggs in more unusual situations and often out of water altogether. *Hyla rosenbergi* lays its eggs in small pools of water retained in a mud basin constructed by the female. The tadpoles live in the basins and, because of the low oxygen content of the water, have very large external gills which float on the surface. See treefrogs.

Tadpoles of *Hoplophryne rogersi* hatch from the eggs in the stems of bamboo or between the leaves of bananas. There is very little water in these situations and the tadpoles probably remain exposed to the air for most of their development. At hatching lungs are already fully developed and external gills are never formed, while the internal ones are very reduced. The tadpole has a triangular flap of skin on either side of the body in the gill region and these are probably locomotory organs, the tadpole being able to push itself along with them.

Many species of frogs have developed similar methods of avoiding the free-swimming tadpole stage by laying the eggs out of water. The tadpoles may remain in the moist earth until they metamorphose as, for example, in *Anhydrophryne*, while in some species they are carried around by the adult. In Darwin's frog *Rhinoderma darwinii* the male carries the tadpoles in its vocal sac where they develop normally although the beaks and horny teeth do not become hardened.

In some species the complete development takes place inside the egg and it is a small frog which hatches out, although the tadpole stage is still passed through inside the egg capsule. In such situations internal gills are of little use and the tadpole is modified to obtain oxygen which diffuses in through the capsule. For example, the tadpole of the Marsupial frog *Gastrotheca marsupiata* has the external gills expanded into large bell-shaped structures while in *Platymantis* no external gills are developed and the tadpole has two large abdominal sacs well supplied with blood for respiration. Such tadpoles do not feed, of course, but depend on a large supply of yolk for the entire development.

Although in some species, for example, the Rain frogs *Breviceps*, the habit of passing the tadpole stage out of water has enabled the frog to become completely independent of water; in most cases it is probably an adaptation to avoid predators. Free-swimming tadpoles are eaten in large numbers by many fish. Water beetles and other enemies and of the large number of eggs laid by most frogs only a small proportion survives the rigours of the tadpole stage and metamorphosis. Frogs which have avoided this dangerous period usually lay fewer eggs than do those with a free-swimming tadpole stage. This is partly because such large numbers are not necessary but in any case the eggs must be larger since they have to contain enough yolk for the whole development. The development of a life-cycle which avoids the free-living tadpole stage would appear to enable such frogs to radiate into many more habitats but this is apparently not the case. The conditions under which such frogs are able to lay their eggs—in holes constructed under leaf litter, for instance—are so specialized that, in fact, the frogs are restricted as to the places in which they can breed. Only a few species have developed such methods and the large majority of frogs possess free-swimming tadpoles.

Although the arrangement of horny beaks and teeth around the mouth described for the Leopard frog is the common pattern, enabling the tadpole to scrape food particles off vegetation, some frogs have a different method of obtaining food. Those of the family Microhylidae have no beaks or teeth and feed on small organisms suspended in the water, filtering them from the water as it passes through the opercular chamber. Tadpoles of *Ooeidozyga* are predaceous and have the horny beaks but lack the teeth. Some species have 'umbrella mouths' in which the lips are produced into a large funnel around the mouth. In *Microhyla heymonsi* it is used in feeding on food particles in the surface film of the water.

This brief review indicates the ways in which tadpoles are adapted to their environment, completely independently of the mode of life of the adult. Nevertheless the variations in tadpoles which lead to the evolution of such adaptations can only be transmitted from generation to generation through the adult frog. Therefore any basic differences under-lying the adaptations should reveal relationships between the tadpoles which parallel those of the adults.

Variations in two characters, the spiracle and the mouth apparatus, have been used to help decide the relationships between different families of frogs. The spiracle may be on the left of the body of the tadpole, as in the Leopard frog, or it may be central or it may be paired, and the mouth may either have horny beaks and teeth or lack these structures, these different combinations giving four types of tadpoles. (Ill. p. 145.)

TAIPAN *Oxyuranus scutellatus*, a slender *elapid snake and the largest and deadliest of Australasian snakes, growing to a little over 11 ft (3·4 m) in length. It has a large head distinct from its neck, a relatively slim fore-body and tapered tail. Its fangs are large and its venom one of the most potent neurotoxins known; death is usually caused by paralysis of the nerve centres controlling the lungs and heart. It is reputed to be the world's deadliest snake. Australian taipans are rich brown above and cream below, while those from New Guinea are usually blackish with a rusty-red stripe along the back.

The taipan is found throughout many parts of northern and north-eastern Australia, ranging from coastal rain-forests to the drier inland regions. In New Guinea it is found largely in the savannah woodlands along the southern coasts. About 16 eggs are laid in a clutch. The taipan is a timid, retiring snake which may become very aggressive when provoked. It may be seen in weather conditions that are too hot for other snakes, and although generally diurnal, it may move about at night if the weather has been excessively hot. It feeds upon small mammals and reptiles.

Specific and polyvalent antivenenes have been developed for the taipan, without which the chances of recovering from a bite are slender. The name taipan is a Cape York aboriginal name for this snake. FAMILY: Elapidae, ORDER: Squamata, CLASS: Reptilia. (Ill. p. 146.)

TEGU *Tupinambis nigropunctatus,* one of the largest of the lizards in the family Teiidae, an inhabitant of tropical South America, is about 3 ft (1 m) long.

TEIIDS, a family of lizard-like reptiles, related to Old World lizards and skinks, with a long tail and a long, narrow, deeply-cleft tongue. Although the front teeth are conical, as is usual in lizards, the lateral teeth of both jaws may assume several different forms according to the species, depending on the feeding habits. For example, the Caiman lizard *Dracaena guianensis* has conical front teeth followed by large, oval teeth adapted for crushing snail shells. The skin of teiids is armed only with superficial epidermal scales; scales of the type present in the dermal layer of the skin of some related families being absent.

The Caiman lizard is unusual among the teiids in being semi-aquatic as most species are definitely terrestrial, arboreal or fossorial. The larger teiids have a tendency to be more active in daylight, whereas the smaller species are largely nocturnal.

The 40 genera are restricted to the American continent, mainly south of Mexico, where they occupy a position corresponding to that of the lizard family Lacertidae in the Old World. Only the genus *Cnemidophorus* reaches as far north as the United States.

The larger species of teiids, known as tegus, may attain a length of nearly 4 ft (122 cm) and superficially resemble Monitor lizards (Varanidae). The Black tegu *Tupinambis teguixin* and the Golden tegu *T. nigropunctatus* range over much of Central and South America but the Red tegu *T. rufescens* is mostly restricted to Argentina.

Ameivas are small, attractively marked teiids which resemble the smaller European lizards in general behaviour and form. The Jungle runner or Surinam lizard *Ameiva ameiva* and the South American Striped

Teiids are mostly carnivorous. In captivity they will feed on insects, lizards, birds, mice and carrion. Some species will also take eggs and fruit, and it has been reported that tegus will drink blood, milk and lemonade as well as water. FAMILY: Teiidae, ORDER: Squamata, CLASS: Reptilia.

TERRAPINS, name given to the seven geographical races of *Malaclemys terrapin* living in the eastern part of North America. They are moderate-sized turtles with a carapace up to about 10 in (25 cm) long. The individual scutes of the dorsal carapace are often in the shape of a truncated cone and clearly concentrically grooved, so that in America they are called 'Diamondback terrapins'. They live in the sea and in salt and brackish water lakes along the Atlantic coast of North America, from Massachusetts southward to the Yucatan Peninsula in Mexico, and the Florida keys. Like many seabirds and like marine turtles, terrapins have special glands behind the corner of the eye to secrete the excess salt from the body. Nevertheless, salt seems to be vital to them, since if they are kept for a long time in freshwater only, they develop ulcers, no longer eat and finally die.

Terrapins usually stay in the water, but are also said to travel considerable distances on land, if they cannot find a promising place to lay their eggs. They live chiefly on small crustaceans and molluscs, but also take a small amount of vegetable food.

Terrapins are highly esteemed delicacies. At one time they were sold on the markets and formed an everyday item of food. In the 18th century there was even a rising of the slaves, who were protesting that they were too often given the fat flesh of these turtles. Owing to the excessive persecution by human beings and the cultivation of the coastal areas the terrapin population has been so drastically reduced, however, that they are now being bred in terrapin farms. They cost about seven dollars each.

In Britain almost any small freshwater turtle of any kind is likely to be called a terrapin. In the United States many people use the word for any edible freshwater turtle. Strictly speaking it should be reserved for one species only, *Malaclemys terrapin*. See turtles. FAMILY: Emyidae, ORDER: Testudines, CLASS: Reptilia.

TESTUDINES, a reptilian order which includes all tortoises, turtles, and terrapins and belongs to the subclass Anapsida. The most obvious feature is the exoskeleton enclosing the body and which is composed of the dorsal carapace and ventral plastron. Typically the exoskeleton consists of an inner bony layer covered by an external layer of horn. The exoskeleton may be much reduced in aquatic types. The trunk vertebrae are reduced in number and together with the ribs become incorporated in the carapace. The jaws of all species, fossil and living, are toothless being covered by horny plates which macerate plant food or soft animal foods.

The oldest known is the Triassic genus *Proganochelys*. This and other primitive chelonians were incapable of retracting the head within the box-like exoskeleton. Two more advanced groups which can retract the head are recognised: the Cryptodira and Pleurodira. CLASS: Reptilia.

THECODONTS, extinct reptiles that lived about 200 million years ago and which probably represent the ancestral stock from which dinosaurs, pterodactyls, crocodiles and birds were derived. They were generally small, a few feet (1 m) long and they received their name because their teeth were implanted in deep sockets, each tooth being hollow at the base with its successor developing in that hollow. Most of them were terrestrial but some lived in shallow water and many of them showed a tendency to become bipedal. Most of them were probably herbivores but there were some at least which were definitely flesh-eaters and these were larger than usual with very large skulls. ORDER: Thecodontia, SUBCLASS: Archosauria, CLASS: Reptilia.

THERAPSIDA, extinct reptiles that lived during the Permian and Triassic period 270–180 million years ago. Their remains have been found mainly in South Africa, but others have been collected from America, Europe and Asia. They ranged in size from that of a rat to massive beasts 13 ft (4 m) long and they are important because their skulls show some of the features of mammalian skulls, especially in the bony arch between the orbit and the openings to the rear of the skull. ORDER: Therapsida, SUBCLASS: Synapsida, CLASS: Reptilia.

THEROPODA, a suborder of carnivorous *dinosaurs 10–50 ft (3·0–15 m) long, with long, strong hindlegs, small front legs and long powerful tail used no doubt as a balancer when the reptile was running bipedally. The teeth, set in sockets in the jaws, were sabre-like, often with serrated edges. ORDER: Saurischia, SUBCLASS: Synapsida, CLASS: Reptilia.

THIRST SNAKES, so called because one of their genera is named *Dipsas,* after a serpent of Greek legend whose bite caused a raging thirst, are small inoffensive snakes that feed solely on slugs and snails. Nocturnal and mostly arboreal, Thirst snakes have long needle-like teeth enabling the snake to grip the soft slimy prey, and they lack the chin groove, a characteristic feature of snakes which makes a wide stretching of the jaws possible. Those Thirst snakes that eat snails are expert at withdrawing the mollusc from its shell.

There are 16 species of Thirst snake in Southeast Asia, nearly all in the genus *Pareas,* and others in Central and South America, including *Dipsas,* which eats snails, and *Sibon,* which appears to eat only slugs. FAMILY: Colubridae, ORDER: Squamata, CLASS: Reptilia.

THREAD SNAKES, superficially similar to *Blind snakes, are burrowers, small and wormlike, 6–10 in (15–25 cm) in length, with only vestiges of a pelvis and hindlimbs. Lower jaw teeth are numerous, but the upper jaw, which is immoveably fixed to the rest of the skull, has no teeth. The eyes are hidden beneath head scales. Thread snakes, of which there is only one genus, *Leptotyphlops*, are found in Africa, southwest Asia, and also in the New World, in savannahs and semi-desert regions. A few elongated eggs are laid. The food of Thread snakes consists largely of termites. FAMILY: Leptotyphlopidae, ORDER: Squamata, CLASS: Reptilia.

TIGER SNAKES, a group of closely related Australian *elapid snakes of the genus *Notechis*. All are restricted to the coast, ranges and wetter parts of the interior of southern Australia, including Tasmania.

They are relatively heavy, thick bodied snakes with broad, rather massive heads. The Common tiger snake of southeastern Australia, *N. scutatus,* averages only a little over 4 ft (1·2 m) and varies considerably in colour and pattern. It ranges through various shades of grey, brown, reddish or olive to almost black. Typically it has numerous light yellowish cross-bands along its length, but these are often indistinct or absent.

A number of isolated populations of Tiger snakes are variously regarded either as distinct species or as geographic variations of a single species. The most distinctive of these populations occur on various small islands in Bass Strait and off the coast of South

The Thirst snake *Dipsas turgidus* seen here feeding on a snail.

Australia. These insular Tiger snakes are generally characterized by melanism, an excessive development of black pigment resulting in snakes which are uniform dark brown or black above and cream to dark grey below, although in many specimens a faint banded pattern persists. The black Tiger snakes of the islands of eastern Bass Strait differ from all others by their larger size, for they average nearly 6 ft (1·8 m) in length.

In southwestern Australia is another isolated Tiger snake population. This Western tiger snake *N. scutatus occidentalis* grows to 7 ft (2·2 m) in length, although it averages only about 4½ ft (1·3 m). It is very dark grey to black above, with or without numerous narrow yellowish cross-bands, while the belly is yellowish to grey.

Tiger snakes are normally shy and inoffensive, but react savagely when provoked. The neck is then flattened like that of a cobra while the first quarter or so of the flattened body is held off the ground in a long, low arc. All are highly venomous, their venoms being among the most potent known. Although they have relatively short, immovable fangs they cause a high proportion of the average of only four deaths which result from snake-bite in Australia each year. Before the development of an antivenine in 1929, the first to be developed for any Australian snake, about 45% of Tiger snake victims died. Like that of other dangerous Australian elapids, the venom of Tiger snakes acts largely on the central nervous system, causing death by respiratory paralysis. The potency of Tiger snake venom varies considerably in different populations, the most potent yet recorded being that from the Black tiger snake *N. ater,* from Reevesby Island in Spencer Gulf, South Australia. It was found to have venom more than twice as deadly as that of Tiger snakes from the mainland of southeastern Australia.

Tiger snakes are found in a wide variety of habitats. In southern Queensland they chiefly inhabit rain-forests, whereas in the southern part of their range they are generally found in wet coastal scrubs and sclerophyl forests. West of the Great Dividing Range they often occur in dense colonies along river banks and flood plains, or around large swamps and lakes. Although frogs constitute the principal source of food, small mammals, birds, lizards and, on occasion, fish are also eaten. For Tiger snakes from the Bass Strait islands, the chicks of the muttonbird or Sooty shearwater *Puffinus tenuirostris* are eaten, while their nesting burrows are utilized for shelter. The Western tiger snake is said to inhabit most damp environments within its range.

Tiger snakes produce living young, an average litter numbering about 50. The young measure about 8 in (20 cm) at birth, and are usually much more strongly banded than the adults. FAMILY: Elapidae, ORDER: Squamata, CLASS: Reptilia. (Ill. p. 146.)

TOAD, a name referring strictly only to members of the family Bufonidae, but the terms 'frog' and 'toad' are the only common names available to describe the 2,000 species of the order Anura. Frog is used for those which have smooth skin and live in or near water while toad is used for those which have a warty skin or live in drier habitats. The terms are used independently of the actual relationships of the animals involved. For example, *Bombina bombina* of Europe is known as the Fire-bellied toad, but belongs to the family Discoglossidae, while *Scaphiopus holbrooki,* the Eastern spadefoot toad of America, is a member of the Pelobatidae. The term 'toad' was originally used for the genus *Bufo* which comprises the Common European toad *Bufo bufo* and the American toad *Bufo americanus* so the family Bufonidae can be referred to as the 'true toads'. The other toads are dealt with under their appropriate families while frogs and toads in general are dealt with under Anura.

In their internal structure members of the Bufonidae are characterized by having an arciferal shoulder girdle (one in which the two ventral halves overlap in the mid-line) and procoelous vertebrae (this refers to the shape of the centra—the spool-shaped bones in the vertebral column). They are distinguished from the Atelopodidae and the Leptodactylidae, which also have these characters, in having a sternum or breastbone (it is absent in the Atelopodidae) and in not having an episternum, a bone on the front of the sternum (it is present in the Leptodactylidae).

There are 17 genera and the family is represented throughout the world except in Madagascar and Australasia.

The genus *Bufo* is the largest and most widespread, more than 200 species occurring throughout the world. Members of the genus are easily distinguished from other anurans. They have a short squat body and short legs and their skin is dry and covered with tubercles or warts. These warts are in fact collections of poison glands. Such glands are present in most anurans but are most prominent in toads. When a toad is attacked it does not rely on long rapid jumps for defence but on these glands. Each wart exudes a milky fluid which acts as an irritant to the mucous membranes of the attacker. A dog, for example, which has picked up a toad in its mouth quickly drops it. It then shows signs of distress and copious saliva flows from its mouth. If larger doses of the fluid are injected into laboratory animals it acts as a cardiotoxin, slowing and eventually stopping the heart. The poison glands do not protect the toad against all predators; most snakes and birds are apparently unaffected by it. Two concentrations of these poison glands form a conspicuous oval ridge behind each eye known as parotid glands.

The hindlegs of toads are relatively shorter than those of some other anurans such as the true frogs *(Rana)* and in general they crawl or progress in short hopping movements. This is not universal however and some species of toad can jump fairly well while others, such as the natterjack *B. calamita,* of Europe, have even shorter legs and only walk or run.

Toads are generally considered to be more intelligent than frogs although this is partly because, not relying on sudden leaps for their defence, they are slower and more predictable in their movements. While a frog will leap blindly off a table regardless of its height above the ground a toad will walk to the edge and look over. Toads learn fairly quickly (after about six attempts) not to eat bees and the lesson is remembered for about two weeks.

Toads have a marked homing instinct. Many species rest each day in a particular spot and, if taken and liberated as much as 1 ml (1·6 km) away, rapidly return to it. The mechanism by which they are able to do this is not fully understood although during the breeding season the calling of other toads certainly guides them back to their pond from a considerable distance.

Bufo bufo is the Common toad of Great Britain and Europe. It is usually brown in colour, sometimes spotted with dark brown, black or red, and females reach a length of about 3½ in (8·7 cm) and males 2½ in (6·2 cm) although in some warmer areas, probably because of the greater abundance of insect food, larger specimens are found, sometimes reaching a length of about 5½ in (13·7 cm). Largely on the basis of such size differences the species is divided into several subspecies.

Toads are nocturnal, spending the day concealed in holes in walls, drainpipes or similar places. They emerge at night and feed on any small animal which moves. They are sometimes found sitting near a lighted window or lamp snapping up the insects attracted by the light. Like other anurans they are only able to recognize food if it moves but the feeding action of a toad is more deliberate than that of some anurans. If a worm is placed a few inches away from a toad, for example, it walks rapidly up to it and looks down at it for several seconds, its nervous energy being shown by a twitching of its toes. The worm is then snapped up, the toad's tongue flicking rapidly out and dragging the worm into the mouth.

Toads hibernate on land, burying themselves in loose soil, either alone or in groups. On emerging from hibernation, usually in March, they migrate to the breeding pond where the males attract the females to them by their calling. They usually call while raising themselves on their front legs in shallow water. The male clasps the female behind the arms and the pair swim about in amplexus until the female comes into contact with some waterweed. Oviposition then commences. The female extrudes the eggs in the form of a long string while the male ejects sperm over them. This continues at intervals for several hours, the female swimming round so that the long string of eggs, about 7–10 ft (2·1–3·0 m) long, is wrapped around waterweed. A total of about 4,000–5,000 eggs is laid. The tadpoles hatch after about 12 days but the time taken to develop into the adult varies considerably, depending on the temperature. About three months is an average period although in warm areas it may be two months while in some cold areas the tadpoles have been known to hibernate and metamorphose the next year.

This description of the habits of *B. bufo* is applicable in general to all the 150 species of the genus *Bufo*. They are all similar in appearance and habits and are not highly specialized for a particular habitat. It is probably this general adaptability which has enabled the genus to become world-wide in distribution. In general toads are found in open country rather than in wooded parts. The skin is thick and resists desiccation and several species are found in desert areas.

The American toad *B. americanus* is found throughout the eastern half of North America in almost any habitat, from gardens to mountains, the only requisites being shallow breeding pools and moist hiding places. It is 3–5 in (7·5–12·5 cm) in length and usually a reddish brown although there is a great variation in the markings. Like several species of *Bufo* the American toad has a pattern of bony crests on the head.

The Southern toad *B. terrestris* is more restricted in its range occurring in the southeast coastal plain from North Carolina to the Mississippi River. It is 1½–3½ in (3·7–8·7 cm) long and the bony crests have two pronounced knobs behind the eyes which give the toad a 'horned' appearance. It is found in most open situations but is particularly abundant in sandy areas. There are about 16 species of *Bufo* in North America although the number of subspecies is uncertain.

It is a characteristic of the genus *Bufo* that because the species are all so similar the taxonomy is not fully worked out. For example, hybrids between some species have been found and some forms which were thought to be a single species are found to be two which can only be distinguished by the call of the male. In southern Africa 21 forms of *Bufo* are found and these can be grouped into five distinct groups but what taxonomic status these groups should be given is uncertain.

The Common or Square-marked toad *B. regularis* is the commonest toad in Africa and is found from the Cape to Egypt. It is up to 4 in (10 cm) in length with a pattern of dark brown blotches on a light background. These are so arranged that there is a conspicuous light-coloured cross between the eyes which is distinctive of the species. It spends the day hiding under logs and stones and emerges to feed at night. It breeds from August to late summer, as many as 24,000 eggs being laid by each female. The tadpoles hatch after four days and change into toads after about one month.

B. anotis is the only toad in southern Africa which is forest-dwelling. Nothing is known of its breeding habits but it is found a long way from water and its eggs are large which may indicate that the development occurs on land. Further investigation may show that it does not in fact belong to the genus *Bufo*.

Some of the smallest members of the genus are found in South Africa. The Striped mountain toad *B. rosei* is an agile little toad about 1½ in (3·7 cm) in length and dark brown with three light stripes running along the body. It is found in marshy areas on open mountain slopes. The Pigmy toad *B. vertebralis* is even smaller, females being about 1 in (2·5 cm) long. They are light brown with dark brown patches and the parotid glands are very indistinct. They are found in open, sandy and grassy areas and the development is very rapid, small toads, about ¼ in (6 mm) long, emerging from the water about 16 days after the eggs are laid.

Another small toad is the Oak toad *B. quercicus* of North America. The adults are ¾–1¼ in (20–32 mm) long with a short fat body. They are dusky brown, with black and white patches and a light stripe down the middle of the back. They are common in the pinewoods of the southeast, preferring sandy areas. They spend some time buried under leaves or in the sand but are more active during the day than other species of toad.

For a long time toads have been generally regarded with loathing as poisonous or evil creatures. They are, of course, completely harmless and are in fact beneficial to man in the enormous numbers of insects which they eat in gardens and farms. This feature has been made use of in the Marine toad *B. marinus*, one of the largest species of toad reaching a length of 9 in (22·5 cm) and found from Patagonia to southern Texas. It has been introduced into several parts of the world such as Puerto Rica, Haiti and Hawaii to control the beetles which cause considerable damage to the sugar cane crops. Following such successes it was introduced into Australia in 1935 to combat the beetle *Dermolepida albohirtum*. This has not been very successful and in the absence of many natural predators the toads are multiplying rapidly and increasing their range.

Other genera of Bufonidae are more restricted in their range. Species of *Pseudobufo* are found in the Malay peninsula and Borneo. Although their skin is rough like that of *Bufo* their toes are completely webbed and they are aquatic. The tip of the snout is turned up so that the nostrils protrude above the surface as they lie in the water.

Nectophryne is another genus which has habits different from those of *Bufo*. Species of this genus are found in southern Asia and have small discs on the tips of their digits which help them to climb bushes and trees.

Species of *Ansonia* from the Philippines breed in fast-flowing mountain streams and the tadpoles have flattened bodies and suckerlike mouths to cling to rocks.

Two species of *Nectophrynoides* are found in Africa and are unique among anurans in that the female gives birth to fully metamorphosed toads. The eggs, about 100 in number in *N. vivipara*, are retained in the oviducts where the tadpole stage is passed through. How the sperms are transmitted from the male is not known as no copulatory organs have been seen. FAMILY: Bufonidae, ORDER: Anura, CLASS: Amphibia. (Ill. p. 145, 147, 148, 149.)

TOKAY *Gekko gecko,* a small common *gecko of the tropics of southeastern Asia. Its common name is derived from its loud call of *to kay.*

TOMMYGOFF, vernacular name used in Panama for the snake also known as *ferde-lance.*

TORTOISES, slow-moving, heavily armoured reptiles which first appeared some 200 million years ago and have remained relatively unchanged for 150 million years. The body is enclosed in a box or shell which in many species is rigid and into which the head, tail and limbs can in many instances be withdrawn. The top of the shell, known as the carapace, is formed from overgrown, widened ribs. The lower part of the shell, called the plastron, is also made up of bony plates. Both carapace and plastron are covered with horny plates or shields known as scutes. The males are usually smaller than the females and often have a longer tail and the plastron may be concave.

The order to which tortoises belong used to be called the *Chelonia but is now known as the *Testudines. The order includes tortoises, turtles and terrapins, three names which tend to be given different meanings in different parts of the English-speaking world, but all have certain fundamental features in common.

For example, they have no teeth, but the jaws are covered with a horny bill which can be used for tearing food apart. They have moveable eyelids which are closed in sleep. Their external ear openings are covered with a membrane and it is doubtful if the Testudines can hear airborne sounds but like snakes they probably can pick up vibrations through ground or through water. They all lay eggs and the aquatic species must come ashore to lay them. In temperate climates land tortoises hibernate in the ground and freshwater species under mud at the bottoms of ponds. As a group they are noted for their long life-spans, the longest recorded being in excess of 158 years, for one of the Giant tortoises, but even the Garden tortoise has been recorded as living 50 years or more.

Tortoises form one family, the Testudinidae of the suborder Cryptodira or Snake-necked tortoises. The carapace is usually rigidly ossified and domed. The only substantial difference from the closely related Pond tortoises, family Emydidae, is in the structure of the feet. Whereas in the Pond tortoises the legs end in free fingers and toes, which are more or less firmly connected with each other by webs, in the tortoises the toes are incorporated in the structure of their club-feet, so that only the horny claws can be seen. Many investigators therefore regard tortoises and Pond tortoises as two subfamilies of a single family, Testudinidae.

In some types of tortoises the outsides of the forelegs and hindlegs are sometimes covered with large, strong scutes, which are partly ossified even at the base. As these parts remain visible when the creature is retracting under the carapace, the large scutes represent a special protection.

The structural arrangement of the carapace or shield of the tortoise is not basically different from that of the other neck-hiding tortoises, but the bony plates are always covered with horny epidermal plates; there is never a thick leathery epidermis such as that of the Mud turtles Trionychidae, the Papua turtle (*Carettochelys*) or the Leathery turtle (*Dermochelys*). On the other hand, in the Flexible-shelled or Tornier's tortoise *Malacochersus tornieri* the horny part of the shield has almost completely degenerated and therefore appears soft, since the creature is covered by practically no more than the horny epidermal plates. The shells of the Giant tortoises of the Galapagos and Seychelles Islands are also quite thin.

In the Pond tortoises, as in some other types of tortoises part of the plastron is hinged. The hinge is usually in the posterior part of the plastron and is found in particular in older females as in the case of the Algerian tortoise *Testudo graeca*; it probably makes its egg-laying easier. In the Spider tortoise *Pyxis arachnoides* of Madagascar, however, the fore portion of the plastron is articulated. As an exception to all other types, in the Flexible tortoises of the African genus *Kinixys* there is a transverse hinge at the posterior part of the dorsal carapace, which can be drawn down like the visor of a helmet.

Nearly all tortoises move very slowly, and therefore they feed chiefly upon vegetable matter. However, many types are also carnivorous, eating such small animals as worms and slugs. The Wood tortoise *Testudo denticulata* and the Coal tortoise *T. carbonaria* feed mostly upon carrion. The predilection of nearly all tortoises for animal or human excrement is remarkable.

Tortoises mate in the spring; the male usually makes squeaking noises during copulation, which often takes hours. The females lay spherical eggs with calcareous shells in holes in the ground which they dig themselves and then cover them again. There is no record of brood care of any kind.

Tortoises live in areas which extend from dry, hot desert regions to the humid jungles; this includes the tropics, subtropics and warmer temperate regions in all the continents except Australia. There are about 35 species and about 30 subspecies, divided among six genera.

The four species (or subspecies?) of the Gopher tortoises *Gopherus* are found only in desert regions in the southwest of North America.

During the intolerable heat of the day they hide in holes which they dig in the ground and which consist of a long passage and a terminal, spacious living chamber. They come out at dusk when the air has cooled down and usually eat cacti. The epiglottal shields on the underside in the male are extended very much forward and are used, when fighting for the female, to lever the rival onto his back and put him out of action. It is questionable whether these extensions are also used as spades when digging the burrow.

The four species of Flat tortoises *Homopus* in southern Africa are characterized by a relatively flat carapace, the short, powerfully distributed epiglottal scutes of the dorsal shield and by the hooked horny beak of the upper jaw. Their dorsal shield shows beautiful yellow, red and even green shades. They seem to live mainly on grass roots or other unusual foods; they can rarely be kept in captivity.

The Flexible tortoises *Kinixys*, already mentioned, which are able to lower the posterior part of their carapace, live in Africa, south of the Sahara. There are three species. When resting they shelter the front part of their shield between stones and protect the posterior soft parts by lowering the rear part of the carapace. These tortoises seem to like to be near water and are even said to be able to hunt swimming fish with skill.

In the East African Tornier's tortoise *Malacochersus tornieri* the bony scutes of the extremely flat carapace have degenerated to such an extent that practically only the flexible horny scutes remain. The animals can run relatively fast and when danger threatens they shelter between clefts in rocks. They then blow up the body and the flexible shell by breathing in, so much that they are firmly clamped and cannot be drawn out of their hiding places.

The relatively small Spider tortoises *Pyxis arachnoides* live in western Madagascar. They have a transverse hinge in the plastron, but in contrast to all other tortoises, this is in the front part of the plastron.

There are about 27 species of the genus *Testudo,* and they make up by far the largest proportion of tortoises. In order to classify the multiplicity of types, many investigators distinguish between several genera including *Testudo, Agrionemys, Chersine, Geochelone* and *Psammobates*. However, until it can be proved to what extent these groups are related to each other and to other tortoises, it would seem more suitable to allow them to be considered merely as subgenera of *Testudo*.

There are three *Testudo* species in southern Europe: the Greek tortoise *T. hermanni*, the Algerian or Iberian tortoise *T. graeca* and the Margined tortoise *T. marginata*. Of these *T. marginata* is found only in the south of Greece and on the island of Sardinia where it was introduced by soldiers during World War II. There are two subspecies of *T. hermanni* ranging from Spain and the south of France as far as Greece and Rumania. *T. graeca* looks quite similar, and there are four subspecies from northwest Africa through southern Europe to southwest Asia. It can be clearly distinguished from *T. hermanni* by the following features: the tail does not end in a horny spine; on the back, next to the root of the tail on either side, there is only a large, wide horny scute at the posterior edge of the dorsal carapace (in *T. hermanni* there is a pair of these).

Southwest and Central Asia is the home of the Four-toed tortoise *T. horsfieldii* in which, in contrast to all other tortoises, the forelegs and hindlegs each have only four claws. This tortoise is not active for more than three months of the year. It spends the remaining time in a dormant state, for which it burrows into the ground.

Some African and Asiatic *Testudo* species have more or less clearly developed radial yellow streaks on a dark background on the shields of the carapace (sometimes also on the plastron) which can also be seen on the Madagascar Spider tortoise. In generalizing, the types coloured in this way are called 'radiating tortoises' although they do not form a group of related species. Among the representatives of this species in Africa are the actual Radiated tortoises *T. radiata* of Madagascar and the Roofed tortoise *T. tentoria* in the south of the continent. In these types there is nearly always an uneven cervical scute on the anterior edge of the dorsal carapace over the neck. On the other hand, it is lacking in the Asiatic species of this pattern type, such as the Star tortoise *T. elegans* and its relatives.

In the New World, the genus *Testudo* is found only in South America; to the north of this the only tortoises are the species of *Gopherus*. The Wood tortoise *Testudo dent-*

iculata and the Coal tortoise *T. carbonaria* inhabit the humid, tropical rain-forest. *T. chilensis* is found only in Argentina and despite its scientific name is not found in Chile.

The carapace of the Giant tortoises *T. elephantopus* of the Galapagos Islands and *T. gigantea* of the Seychelles is up to 4 ft (1·2 m) long. The Galapagos types lack the uneven nape scute on the front margin of the carapace, which is developed in the Seychelles species. Several strains of both species inhabit the small islands of the two archipelagos, but some have died out or are threatened with extinction. In some of their subspecies the front part of the carapace curves upwards in the shape of a saddle. This enables the animals to stretch the head and neck up farther than other tortoises and thus to feed on plants higher up. These island tortoises originally had no natural enemies and their shield has become relatively thin.

Many people keep tortoises in captivity, but unfortunately often in unsuitable conditions. These animals should in no circumstances be allowed to run around freely on the floor of a room, since it is too cold and draughty there. It is far better to give them a roomy, light and sufficiently warm terrarium, with a drinking vessel and hiding places, and which is always kept clean. Lettuce (well-washed!), dandelion, fruit, tomatoes, bananas and sometimes a little meat or fish are suitable food. To prevent the tortoises from becoming rickety lime and vitamin preparations are added to their food (bread, macaroni or cake soaked in milk). Take care! they eat it with relish, but it causes digestive trouble. At least once a week the tortoises should be bathed in shallow warm water at 77–80°F (25–27°C), so that they can drink and evacuate therein. In summer it is essential for them to spend some time regularly in a well fenced-in open space, so that they get unfiltered sunlight; together with the lime in their food they need it to build the bones of their skeleton and of the carapace. This applies also to the tropical types; they should enjoy direct sunlight at least during the midday hours.

Only those species coming from the far north (but not the south!) of the tortoises' range of distribution should be allowed to hibernate cold. If they have thoroughly evacuated in the autumn and have become comatose at temperatures around 50–47°F (10–8°C) put them in a well ventilated box with peat moss (not peat mull) and transfer them to a dark cellar which must, of course, be free of rats or mice. The temperature should not be more than 40–47°F (4–8°C) so that they will neither freeze nor become lively. The moss must be slightly moistened now and again so that the tortoises do not dry up. In March or April gradually move the tortoises to warmer, lighter rooms, so that they awaken from their winter sleep. If they have become

lively, after two or three days bathe them in moderately warm water, to compensate for the loss of fluid and to help them evacuate.

It may be mentioned that probably only the Four-toed tortoises *Testudo horsfieldii* actually need such hibernation. All other species can or even should be kept fully active during the winter in suitably equipped containers. SUBORDER: Cryptodira, ORDER: Testudines, CLASS: Reptilia. (Ill. p. 149, 150.)

TORTOISESHELL, the name given to the horny scutes on the shell of Sea turtles, especially to those of the Hawksbill turtle *Eretmochelys imbricata,* which are renowned for their vivid pattern of amber, reddish-brown, blackish brown and yellow.

One of the idiosyncrasies of the English language is that we call a land chelonian a tortoise and a marine chelonian a turtle, but we call the shell from a turtle 'tortoiseshell'. The word 'turtle' is from a corruption by English sailors in the 16th and 17th centuries of either the French *tortue* or Spanish *tortuga,* meaning in both cases tortoise, the animal with the tortuous or twisted feet. More confusing still, in North America the name tortoiseshell is used although practically all chelonians are called turtles. Paradoxically, the flippers (or feet) of turtles are anything but twisted.

When taken from the turtle the scutes can be welded together by applying heat and pressure and thus thicker pieces of tortoiseshell can be made, which can be used to make combs, tortoiseshell boxes and trinkets. The horny scutes of the hawksbill overlap like the tiles of a roof and they are thicker than the scutes of other species.

To strip the scutes from the turtle, heat has to be applied and in some areas the turtle used to be held over glowing embers or hot water was poured onto it. Of course, the scutes can also be removed from a freshly killed turtle, but it used to be said that the quality was superior if the scutes were taken from the living animal. Moreover, it is believed that if the turtle, after careful stripping, is put back into the sea it will develop a new set of scutes. Indeed, Deraniyagala did show that in a young hawksbill which had lost a scute, this was replaced by a new one in about eight months. There is no proof, however, that if all scutes are stripped from the turtle it will survive and form a completely new set of scutes.

The tortoiseshell from various parts of the world differs in colour and quality. That from the West Indies is usually more reddish, that from the Indian Ocean more dark in colour. A large hawksbill with the carapace 30 in (75 cm) long will yield 8 lb (3·6 kg) of tortoiseshell. The trade in tortoise-shell has declined through the years being partly replaced by synthetic materials, but is still exported from the Caribbean.

The scutes of the Green turtle and those of the Loggerhead turtle are too thin to be of much use and they do not show the vivid pattern that makes real tortoiseshell so attractive. Still it seems that in the past even the scutes of the Green turtle and of the Loggerhead turtle were used to some extent. 18th century authors mention them as being used for panes of lanterns and for inlay.

TREEFROGS, strictly only those frogs which belong to the family Hylidae. The habit of living in trees from which they are named has in fact been adopted by many species belonging to other families of frogs, while some members of the Hylidae do not have this arboreal habit. Nevertheless the Hylidae contains the largest number of arboreal genera and the family is best dealt with on its own because, although the tree-living frogs of different families may look rather similar, details of their internal anatomy reveal that they are not closely related.

Members of the Hylidae are characterized by having a pectoral girdle in which the two ventral halves overlap in the mid-line (the arciferal condition) and an extra disc-shaped element of cartilage in each finger and toe. Two other small families, the *Pseudidae and *Centrolenidae, also have these characters and are sometimes included in the Hylidae. The Hylidae differ from them in having the extra element disc-shaped (it is rod-shaped in the Pseudidae) and in having the end-bone in each digit claw-shaped (it is T-shaped in the Centrolenidae).

The extra element in each digit is found also in the treefrogs of other families and is an adaptation to their arboreal habits. It occurs between the last two bones in each digit and enables the last bone to move through a large angle relative to the rest of the digit. This last bone supports an adhesive disc and its mobility means that the disc can remain pressed flat against the surface while the hand or foot is at an angle to it. The adhesive discs, formed by an expansion of the tip of each finger and toe are a distinctive feature of treefrogs and enables them to cling to vertical surfaces. In structure a disc consists of a soft pad of tissue under the curved bone. The skin of the pad is thickened and contains many modified mucous glands which secrete a sticky fluid onto the surface.

The Hylidae is a large family, containing about 34 genera, but, with two exceptions, *Nyctimystes* and *Hyla,* they are only found in the New World. *Nyctimystes* occurs in New Guinea while *Hyla* is almost world-wide, but is absent from the Arctic and Antarctic and most of Africa.

Hyla arborea is the European treefrog and is found throughout Europe and most of Asia. On the basis of differences in colour pattern and the length of limbs it is divided into several subspecies. The typical form is a small frog, about $1\frac{3}{4}$ in (43 mm) long, bright green with a dark stripe, edged with yellow, running along the side of the body; a small branch of the stripe projects forwards over the back from just in front of the hindlimb. It spends the day sitting on the leaves of trees and bushes and relies on its colouration for protection. If approached it does not jump away but crouches lower onto the leaf. It leaps at any insect which flies within reach, catching it in its mouth. In jumping it takes no account of its height above the ground or the position of other leaves and depends on its outstretched hands and feet catching onto a leaf or twig to break its fall. Most of its hunting, however, is done at night when it is more active.

During the last century European treefrogs were thought to be useful weather prophets and were often kept in small jars with a pool of water in the bottom and a small ladder. At the approach of fine weather the frog was supposed to sit at the top of the ladder while, when rain was imminent, it moved to the bottom. Experiments have shown that this is unreliable although, like most frogs, it will call more readily in dark rainy weather than on sunny days.

It hibernates in the mud at the bottom of ponds and breeds in April and May. About 800–1,000 eggs are laid in several lumps attached to water plants below the surface of the water. The tadpoles reach a length of about 2 in (5 cm) and change into frogs after about three months.

There are several hundred species of *Hyla* but they are all rather similar in habits to the European treefrog. There is, however, considerable variation in the general shape and colour. *H. versicolor,* the Common or Gray treefrog of North America, is a short squat frog about 2 in (5 cm) long, with a rough warty skin. Although, like most treefrogs, it is able to vary its colour quite considerably, it is usually grey or brown with irregular dark patches on its back and difficult to see when sitting on the lichen-encrusted bark of a tree.

The Green treefrog *H. cinerea,* also of North America, is also about 2 in (5 cm) long, but is a very slim, long-bodied frog with a completely smooth skin and long legs. Its colour is usually bright green but may occasionally be grey.

About 21 species of *Hyla* occur in Australia. Several of them are able to live in the hot, dry parts. *H. caerulea* for example, can tolerate a loss of water equivalent to 45% of its body weight while *H. moorei* from the more temperate areas can only tolerate a 30% loss. Some species, such as *H. rubella* and *H. aurea,* show a tendency away from an arboreal habit and spend much of the time in or near water.

Three species of *Hyla* have been introduced into New Zealand where they form the only amphibian population besides the three species of *Leiopelma* (see Amphicoela).

Although treefrogs live in trees, usually some distance from water, most of them have to return to water to breed and have the pattern of development characteristic of most frogs, with a free-swimming tadpole stage. Some species, however, have developed breeding methods in which the vulnerable eggs and tadpoles are protected to a certain extent from predators.

The females of *Hyla rosenbergi* construct small pools of water in the shallows of ponds. They collect small quantities of mud from the bottom of the pond and build them into a wall. They continue until the wall is higher than the surface of the water and a small pool about 1 ft (30 cm) in diameter is cut off from the rest of the pond. The frog uses its hands to smooth the insides of the wall. The eggs are laid in these basins and the tadpoles hatch after about four or five days. They have large external gills which float on the surface of the water and enable them to obtain sufficient oxygen, since there is only a limited quantity dissolved in such small bodies of water.

Hyla goeldii avoids laying the eggs in water altogether. The skin on the female's back has a fold down each side which forms a small hollow. About 25 large eggs are carried in this until hatching when the female moves to the small pools of water held in the bases of bromeliad leaves. The tadpoles complete their development in these pools.

All the species of *Hyla* which occur in Jamaica also lay their eggs in these bromeliad aquaria and the tadpoles show interesting modifications to such a habitat. They feed on the other eggs, either of their own or of other species, which are lying in the same pool and the horny teeth around their mouths are adapted to such a diet.

Other genera of treefrogs appear to have carried the adaptation shown by *H. goeldii* a stage further. In the Marsupial frogs *Gastrotheca* the brood pouch is a completely enclosed sac on the female's back and opens by a small slit-like opening over the cloaca. As the eggs are released and fertilized the female tilts her body so that they slide forward into the pouch. The pouch then seals up and the eggs are carried around and develop inside it. In some species, such as *G. marsupiata,* the young are released as tadpoles while in others, such as *G. ovifera,* the complete development takes place inside the brood pouch and the young emerge as froglets. The female uses the toes of her hindfeet to open the pouch, enabling the young to escape.

Frogs of the genus *Phyllomedusa* belong to another group of hylids that have an interesting breeding method. In this case the eggs are laid in a tube formed from leaves. The female, carrying the male on her back, selects a leaf overhanging water. She climbs onto it and both she and the male hold the two edges of the leaf together at the bottom. The eggs are released into the funnel thus formed and the jelly of the eggs holds the two leaves together. The frogs move up the leaf, laying more eggs as they go, until the whole leaf is formed into a tube containing about 100 eggs. The tadpoles hatch after about six days and drop into the water to complete their development. *Agalachnis* has similar breeding habits.

Some genera of hylids have the bones of the skull enlarged to form a bony shield covering the head. In *Hemiphractus scutatus* which occurs from Ecuador to Brazil the helmet is extended to form a triangular horn behind each eye. In some, for example, *Flectonotus,* the skin of the head fuses with the bone. The function of these bony helmets is not fully known. They are probably defensive although in some genera, such as *Diaglena,* in which the flat, bony snout protudes in front of the mouth, it has been suggested that it may be used to dig for insects in rotten wood.

Although most genera of hylids are arboreal in their habits there are exceptions. The Chorus frogs belong to the genus *Pseudacris* which is found only in North America. Most of them are small and delicate, about 1 in (2·5 cm) long, patterned with brown or green stripes or spots. They do not climb very much and the adhesive discs on their fingers and toes are small. Their toes are only slightly webbed and they are poor swimmers. They only call during the breeding season, which is in the Spring in the north but during the winter rains in the south. After that they are rarely found due to their small size and the effective camouflage of their colouration among vegetation of the same colour.

The Cricket frog *Acris gryllus* is a representative of a genus which has progressed even further from the arboreal habits of most hylids. It is small, $\frac{1}{2}$–$1\frac{1}{4}$ in (13–31 mm) long, with a pointed snout. Its toe discs are very small and it resembles a true frog *(Rana)* more than a treefrog. It is very variable in colour and may be grey, brown, reddish tan or green. It never climbs but lives always on the ground among the grass bordering streams and swamps. Its name refers to its chirping call which is heard in chorus during the Spring. Unlike most frogs it is active during the day. FAMILY: Hylidae, ORDER: Anura, CLASS: Amphibia. (Ill. p. 151, 152.)

TREE SNAKES, very slender snakes living in trees in Malaya and the East Indies. They are reputed to launch themselves and glide from trees to the lower bushes and are sometimes referred to as *flying snakes, especially the species of *Chrysopelea.* The Golden tree snake *C. ornata* can climb a tree by forcing the sides of its body against irregularities in the bark, as if crawling up a shallow trench. In this it is helped by its belly scales being keeled at their sides. Tree snakes have only a weak venom and some species at least also constrict their prey. FAMILY: Colubridae, ORDER: Squamata, CLASS: Reptilia.

TRICERATOPS, the best known but not the largest of the horned *dinosaurs, it was 20 ft (6·2 m) long with a skull 6 ft (2 m) long bearing a short horn on the snout and a larger horn over each eye. The rear part of the skull was carried backwards in a bony frill over the neck.
ORDER: Ornithischia, CLASS: Reptilia.

TRITYLODONTA, extinct mammal-like reptiles, or 'near mammals' of the Triassic-Jurassic period. See *Oligokyphus*.

TUATARA *Sphenodon punctatus,* belonging to the otherwise extinct reptilian order, Rhynchocephalia. The rhynchocephalians are characterized by the presence of a 'beak-like' upper jaw, and first appeared in the Lower Triassic some 200 million years ago. The group was virtually extinct by the Lower Cretaceous about 100 million years later. The members of the group formerly had a widespread distribution, and fossils have been found from all the continents except North America. The order is now represented only by a single genus with one species, the tuatara, which is restricted to approximately 20 islands off the coast of New Zealand. The ancestry of the tuatara may be traced back to the fossil reptile *Homoeosaurus* from the Upper Jurassic and the similarities between the two forms are striking. It seems, therefore, that the structure of the tuatara has remained virtually unchanged for some 130 million years. The existence of the tuatara is just as astonishing as the discovery of a large dinosaur would be. Perhaps even more so since the tuatara is the sole survivor of a group which reached its peak about 180 million years ago whereas the dinosaurs were at their peak about 140 million years ago in the Jurassic and Cretaceous.

The tuatara is 'lizard-like' in general appearance but is distinguished from the lizards by several skeletal features involving the skull and the ribs. The generic name *Sphenodon* means 'wedge tooth' and this refers to the chisel-like teeth on the upper and lower jaws, which are fused to the jawbone, not set into sockets. The Maori word tuatara means 'peaks on the back' and this describes the triangular folds of skin which form a conspicuous crest down the back and tail of the male. The female has only a rudimentary crest. Tuataras vary in colour from black-brown to dull green, while some may have a reddish tinge. The upper part of the body is covered with small scales that may have small yellow spots. The feet have five toes each with sharp claws and are partially webbed. A vestigial parietal 'eye' is found on the top of the head in very young animals, but soon

becomes covered over, and is invisible in adults. The presence of this 'eye' is considered to be a very primitive feature since it also occurs in the ancestors of the rhynchocephalians. It is usually further reduced or even absent in modern lizards. The parietal eye retains some traces of a lens and a retina, but there is doubt about its function. It may be that it acts as a register of solar radiation and controls the amount of time the creature spends in the sunlight. This is important since the tuatara, like all reptiles, has a body temperature which is affected by the temperature of its surroundings, and is said to be ectothermic. The body temperature may therefore be controlled to some extent by basking in the sun or seeking the shade. Nevertheless, the tuatara spends most of the daytime in its burrow leaving it only occasionally to sunbathe, mainly in late winter and spring. It is therefore largely nocturnal and is active at temperatures which are much lower than those favoured by lizards. Available reports indicate that the tuatara may be active at temperatures as low as 45°F (7°C) and, further, that even in winter it only hibernates lightly. Allied to its low body temperature is the fact that it has a very low metabolic rate. This means that it requires very little energy to keep the vital body processes, such as excretion and digestion, 'ticking over'. The tuatara is reputed to grow very slowly and probably does not breed until it is 20 years old. Growth may continue until the age of 50 or beyond and the animals are said to be extremely long-lived. Estimates of the life span vary from about 100 to 300 years.

The mating habits of the tuatara are also remarkable in that the male has no copulatory organ and mating is accomplished by the apposition of the male and female urinogenital openings (known as cloacal apposition). Pairing usually takes place in January but the sperm is stored within the female until October-December. She then scoops out a shallow nest in the ground and lays 5–15 eggs with soft white shells. These remain in the nest for a further 13–15 months before hatching, the longest incubation period known for any reptile.

At the present time the tuatara is found only on some small islands off the east coast of the North Island of New Zealand and in Cook Strait between the North and South Islands. These small islands also have large colonies of birds such as petrels and shearwaters which nest in burrows. The tuatara is capable of digging its own burrow, but seems to prefer ready-made ones, and therefore frequently shares a burrow with a seabird. The two inhabitants of the burrow have an amicable co-existence on the whole although the tuatara will occasionally eat the eggs and even the chicks of these birds. The normal diet of the tuatara is moths, beetles, crickets

and other small invertebrates. It is evident that it was also found on the North and South Islands of New Zealand since the animal was so well known to the Maoris. In fact the tuatara figures very prominently in the traditional wood carvings which ornament Maori meeting houses and is a symbol of death or misfortune. This stems from the Maori myth that the tuatara, and lizards, were the close associates of the goddess of fire who originally brought death into the world by slaying her own grandson.

The reason for the survival of the tuatara in New Zealand is one of isolation. The separation of New Zealand from other land masses occurred long before the evolution of the predaceous land animals and therefore the tuatara has been able to survive in New Zealand in the absence of predators, but has been wiped out in other parts of the world.

Subfossil remains show that the tuatara was originally found in a number of parts of the North and South Islands of New Zealand, but they have long since disappeared from the mainland. This was probably due to a gradual change in climatic conditions, vegetation and perhaps also the avifauna, before and for some while after the arrival of the Maoris. There is little evidence to support the suggestion that either Europeans or introduced animals were to blame for the elimination of the tuatara from the mainland.

Although the tuatara is found on about 20 offshore islands, it appears to be maintaining a satisfactory replacement rate and age distribution on only a few of these. On many islands the population seems to consist only of adult animals, although the reasons for this are not clear. The species is very strictly protected by the New Zealand Government, and it is to be hoped that such measures will ensure the continued survival of this fascinating relic from Triassic times. FAMILY: Sphenodontidae, ORDER: Rhynchocephalia, CLASS: Reptilia. (Ill. p. 153.)

TURTLES, aquatic relatives of *tortoises and divisible into freshwater and marine turtles (see turtles, marine). Some of the smaller species of freshwater turtles (dealt with here) are called *terrapins and Pond tortoises. In most of them the carapace is rather flat. In some species also it does not completely ossify when the animal gets older, so that more or less large fontanelles are left near the margin of the carapace. The legs are laterally flattened and end in free fingers and toes which are webbed at least at the base. It is only in the Soft-shelled turtles and Papuan turtles that the legs are transformed into wide flippers, from which only two or three claws protrude.

The time spent in the water by the various species varies considerably. Many of them only leave the water in order to lay their eggs or to sun themselves for a short while; others go for more or less extensive walks on land or even live there for months; the Box turtles scarcely go into the water at all. Their feeding habits also differ greatly. There are all gradations from species which are entirely carnivorous to others which are almost entirely vegetarian.

It is not always possible to tell the difference between the sexes. The tail of the male is often relatively longer than that of the female and is somewhat thickened at the base. The plastron of the male is usually slightly concave, while that of the female is rather convex. With the exception of the terrestrial Box turtles, mating takes place in the water, usually in the spring. The female goes on land to lay her eggs and uses her hindlegs to dig a hole in the ground near the bank. She then softens the soil by evacuating the fluid contents of her anal sacs, which empty into the cloaca at the end of the intestine. Finally, she hangs her tail in the hole and then lays the eggs, one by one; she picks them up, using the hindlegs alternately and carefully allows them to slide to the ground. After depositing them she fills up the hole again and smooths the surface with her plastron until it is no longer noticeable. Finally she returns to the water and forgets about her eggs.

The eggs are incubated by the heat of the soil alone, and the young hatch out towards the end of the summer. In northern latitudes there is sometimes not enough heat to complete the development of the embryos in the same year. In that case they may hibernate in the eggs so that the young do not hatch out until the next spring. This applies to the European pond tortoise and some of the North American types.

The adult turtles of the types found in northerly areas also hibernate, digging themselves into the mud of their home waters. Since their metabolic processes are very greatly slowed down at the prevailing temperatures of 39·5°F (4°C), they do not need to come up to breathe during this period, but obtain oxygen from the water through their anal sacs.

Aestivation has been observed in some species of *Pelomedusa* and *Pelusios* in tropical Africa. When their ponds dry up, the turtles lapse into a state of rigidity. They do not stir again until the rainy season sets in and the dried up lakes and rivers fill with water.

There is little exact information available about the maximum age that turtles can reach. We do know, however, that some species can be over 100 years old. A maximum age of about 120 years has been established in the European pond tortoise.

Most freshwater turtles belong to the Snake-necked turtles, suborder Cryptodira. These hide the head or neck under the front part of the carapace retracting the neck and vertebral column in a vertical S-shaped curve;

the pelvic girdle is not connate with the plastron.

The two American species of *Snapping turtles, family Chelydridae are related to the Mud turtles and Musk turtles, family Kinosternidae, which are also to be found in both the Americas, but unlike the Snapping turtles, they usually remain small. They also swim very little, but wander quietly around the bottom of their usually shallow, undisturbed ponds and eat fish, small invertebrates, chiefly snails, but also vegetable matter or even carrion. The scutes of the plastron are separated from those of the carapace on both sides by a more or less complete longitudinal row of horny inframarginal plates, thus showing a really original structure of these turtles. The smooth skin of the visible soft part, which has hardly any scutes, is also characteristic.

In the Mud turtles *Kinosternon* the large plastron has an anterior and a posterior transverse hinge so that the turtles can raise the front and rear lobes of the plastron to protect their soft parts. The plastron of the other genera *Clardius* and *Staurotypus*, of Mexico and Central America, and also of the North American musk turtles of the genus *Sternotherus*, is small and cruciform. The Musk turtles get their name from the strongly odoriferous excretions which they expel from the cloaca when they are molested; for this reason Americans call them 'stinkpots'.

A complete series of inframarginal scutes on either side between the dorsal and ventral shield is also to be found in the Tabasco turtle *Dermatemys mawii* in Eastern Mexico as far as Guatemala and Honduras; it is the only species of the family Dermatemydidae. These highly aquatic turtles, up to 16 in (40 cm) long, are excellent swimmers and are entirely vegetarian.

Inframarginal scutes are also present in the Big-headed turtle *Platysternon megacephalum* of Southeast Asia, the only species of the family Platysternidae. The enormous head of this turtle ends in a downwardly hooked horny beak and is armoured with large horny scutes. It contrasts remarkably with the extremely flat dorsal carapace and cannot be retracted under it. This turtle lives in flat, stony and very cold mountain streams and its chief food is molluscs. The tail is about the same length as the carapace and covered with strong, knobby, horny scutes; with the help of the tail the turtle is an excellent climber.

The Pond turtles, Emydidae, are by far the largest family of turtles, with about 25 genera and 80 species and also a large number of subspecies. In these there are many differences in the shape of the carapace and also the living habits. There are also transitions between aquatic and terrestrial and between carnivorous and vegetarian types.

The genera *Kachuga, Hardella, Callagur*

and *Batagur*, of southern Asia, stay in the water almost exclusively. They are preponderantly vegetarian and have parallel, long masticating strips on the horny jaws for chewing their food. The lungs are in bony chambers formed by the inner walls of the shield, to protect them from excessive pressures when diving in deep water. In at least some of these types the females are considerably larger than the males. The Temple turtles *Hieremys annandalei* which are looked after in their native countries in special turtle temples, are also predominantly vegetarian. *Notochelys platynota*, also indigenous to that part of the world, has similar feeding habits; the number of vertebrals on the carapace is regularly increased by one or two.

Most species of Emydidae, however, live in the same way as the European pond tortoise *Emys orbicularis*, which usually stays in the water but occasionally comes out to sun itself and also travels short distances on land. Usually black spotted or striped with yellow, this is one of the species most widely distributed northwards; it is still found in Holland and northern Germany, near Hamburg. In the south its range extends to northwest Africa, in the east to western Asia. Its North American relative Blanding's turtle *E. blandingii* is much more terrestrial, but according to more recent findings it merits its own genus, *Emydoidea*.

In North America the turtles of this family are represented by the greatest number of species and subspecies. There, the species of *Pseudemys* are called cooters and sliders, like the Red-eared turtle *P. scripta elegans* which has a bright red stripe along the head and is often offered for sale in the pet shops. The Map turtles *Graptemys*, in which the carapace usually has a pattern like a map, are characterized by a knobby keel along the middle of the carapace. The carapace of the Painted turtles is brown and the sutures are often bordered with red. All these species have much the same way of life as *E. orbicularis*.

The North American diamondback terrapin *Malaclemys* is closely related to the Map turtles *Graptemys*. Since these terrapins lead a special kind of life and have a special significance for human beings, they are dealt with in a separate article. See terrapins.

The River turtles of the genus *Clemmys* are indigenous to North America and also Europe, northwest Africa and Asia; the old-world types have recently been assigned to the genus (or better, the subgenus) *Mauremys*. The majority of these species stay most of the time in water, like the Caspian river turtle *C. caspica* indigenous to the Mediterranean area, the East Asian ocellated turtle *C. bealei*, which has one or two pairs of yellow ocelli on the neck; or the beautiful North American spotted turtle *C. guttata*, which has bright yellow, round spots. The

Wood turtle *C. insculpta* also indigenous to North America, however, leaves its watery home for months during the summer and travels on land, only returning to water to hibernate.

The species of the large genus *Geoemyda*, of Asia, Central America and northern South America, lead a different terrestrial life. Their way of life, even the shape of the carapace, may change during the lifetime of each individual. In the young of the Spiny turtle *G. spinosa*, which mainly remain on land, each marginal scute of the carapace is continued laterally in a long pointed spine; each costal scute also has a pointed spine. As the turtle grows the spines disappear completely and it then lives mostly in the water.

The carapace of the Asiatic box turtles is strikingly domed. These belong to the genus *Cuora*, in which the plastron is divided by a ligamentous transverse hinge into a movable front and hind flap; these truly terrestrial turtles like to eat sweet fruit. The true Box turtles *Terrapene*, of North America, have the same shell structure. *T. carolina* is the best known species, another is the Ornate box turtle *T. ornata* whose darker carapace has yellow rays on every scute, reminiscent of the Star tortoise *Testudo elegans*. These turtles remain on land and do not even go to water to breed; they feed for the most part on vegetable matter, and are alleged even to eat fungi. These Box turtles are only recognizable as members of the family of Emydidae by their free fingers and toes.

The Land tortoises of the family Testudinidae, are very closely related to the Pond tortoises family Emydidae, and some herpetologists regard the two as subfamilies only, the Emydinae and Testudininae of the family Testudinidae.

The Soft-shelled turtles of the family Trionychidae in Africa, South and East Asia and North America form a highly aberrant group. Their carapace is not covered with horny scutes, but with a thick leathery skin which projects far beyond the edge of the bony shield beneath. The marginal plates of the bony carapace have almost or even entirely disappeared; the plastron consists only of some bony scales. The elongated head ends in a fleshy proboscis; the jaws are covered with thick lips. The legs have become paddle-shaped flippers, from which only three claws still project freely. All the Soft-shelled turtles are extremely irascible and almost entirely carnivorous. Usually they keep to freshwater, a few also go into brackish water or the sea, such as the Southeast Asian *Dogania subplana*.

Most of the species belong to the genus *Trionyx* distributed over Africa, southern Asia and North America. In the genera *Cyclanorbis* and *Cycloderma* in Africa and *Lissemys* in southern Asia there are lateral movable flaps under the hindlegs in the rear part of the plastron and the turtles can flip them up for protection.

The Papuan turtle *Carettochelys insculpta* occupies an intermediate position between the 'normal' Pond turtles and the Soft-shelled turtles, and is the only representative of the family Carettochelyidae. It lives mainly in the region of the Fly River in New Guinea, but quite recently it has also been discovered in the Northern Territory of Australia. In this species the bony part of the carapace is completely developed, but it is covered with a leathery skin and not with horny scutes. The snout terminates in a fleshy proboscis, but there are no fleshy lips to the jaws, which are fully exposed. The legs have also become paddle-shaped flippers, but each terminates in only two claws. The Papuan turtle is mainly vegetarian and not very irascible. It is found not only in freshwater, but also in the brackish water of river mouths.

The remaining turtles belong to the second suborder the Side-necked turtles, Pleurodira. When they withdraw the head they bend the, sometimes very long, neck in a horizontal S-shaped curve. The pelvis is firmly attached to the plastron. Most of the Side-necked turtles are dark, fully aquatic species and very fierce. They are to be found only in freshwater in the southern hemisphere and are distributed over Africa, Madagascar, New Guinea, Australia and South America.

Hidden-necked turtles of the family Pelomedusidae can withdraw the head a little way into the neck before turning it sideways. The species of *Pelomedusa*, with a rigid plastron, and *Pelusios*, in which the plastron has a cross-joint, are found in Africa. There are only four claws on the hindlegs of the species of *Podocnemis*, which are mostly distributed in South America. One species, *P. madagascariensis*, also appears in the African region. The giant Arrau turtle *P. expansa* of South America is characterized by particularly large batches of eggs; the Terekay turtle *P. unifilis* is smaller and is sold in pet shops.

The second family of Side-necked turtles are the Chelidae, in Australia and South America, containing species with an extremely long neck, like the Australian snake-necked turtles of the genus *Chelodina* and the South American snake-necked turtles of the genus *Hydromedusa*, with head and neck approximately the same length as the carapace.

The peculiar *matamata *Chelys fimbriata* of South America also belongs to this group, and its extremely flat head looks triangular because of the lateral flaps of skin, and it terminates in front in a fleshy proboscis. The head and neck are decorated with long fringes of skin and the carapace has three knobby keels. It has much the same way of life as the Alligator snapper *Macroclemys temminckii* of North America. It also does not actively hunt its prey, but lies in wait for it. When a fish is lured by the skin-fringes, the matamata opens its enormous jaws at lightning speed, causing a strong rush of water which draws the prey far into the mouth.

In addition to these unusual long-necked turtles, there are also numerous species of the family Chelidae with necks of normal length, like the species of *Emydura* in Australia and New Guinea or the *Platemys* species in South America. In these the neural plates of the bony carapace have wholly or partially disappeared, so that the pleural plates meet directly in the centre-line. ORDER: Testudines, CLASS: Reptilia. (Ill. p. 150-152, 154-156.)

TURTLES, MARINE, tortoises adapted to life in the sea. Like the land tortoises their body is encased in a shell, which consists of a dorsal part, the carapace, and a ventral part, the plastron, joined together on either side by the bridge. From land tortoises and terrapins, they differ in the shape of the limbs, which have developed into flat flippers. These make turtles good swimmers, but make their movement on land very cumbersome. The head and neck cannot be completely withdrawn within the shell.

Seven species of turtle are known. The largest is the Leathery turtle or leatherback *Dermochelys coriacea*, the carapace of which may reach a length of 6 ft (1·8 m). The bony carapace, which is in no way joined to the vertebrae and ribs, consists of a mosaic of bony platelets covered with a leathery skin. The species is easily recognized by the presence of seven ridges, often notched, running lengthwise over the back. The plastron consists of four pairs of bony rods, arranged to form an oval ring; more superficially six rows of keeled platelets are present. The Leathery turtle is blackish above with numerous scattered, small, irregular whitish or pinkish spots; below it is white with black markings. It is found in all tropical and subtropical seas, and from there it wanders far to the north and south into temperate regions. It is a fairly regular visitor to British and French waters; in Norway it has been found up to 70°N. The food of the Leathery turtle consists mainly of jellyfish and salps. Although it breeds all through the tropics, only a few nesting beaches are known, where large numbers of females come ashore to deposit their eggs, for example, on the east coast of Malaya and in French Guiana.

In the rest of the Sea turtles the bony shell is of a more solid construction. The carapace consists of bony plates, which are firmly joined to the vertebrae and the ribs, and of a series of smaller bones around the margin; the plastron consists of nine flat bones, which leave some openings between them. Both the carapace and the plastron are covered with horny scutes. On the carapace, the horny scutes are arranged in three longitudinal

Above: common snapping turtle laying her eggs.

Below: young snapping turtles hatching.

Chelonia species are mainly vegetarian, with a preference for sea grass. However, the hatchlings are carnivorous, and adult Green turtles, in captivity, can be fed with fish. Due to the unlimited harvesting of eggs, and to a much lesser extent to the killing of adult turtles, the populations have declined. In some areas the freshly-laid eggs are taken from the nests, to be buried once more in hatcheries, where they are protected against predators. The hatchlings are kept in tanks of seawater until they have digested the remaining yolk, and until they are able to dive. Then, at night, the young turtles are released at sea over a fairly wide area, to obviate their being taken by the large numbers of predatory fish that usually lie in wait off the nesting beaches. It is hoped that in this way the populations will regain their full strength. Important nesting beaches of the Green turtle are found on the islands of the Great Barrier Reef, small islands off Sarawak, in the Seychelles, on the island of Ascension and on the coast of Costa Rica.

The Hawksbill turtle *Eretmochelys imbricata*, like the Green turtle, has four pairs of costal scutes, but the scutes of the carapace overlap, like the tiles on a roof. The carapace may reach a length of 36 in (91 cm). Moreover, this species has two pairs of prefrontal shields on the snout. The Hawksbill is the species that yields tortoiseshell. In some areas, as in the Caribbean, it is also much appreciated as food, but in other areas, for example, New Guinea, the meat is known to be highly poisonous. The Hawksbill is carnivorous, feeding on various kinds of small marine animals. It is believed never to move far from the nesting beaches. It is found in all tropical and in some subtropical seas, for example, the Mediterranean. Those from the Indian and Pacific Oceans are more darkly coloured than those from the Atlantic.

The Loggerhead turtle *Caretta caretta* has five pairs of costal scutes; the snout is covered with two pairs of prefrontals, which often have one or more scales wedged in between them. Its general colour is reddish brown above, yellowish below. The Loggerhead occurs in all oceans, also in the tropics, but it is more common in the subtropics, where it breeds. It is often found far from land in mid-ocean and on its wanderings it comes to temperate seas; it is a fairly regular visitor to the Atlantic coasts of Europe, and it even has been found at Murmansk in northern Russia. The Loggerhead feeds on a variety of marine invertebrates, such as shellfish, squids, Goose barnacles and jellyfish. The carapace may reach a length of 40 in (101 cm).

The Olive Ridley *Lepidochelys olivacea* and Kemp's Ridley *Lepidochelys kempi* are characterized by minute openings (pores) on the hind borders of the scutes that cover the bridge. Both species have the snout covered by two pairs of prefrontal shields. Kemp's

rows, one row consisting of the nuchal scute (or precentral) and a number of vertebral scutes (centrals) along the middle of the back, with a series of costal scutes (or laterals) on either side, and with a series of small marginal scutes along the border of the shell. The number of scutes in the various series are used to identify the species.

The genus *Chelonia* contains two species: the Green turtle *Chelonia mydas,* occurring in all tropical and subtropical seas, and the

Flatbacked turtle *Chelonia depressa,* which is found only along the north and east coasts of Australia. Both species have four pairs of costals, and a single pair of prefrontal shields on the snout. The Green turtle is the larger of the two; the carapace may reach a length of 55 in (1·4 m). It is this species that is in demand for preparing turtle soup; for this one uses not only the meat, but also the gelatinous cartilage ('calipee'), which fills the openings between the bones of the plastron. The

143

Ridley has five pairs of costal scutes. It is a small turtle, the carapace reaching a length of only 27½ in (69 cm). Its only known nesting beaches are on the Gulf Coast of northern Mexico. There, the females may arrive in large 'arribadas', hundreds and sometimes thousands coming ashore at the same time. Some individuals wander through the Florida Strait into the Atlantic Ocean, going northwards along the east coast of North America, and crossing the ocean to Europe, the Azores and Madeira. In the Olive Ridley the number of scutes on the carapace is strongly variable; it usually has six to nine vertebral scutes, and six to nine costal scutes on either side (the numbers on the left and right often being different). Its carapace may attain a length of 30 in (76 cm). It has a wide distribution in the Pacific and Indian Oceans (but it has not yet been found on the east coast of Africa); in the Atlantic Ocean it is found on the west coast of Africa northward to Senegal, and on the coast of South America from the Guianas to Trinidad. As in Kemp's Ridley the females arrive at the nesting beaches in large numbers. Well known nesting beaches are found on the Pacific coast of Mexico, and in the Guianas; without doubt important nesting beaches will still be found on the west coast of Africa, and in the Indo-Pacific area. The Olive Ridley wanders far into temperate seas, for example, to Japan and to New Zealand. Both species are carnivorous.

Although turtles spend practically their whole life in the sea, the females have to go ashore to deposit their eggs, the young turtle begins its life on land, and in some areas, as in the Hawaiian Islands, Green turtles are known to leave the water to bask in the sun. Usually the eggs are laid during the night, but Kemp's Ridley prefers daylight. There are differences between the species in the way in which females move on the beach and in the way the nest is dug, but in general terms the process can be described as follows. After emerging from the surf, pausing from time to time, the female moves across the beach until a suitable site is reached above the high water line. With alternate movements of the fore flippers a shallow pit is dug into which the body fits. This is the body pit. Then the hind flippers are used alternately to dig the egg chamber. When this is completed, the eggs are laid; in groups of two, three or more, the spherical eggs are dropped in the hole. The number of eggs in the clutch varies greatly. In Sarawak the clutches of the Green turtle were observed to vary from 3 to 184, with an average of about 104 eggs per clutch. After the eggs have been laid, the hind flippers shovel sand into the egg chamber to fill it up; the sand is firmly pressed down and the female starts to move away, and in doing so, it throws sand over the nesting site with the fore flippers; in this way the exact position of the egg chamber is obscured. During one breeding season a female will return to the beach several times, at intervals of 12–14 days, to lay new clutches. Females of the Green turtle have a breeding season once in every two or three years; the Ridleys lay every year.

It is left to the heat of the surroundings to incubate the eggs. The incubation period varies according to the species, and according to the external circumstances. In Sarawak in January to March 56–80 days may elapse before the hatchling Green turtles emerge from the nest, but from April to December this period varies from 48 to 63 days. After hatching at the bottom of the egg chamber, by joint efforts, the hatchlings move close to the surface. There they wait until night has fallen, to emerge together, to scramble to the sea, and to disappear from view. Usually they are not observed again until they are at least a year old. Very little is known as to where the young turtles spend the first year of their life, but there are indications that the young (at least of some species) move out into the open sea, to stay there far from the coasts for a year or more. Only tropical and subtropical regions have a climate that allows the eggs to develop, and it is there that the nesting beaches are found. The Loggerhead turtle apparently needs less high temperatures, and its nesting beaches are found farther away from the equator than those of any other species.

In the breeding season the turtles have to move from the areas where they find food to the nesting beaches and back, and in some instances this means migration over long distances. This migration is especially marked in the Green Turtle. This species feeds mainly on sea grass ('turtle grass') and the pastures are often far from the nesting beaches. The most remarkable migration is that of the Green turtles that cross a long stretch of open ocean, and against a fairly strong current, from Brazil to the island of Ascension. How these turtles orientate themselves, and how they navigate to pinpoint this small island is as yet unknown. The long distance movements are demonstrated by females which were tagged on the beaches of Ascension and which were recaptured off the Brazilian coast. Females tagged on the Caribbean coast of Costa Rica have been recaptured over a wide area, extending from the south of Florida to the island of Margarita off the Venezuelan coast; the majority of the Green Turtles nesting on the beaches of Tortuguero, Costa Rica, have been recaptured on the sea grass pastures off Nicaragua. Tagging experiments have also shown that a female will nest several times in one breeding season, and that after an interval of two or three years will return once more to the same beach.

Of the distance over which other species migrate little is known. It is reasonable to suppose that the Ridleys which nest every year, do not normally move away from the nesting beaches over very great distances. Along the Atlantic coast of North America, Leathery turtles seem to migrate northward regularly to Nova Scotia and Newfoundland during summer, to pass southward once more in autumn. The long voyages across the ocean undertaken by juvenile turtles, and which are to be distinguished from the breeding migrations, are well known. Loggerheads move northward along the Atlantic coast of North America, and many of them cross the ocean to the coasts of Europe and to the Azores; a juvenile Loggerhead even got as far as Murmansk in northern Russia. Kemp's Ridley, the only known nesting beaches of which are found on the Gulf Coast of northern Mexico, occasionally passes through the Florida Strait into the Atlantic Ocean, to travel northward along the American Atlantic coast, and to cross the ocean to European shores to the Azores, and to Madeira. The Leathery turtle also seems to roam widely across the oceans.

A number of nesting beaches, which in the past were frequented by large numbers of turtles have since been deserted, due to the decline in the populations.

The dangers that threaten the nests and the hatchling turtles are many. On nesting beaches where a great number of females concentrate, the later arrivals may disturb nests that have been made earlier. Ghost crabs will burrow down into the egg chamber; stray dogs, cats and Monitor lizards will dig up the nests, and all these predators feed upon the eggs. When the hatchling turtles move across the beach, many will be taken by the same predators, and if the young turtle is still on the beach in daylight birds will take their toll. In the shallow water, just offshore, small sharks and other predatory fish are lying in wait for them. J. R. Hendrickson estimates that one female Green turtle may lay 1,800 eggs in her lifetime; of these only 405 fully develop; of the emerging hatchlings only 243 enter the sea, and of these only 31 will survive the first week at sea. But even adult turtles are not safe from predators. Tigers and jaguars are known to kill turtles on the beach. A Tiger shark can snap an adult Loggerhead turtle in two; there are numerous records of turtle remains found in the stomachs of Tiger sharks. Often turtles are found of which one or two flippers and part of the shell has been bitten off. Remains of a Leathery turtle have been found in the stomach of a Killer whale.

Taking into account predation on adult turtles, and death from disease and parasites, Hendrickson estimates that the 1,800 eggs laid by a female Green turtle result in only three turtles completing a full life-cycle. The great number of eggs will thus be just sufficient for the species to hold their own. However, to all the dangers must be added the

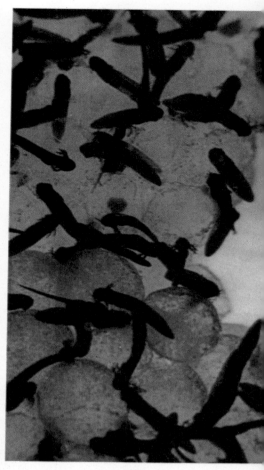

Tadpoles of Common frog of Europe.

Male and female of the European Common toad, in amplexus.

Metamorphosing tadpole of *R. temporaria*, with limbs complete and just before absorption of tail.

The taipan of Australasia, reputed to be the most dangerous of all snakes.

A Tiger snake trying to eat a frog the wrong way round.

Black-spined toad *Bufo melanostictus*, with its vocal sac extended.

The natterjack, the European Toad that runs.

Algerian tortoise named *Testudo graeca*!

When confronted by a Grass snake its natural enemy, the European Common toad blows itself up and rises high on stiff legs, making it difficult for the snake to swallow it.

Spawn of the European Common toad.

Not a prehistoric monster in an antediluvian forest but one of its surviving descendants, a Giant tortoise.

In spite of its name, *Terrapene carolina*, this is the Eastern box turtle, not one of the species normally referred to as a terrapin.

Snapping turtle on land adopts an aggressive posture. Although lacking teeth, turtles can bite hard, with the horny covering to the jaws.

One of nature's paradoxes is that tropical treefrogs are pale or cryptically-coloured when resting by day, but become marvellously coloured when active – by night.

White's tree frog *Hyla caerulea*, swallowing a mouse.   The South American treefrog.   Tuatara, the living fossil of New Zealand.

In the Malayan mud turtle *Trionyx cartilggineus* the shell is flattened and covered with a soft skin instead of the usual horny plates.

havoc caused by man. In some areas turtles are used for food by the local population, and turtles are taken to prepare turtle soup for the gourmet. If the turtles are taken at sea some damage may be done to the turtle population (and it is especially the Green turtle that suffers), but it is believed that the world population of turtles can stand this. It becomes worse when the females are killed on the nesting beaches, often before eggs have been laid. The greatest damage to the populations of all species is caused by unlimited harvesting of the eggs. All over the world millions of turtle eggs are dug up every year and used for human consumption. Even if the number laid by each female were higher than estimated by Hendrickson, and even if more turtles survived to breed, it is clear that the harvesting of eggs gives the death-blow to the turtle populations. A further danger to turtles is the new fashion of making lady's bags out of skin from the neck, shoulders and flippers of turtles killed on the beaches and skinned. This wanton destruction leads to a further decline, and much useful food for man is left unused.

In many countries measures have been taken to protect the turtles on and just off the nesting beaches, and the unlimited harvesting of the eggs is prohibited. The conservation measures often will have to aim at a compromise, allowing of a reasonable exploitation of this important source of animal protein, at the same time to try and safeguard the future of the world's turtle populations. In the Cayman Islands an attempt is made at

Head of the Narrow-bridged mud turtle.

Hawksbill turtle *Eretmochelys imbricata*.

The Hawksbill turtle yields the valuable tortoiseshell of commerce.

Above: female leathery turtle on her way down the beach, having laid her eggs.
Below: tracks in the sand made by a female leathery turtle going up the beach to lay.

'ranching' turtles; eggs are imported from Costa Rica and Ascension Island and placed in hatcheries, to raise the turtles in captivity until they have reached a sufficient size to be slaughtered. Still, this means that thousands of eggs have to be taken each year from the beaches. A more adequate solution would be if one could 'farm' turtles, that is raise turtles from the egg, and to have them breed in captivity, safe from predators. In this way the heavy toll on the turtle populations in the world's seas might be lessened considerably. ORDER: Testudines, CLASS: Reptilia.

TWIG SNAKE, a species of *Thelotornis,* which appears to be most closely related to the *boomslang. These snakes are characterized by a diamond-shaped head with a large eye which has a peculiar keyhole-shaped pupil; the body is slender and the tail long. The top of the head is green, with or without black and pink markings, the body and tail are mottled grey, pink and white and resemble a lichen-covered branch or twig.

Kirtland's vine snake *T. kirtlandii* occurs in the evergreen forests of West Africa, the Congo, Uganda and northern Angola. The Cape vine snake *T. capensis* has a wide range from southeastern Kenya south to Natal and west to Angola. It usually inhabits dry savannah, but is sometimes found on the edge of evergreen forest. The largest Cape vine snake recorded is a Rhodesian specimen of 5½ ft (1·6 m) long.

The female Vine snake lays 5–13 eggs during the summer months.

The Cape vine snake is often found in bushes only a few feet above the ground. Here it remains motionless for hours until its excellent eyesight spots a lizard, frog or small snake in the vicinity. The snake then stalks its prey, climbing down very slowly and then creeping up very close to the prey before striking. The diet consists mainly of lizards, especially chameleons, small snakes, fledgling birds and birds' eggs; frogs are taken, but rarely.

The venom of the Vine snake is similar to that of the boomslang, but less toxic; it causes haemorrhage, but the bite is rarely fatal to a man. SUBFAMILY: Boiginae, FAMILY: Colubridae, ORDER: Squamata, CLASS: Reptilia.

TYRANNOSAURUS, the largest of the extinct reptiles belonging to the subclass *Theropoda, the carnivorous *dinosaurs. Its hindlimbs were powerful and bore three toes, with a fourth very small digit, their skeletons recalling those of birds. The forelegs were ridiculously small by comparison and ended in two tiny fingers. ORDER: Saurischia, CLASS: Reptilia.

URODELA, alternative name for the tailed amphibians or *Caudata, which contains the newts and salamanders.

V

VIPERS, a family of snakes with a highly developed venom apparatus, comparable with that of the nearly related *Pit vipers. The true vipers are found in Africa, where they are most numerous in species, Europe and Asia. The best known species is the European viper or *adder *Vipera berus*. The smallest is Orsini's viper *V. ursini* of southern Europe, less than 1 ft (30 cm) long. The largest is the Gaboon viper *Bitis gabonica,* up to 6 ft (2 m) long and 6 in (15 cm) diameter.

Most vipers are short and stoutly built, with a short tail, and are typically terrestrial. Some, like the Mole vipers, burrow in the ground or, like the Horned vipers, burrow in sand. Few climb, although some of the Puff adders climb into bushes and the Tree vipers are arboreal and have a prehensile tail. Characteristically, vipers do not pursue their prey but lie in wait for it. They strike, wait for a while then track down the victim that has crawled away to die. Their prey is mainly lizards and small mammals. The dead prey is tracked by flickering movements of the forked tongue which picks up molecules of scent in the air, testing these by withdrawing the tongue into the mouth and placing the tips of the fork into the taste-smell organ, in the roof of the mouth, known as Jacobson's organ.

The fangs of a viper are hollow, efficient and large, and are typically folded back when not in use. They are automatically erected as the mouth is thrown wide open for the strike. The poison flowing through the hollow fang comes from a venom gland, a modified salivary gland, at its base. This can be very large and vipers typically have broad heads to accommodate them. In some species the venom glands extend behind the head, to as much as one-fourth the length of the body in Night adders.

Species additional to the European viper (see adder), which rarely exceeds 2 ft (60 cm) in length, with a record of 32 in (80 cm), are the Asp viper *V. aspis,* Lataste's viper *V. latasti* and the Sand viper *V. ammodytes,* all of southern Europe, and all slightly larger than the adder. They have the dark zigzag line down the back as in the adder. In *V. palestinae,* the Palestinian viper, the zigzag has become a continuous line of dark diamond-shaped markings.

Russell's viper *V. russelli,* up to 5 ft (1·6 m) long, the most feared snake of the Indian Peninsula eastwards through Southeast Asia to Java, has a row of large oval spots along the back and a row along each flank, the spots being reddish-brown bordered with black and

The European viper, also known as the adder.

a white border beyond the black. Although its natural food is frogs, lizards and small birds it is a danger because of the many people who go bare-footed in this region.

The four species of Night adder living in, Africa south of the Sahara are all small, rarely exceeding 2 ft (60 cm) long. Although nocturnal the pupil of the eye is rounded, not

vertically elliptical as in other nocturnal species. Their food is frogs and toads, also mice and rats, and they are generally inoffensive although one species *Causus rhombeatus* is named 'Demon adder'. This is because when aroused it coils up, blows itself out, hisses loudly, sometimes even flattens its throat cobra-fashion, and strikes.

Mole vipers of Africa are less than 2 ft (60 cm) long, slender and with only a slender head, unlike other vipers. They spend their lives underground coming out sometimes at night or after heavy rain, to feed on other small snakes, legless lizards, rats and mice.

Puff adders range in size from Peringuey's viper *Bitis peringueyi* of South Africa, less than 1 ft (30 cm) long, to the Gaboon viper 6 ft (2 m) long. They are named for the loud exhalation of air, which produces a puff rather than a hiss. Puff adders living in desert or savannah are brownish but those living in the rain-forests are beautifully coloured. The Gaboon viper is gaudy, with yellow, purple and brown patches in a geometrical pattern, yet it fails to catch the eye on its natural background of leaves on the forest floor. The Rhinoceros viper *B. nasicornis* is so called for the erectile scales at the tip of its snout. It is even more gaudy, with green triangles margined with black and blue added to extensive areas of purple and blue. Puff adders are sluggish, apt to be trodden on, and with a venom almost as potent as that of a cobra or a mamba to livestock or human beings. Their venom is slow acting and may take 24 hours to cause death in a large animal or a man.

Two species of Puff adder, *B. cornuta* and *B. caudalis,* have a hornlike scale over each eye and they are *sidewinders. Species of another African genus *Cerastes* also have these hornlike scales and are known as Horned vipers. Some of them sidewind and all live in sandy deserts in northern Africa and southwest Asia. The scales along their flanks have sawlike edges. As the snake wriggles into the sand these shovel the sand aside and over the snake's back. Horned vipers do this while coiled, and their coils 'modelled' in sand are characteristic.

The counterpart of the Horned viper in the deserts of Pakistan, India and Ceylon, and also in North Africa, is the Saw-scaled viper *Echis carinatus,* less than 2 ft (60 cm) long but extremely numerous. When disturbed it goes into almost a figure of eight with its head in the centre and rubs its saw-edged scales together, making a hissing sound. The warning is appropriate since this species has the most potent venom of all vipers. FAMILY: Viperidae, ORDER: Squamata, CLASS: Reptilia.

The only arboreal viper, the Tree viper *Atheris squamiger*, of Africa.

W-X

WALL LIZARD, name used for several European species of typical *lizards, the best known being *Lacerta muralis*. Their natural habitat is among rocks but when living in gardens they use walls instead. FAMILY: Lacertidae, ORDER: Squamata, CLASS: Reptilia.

WART SNAKES, are unique in being covered with a skin that is like sandpaper to the touch. The two species are the Elephant's trunk snake *Acrochordus javanicus* and the File snake *Chersydrus granulatus*. Both are harmless and highly specialized for aquatic life. They differ from other snakes in a number of features. Both the right and the left carotid arteries are present. The left lung is absent but the right is highly developed and extends the length of the body. Adaptations to aquatic life include a small head with nostrils facing upwards and tiny eyes. The nostrils

The clawed frog *Xenopus laevis* of southern Africa, also known as the 'pregnancy frog'.

can be closed when the snake is submerged by a flap of cartilage in the roof of the mouth. There are no enlarged belly scales and the skin consists of small almost uniform granules. The scales do not overlap each other as is usual in snakes but instead lie side by side, sometimes with skin showing between them. Each body granule is wart-like and has a central tubercle which gives the snake a granular appearance and abrasive texture. The skin of the Elephant's trunk snake is flabby, and this and the snake's girth account for its common name. Occasionally the Elephant's trunk snake grows to 6 ft (1·8 m) long, with a girth of 1 ft (30 cm). The File snake grows to only half this size and has a shorter and more compressed, rudder-like tail. Its eyes are more lateral and its nostrils more dorsal than those of the Elephant's trunk snake. Wart snakes are the only primitive snakes so well adapted to aquatic habits.

The Elephant's trunk snake occurs in Southeast Asia from Cochin-China to new Guinea and also in northeastern Australia. It is found in streams, pools, canals and estuaries. The File snake is almost entirely marine and more widespread; it is found round coasts and estuaries from Ceylon and India across southern Asia as far as the Solomon Islands.

Along the belly from throat to vent is a longitudinal row of slightly fringed scales which may act like a fin and increase the File snake's swimming ability.

Both species produce their young alive and in the Elephant's trunk snake litter sizes from 25 to 32 have been recorded whereas the File snake produces only 6–8 young at a time. The Elephant's trunk snake is sluggish, mostly nocturnal, and feeds on fish. It can remain underwater for over half an hour and swims slowly but well. On land it is practically helpless due to the fact that, lacking large belly scales, it is unable to gain much purchase on the ground. If provoked it may deliver fierce slashing sideways bites.

Wart snake skins with their non-overlapping scales are suitable for leather, which is known as karung. They are used in their native countries for drum skins but are

also exported for use in ladies' shoes and handbags. In some years no less than 300,000 skins have been used. The skins can be bleached, tanned, and then crushed smooth to give a highly polished end product with a pleasant mottled appearance. FAMILY: Acrochordidae, ORDER: Squamata, CLASS: Reptilia.

WATER SNAKES, nearly 80 species of the genus *Natrix,* to which the *Grass snake, of Europe, belongs. Two-thirds of the species live in southern and Southeast Asia, and all are alike in habits, as described under Grass snake, except in their breeding. All Old World Water snakes lay eggs. The two North American species *N. sipedon* and *N. taxispilota,* the only New World water snakes, are viviparous, the females giving birth to 6–58 young. FAMILY: Colubridae, ORDER: Squamata, CLASS: Reptilia.

WHITE DRAGON, see Chinese Salamander.

XENOPUS, a genus of amphibians with four species restricted to Africa: the Clawed frog *Xenopus laevis* is the most widely known. This 5 in (12·5 cm), purely aquatic frog is limited to southern Africa where it is found in pools or streams that dry up in summer causing the animals to aestivate. Claws on the inner three toes of each foot give this frog its common name. The Clawed frog is best known to doctors as the 'pregnancy frog' as it was once used extensively to test suspected pregnancy in women. Other species are: *X. gilli* of South Africa, and *X. mulleri* and *X. tropicalis,* of tropical Africa. FAMILY: Pipidae, ORDER: Anura, CLASS: Amphibia.